D1394991

# Look Behind the Ranges

HAMISH MacINNES

# Look Behind
# the Ranges

*A mountaineer's selection*
*of adventures and expeditions*

HODDER AND STOUGHTON
LONDON SYDNEY AUCKLAND TORONTO

British Library Cataloguing in Publication Data

MacInnes, Hamish
  Look behind the ranges.
  1. MacInnes, Hamish
  2. Mountaineers – Scotland – Biography
  I. Title
  796.5'22'0924     GV199.92.M/

ISBN 0 340 18949 5

# Contents

# ILLUSTRATIONS

## CREDITS

1 New Zealand House
2 John Cleare/Mountain Camera
3 Swiss Air Photographs, Zurich

## Maps and drawings

The hill, though high, I covet to ascend,
The difficulty will not me offend;
For I perceive the way of life lies here.
Come, pluck up heart, let's neither faint nor fear!
Better, though difficult, the right way to go,
Than wrong, though easy, where the end is woe.

JOHN BUNYAN, *The Pilgrim's Progress*

# 1

# Impecunious Peregrinations

Till a voice, as bad as Conscience, rang interminable changes
On one everlasting Whisper day and night repeated-so:
"Something hidden. Go and find it. Go and look behind the Ranges –
Something lost behind the Ranges. Lost and waiting for you. Go!"
[Rudyard Kipling, from 'The Explorer']

"FER CHRIST'S SAKE, MOVE over, MacInnes," said Bill Smith in exasperation. "You're taking up enough room for two!"

"Sorry, old fruit," I apologised, shifting slightly at the same time in order to consolidate my position. "It's this bloody wee bed you've got; it's designed for a Glaswegian dwarf!"

"Well, if you don't like it, you know what to dae," Bill muttered. Turning over with finality and using his rear quarters as a lever, he almost succeeded in displacing me from my precarious situation on the edge of the bed.

That night we had both been through to Edinburgh to hear André Roche deliver a lecture in the Usher Hall. I knew a girl who was a secretary in the Scottish R.G.S. and she had sent me two complimentary tickets, knowing full well that I would never have bought them. Bill Smith, a stolid, unperturbable Glaswegian of immeasurable patience and a member of the famed Creagh Dhu Mountaineering Club, had decided to come over with me to the lecture for, as he casually remarked:

"We could always think o' a visit to Everest during the Glasgow Fair Holidays . . ."

Little did I know then that this lecture was to play a significant part in my future. André Roche was talking about the Swiss attempt on Mount Everest during the autumn of 1952 a few months previously and mentioned, quite casually, that their expedition had left large quantities of food and equipment at the bottom of the slopes leading up to the South Col. Afterwards, some of us were having a drink in the bar, and I had questioned André about this cache of goodies. It was, as he so nicely phrased it, 'a Scotsman's heaven'!

"Hey, Bill." I prodded my bedcompanion. "All that grub – I can't wait."

"Don't tell me you're hungry again!" muttered Bill. Though heavy with sleep, a note of disgust was apparent in his voice. "You've already had five pokes o' fish and chips."

"All that food on Everest, you idiot," I retorted, exasperated by such total lack of comprehension. Somehow or other, my companion fell out of bed that night, which must surely illustrate my somnambulistic prowess. It was my last visit to Bill's house.

I must digress somewhat to explain my association with the Creagh Dhu Club. I first started to climb with them after I returned from National Service; with my usual good fortune, I had spent eighteen months in the Austrian Tirol at an Army Holiday Camp. It was one of the most enjoyable periods of my life and I still keep close contact with friends in Ehrwald. Before my Army days, I had climbed with a lad called Charlie Vigano. I was never very sure of Charlie's nationality – at one stage he couldn't accompany us to France in case they enlisted him for military service; he felt he was unsuited to the uniform of the Foreign Legion preferring a more casual line in clothes! So while I was away in the Army, he had made the acquaintance of the Creagh Dhu through John Cunningham and Bill Smith. These two climbers emerged at the start of the 1950s as the strongest rock climbers that Scotland had produced. Bill, built like a tank, tremendously powerful; John, slight and tough with superb movement, even on the hardest climb. John was then the West of Scotland catch-as-catch-can wrestling

14

champion. Three friends with whom Charlie and I had started climbing – John Black, John Bradburn and Sid Tuinion – had all died together in a blizzard and it was therefore natural that we should seek new climbing companions.

The Club started in the years of the depression and was essentially a working man's club; or perhaps it would be more accurately defined as an unemployed man's club, for there wasn't much employment available then. Some of the lads used to walk to the Cobbler at Arrochar and even as far as Glencoe in order to climb. As most of the Club members were born and bred within Glasgow's City boundary, it may be taken for granted that they could look after themselves in a rough-and-tumble, and the fact that many of them were wrestlers of considerable ability added an unfounded reputation for unruly behaviour.

In the early 1950s, we all possessed motor cycles and sorties to the mountains invariably ended with a race down Loch Lomondside; then, and even now, a particularly tortuous stretch of road hugging the western bank of that scenic loch. We were offered fierce competition by other weekenders, several of whom were well-known racing men, and at least one a T.T. champion. Bill Smith was one of the best riders I ever knew; despite owning only a standard machine, he was faster than anyone else. My usual view of him was from the rear as I vainly tried to emulate his style. Exhaust pipe or footrests would be emitting sparks on tight corners as his machine – generally laden with ropes and rucksacks – banked at what looked to be impossible angles.

Charlie, a swarthy placid character whose native tongue – Scots – had French intonations, was a chef at the time, though he adamantly refused to cook at weekends. He never could master changing gear and burned out the clutch with monotonous regularity before he understood the intricacies of the gearbox. Bill Smith, always a master of innovation, used up most of Charlie's rucksack straps by threading them through the clutch plates in place of the cork inserts. One day I felt I had to warn him.

"Charlie, you'll have to give up climbing – at least with a

rucksack – unless you get the hang of riding your bike!"

"Yes, yes," Charlie agreed in his endearing way. "I've got the message . . ."

My first motor cycle was a 350cc Panther, a somewhat 'tired' middle-weight athlete. I manufactured the teledraulic forks for this machine out of boiler tubing, but somehow never completed the job. When travelling too fast over a pothole, there was a distinct danger of the lower ends of the forks falling out of the top section, since I had neglected to fit retaining rods. I vividly recall one weekend when, by some freak of luck, I had stolen the lead off Bill Smith down Loch Lomondside and was determined that he shouldn't pass me. A heavy stream of traffic was returning to Glasgow after a fine spring Sunday. I suspected Charlie's affliction – clutch trouble – as my machine periodically slowed for no apparent reason; it was as if an enormous hand had grabbed me by the collar. Happily, the answer was much simpler: tied to my bike's rear mudguard was 150-foot of climbing rope, one end firmly attached to the frame of the machine. The knot had held, but the rope itself had uncoiled and was dragging along the road! Cars from both directions were running over it but, thanks to the elasticity of the nylon, there were no disastrous effects.

A little later I became interested in hotting up motor cycle engines. Possibly I had a sub-conscious desire to shatter Smith's supremacy on two wheels, but to no avail. I had more success in designing an all-metal ice hammer – the first of its kind – appropriately called 'the Message'. Many years later I was to manufacture them in a more presentable form. The harder climbs we were now tackling required more sophisticated equipment; I remember persuading a fellow weekend climber, nicknamed 'The Mank' due to his somewhat dishevelled appearance, who was a first-class welder, to tip our crampon points with stellite, a very hard material. Twenty years later a German company adopted the same technique.

One weekend Bill Smith was attempting a new route on the Cobbler, a compact rock peak some twenty miles north-west of Glasgow. The route was a hard one and, after a series of attempts on an overhang, Bill complained of a sore wrist. Later he discovered that his wrist was actually broken. Wearing a plaster cast, he was climbing difficult routes a few weeks later, and he put it to good use in evicting me from his tent when he thought I was taking up too much room. Needless to say, the plaster had to be replaced more than once.

Some time after this, when the winter snows came, we were attempting to scale Raven's Gully in Glencoe, a dark slit high on Buachaille Etive Mor, then unclimbed in winter. For some reason or other, though halfway up, we were still unroped when the ice broke beneath Bill's crampons and he shot down the narrow vertical defile. I remember thinking ungraciously as I watched him fall – 'Hell, I haven't got a black tie!' Bill survived his 500-foot drop between the gully walls, narrowly missing ugly boulders below, and landed in the steep bed of Great Gully. As he shook himself free of the snow, he looked up and shouted:

"Come on down, it's great!" Next day, his arm was back in plaster!

One weekend, as I was about to set off on the uphill hike to the howff at the Shelter Stone of the Cobbler, one of the lads cunningly concealed a rock in my pack. At the doss my unpacking was greeted with howls of derision. However, revenge was sweet, as I secreted the same rock in the practical joker's pack before we returned to our motor cycles on the Sunday evening. There it remained all the following week, only to be carried back up to the Shelter Stone the next weekend!

I never joined the Creagh Dhu Club, though I had a long and memorable association with it. Charlie Vigano once wrote, "MacInnes was never an official member of the Club. Many climbers in Scotland wanted to join the Creagh Dhu, so naturally MacInnes didn't want to . . ."

The period of 1950-54 was important in Scottish mountaineering. During this time the standard of climbing was raised appreciably and many great routes were done. Later, the impetus was maintained by men such as Robin Smith, Jimmy Marshall, and Dougal Haston, all from Edinburgh.

17

Quite a few of the lads were, and still are, ardent skiers. Both pitons and ski sticks were manufactured in the Glasgow ship-yards where many of them worked. One skier, requiring two lengths of stainless steel tubing for 'poles' (as ski sticks were called), memorised – as he thought – the position of two suit-able pieces on the rack. When the knocking-off whistle blew at 5.30 p.m. he grabbed the tubes and broke into a sprint for the main gate where several thousand fellow workmates were dis-gorging into the streets of Glasgow, a stampede of humanity. Unfortunately, he had grabbed the wrong lengths; instead of taking two four-foot pole sections, he had lifted 30-foot lengths! The die was well and truly cast so he kept going, hell for leather through the main gate, cursed alike by his stumbling workmates and the pursuing gatekeepers. He leapt onto a passing tram, the tubes clanking on the rails behind, but still held in a vice-like grip. Our personal equipment was still at a minimum. No one wore crash helmets for motor cycling, let alone for climbing, we all wore bonnets – even slept in them! Our essential gear was generally acquired at the Glasgow Barrows, the weekly market where at that time ex-W.D. gear included bargains such as ice axes, advertised as 'Coal picks, guid for the cellar: 5/–'.

Many of the climbers of that period emigrated, establishing themselves in far corners of the world. From time to time these stalwarts return to the 'old country', usually for a poaching holiday. As one of them told me on a recent visit, "things get a bit dull when hunting's legal!" One of the climbers who used to come away with us had a girlfriend who was a blackpudding bender, but I never had the pleasure of meeting her.

Some time before André Roche's Edinburgh lecture, John Cunningham had emigrated to New Zealand. Bill Smith didn't really see the free food cached in the Western Cwm as a stepping stone to Everest so I wrote to Johnny instead. He was interested and I decided, rather illogically, that the best way to organise the trip was to travel to New Zealand and discuss plans on the spot; so off I went by sea. I told my parents that I was going out to live there and seek my fortune: not really a lie as, after the expedition, I did stay there. But, despite much enterprise, I failed to return a millionaire.

Though I love the sea, especially in its more truculent moods, I do get bored on long voyages with having nothing to do. At the dead of night on the 1st April, I bestirred myself and climbed the topmast, fixing a Jolly Roger there to the amusement of the passengers and the annoyance of the Captain! A Swiss friend and fellow passenger was equally bored by the voyage. Sleeping on deck one night, I was awakened by Walter practising his English, or so I thought. "Sixty-one, sixty-two, sixty-three . . ." Eventually my curiosity got the better of me and I went round to the rear of the poop deck to find him recklessly throwing deck chairs overboard!

Johnny's base was at Christchurch, in the South Island. Initially I shared his flat, much to the consternation of his landlady who, we were agreed, was the only animal of importance missing from Auckland Zoo! In Christchurch too were some older Scottish climbers; namely, 'Big Blondie' Cameron and John Kay. They used to congregate every Saturday in the Gladstone Bar to sing rebel songs and Scottish ballads and were justly famed for their performance.

Since we didn't plan to set off to the Himalayas for another five weeks it was essential for me to get fit again and, at the same time, earn a crust. I decided to seek heavy employment and, with this laudable intention in mind, made my way to the Labour Exchange.

"There's no shortage of jobs in New Zealand," the man behind the desk assured me. "There are sixteen jobs to every person . . ."

"They must be a bit overworked," I muttered under my breath.

"What was that?" he snapped back.

"I said I wanted some heavy work – I want to get fit." He eyed me appraisingly.

"Well, we have a job here, carrying 100-lb concrete blocks up a ramp. Would that suit? or moving carcases at the freezing works?"

"Not really heavy enough," was my reply. "The cement block job's the sort of thing, but it would ruin my hands . . ." I finally settled for a job felling trees, using a cross-cut saw and started the very next morning.

I now decided it was time to find some accommodation of my own, so I moved into a house where the landlady was a health food maniac. I had raw turnips for breakfast, molasses and figs to take to work, and a large cabbage salad washed down with milk at night.

"She's just too bloody lazy to cook for you," one of the lads pointed out one day, catching sight of her tackling a large and well-cooked chop in the back room. "Health foods! Hell, you'll wither away . . ."

There was little time for climbing during that brief stay in New Zealand, other than a trip to the Southern Alps that almost ended with our missing the boat. We had accepted an invitation to go up with Kay and Blondie in their ancient van – a machine of unknown vintage. Pat MacDonald, another former weekender from Glasgow was also in the party; he had just got up from his holidays, two weeks in bed reading Karl Marx. At the edge of a precipitous gorge the van decided to retire from public life. Immediately, a 'meeting of the share-holders' was convened, and a motion was passed that the persistent trouble-maker should be pushed into the river far below. Pat chipped in and nobly presented our case, pointing out that we had to catch the boat at Lyttleton the very next day. So the van was duly pushed on not over and, as if sensing its narrow escape from a watery grave in the Waimakariri, coughed obligingly into life. We finally caught the Tasman Ferry, clutching a tent (donated by Pat) and a rucksack apiece. And so we left the Antipodes.

So I went worn out of patience; never told my nearest neighbours –
Stole away with pack and pony – left 'em drinking in the town;
And the faith that moveth mountains didn't seem to help my labours
As I faced the sheer main-ranges, whipping up and leading down.

[from 'The Explorer']

Our journey to the Himalayas was to take us via Australia and Ceylon before reaching Bombay. Even the start, the crossing of the Tasman Sea to Sydney, was not without incident. I have always found fresh air essential but since we were as usual travelling by the cheapest possible means, our cabin was situated in the depths of the ship. The porthole was only a few inches above the waterline, although securely fastened by two large nuts. Our cabin mate was a man we called 'Bish' (I don't think we ever knew his name), a congenial individual with a bald head and a shy smile; when I found a large bulkhead spanner which fitted the nuts securing the porthole, he kindly agreed that the cabin did smell a bit musty.

The Tasman Sea is notorious for its squally weather and our particular voyage was no exception. Both John and I slept soundly, lulled by Bish's snoring, he slept with his mouth wide open. It must have been about 2 a.m. when a large wave hit the side of the ship and Bish, his lungs, and the cabin were awash. His suitcase floated, as buoyant as a liferaft. Fortunately there was a step at the cabin door entrance which prevented the water running down the passage – but there was all hell to pay next morning when the flood was discovered.

By this time we had heard that Everest had been climbed by Ed Hillary and Sherpa Tensing, somewhat despondently, we altered our plans and decided to attempt Pumori, 23,550 feet, an elegant snow peak close to Everest. Now we would be unable to make use of the food left by the Swiss and later I heard from John Hunt that they had used most of it for their own expedition anyway.

The voyage from Sydney to Bombay was also memorable. We kept ourselves fit playing deck tennis and running round

21

the decks at night. There were plenty of girls, and quite a few oddities, apart from ourselves. One whom we nick-named 'the Professor' was travelling to Dar-es-Salaam; his hobby was collecting personal objects of great composers. He had the key to Beethoven's lavatory and a string from Paganini's violin besides many other 'objets d'art', so he assured us. We spent our spare time sewing a ground sheet into the Boy Scout tent we had acquired from Pat, and learning Urdu coached by a stunning Anglo-Indian girl. I think it was due to her charm that I failed to realise that they spoke Nepali where we were heading, not Urdu.

After we had paid our single fares to Bombay, and allowed for other vital expenses, I worked it out that we would have sixty pounds left. Not a great deal. John observed dryly that we had better start having a third sitting each mealtime, instead of two, as it might be some time before we got a good meal once we'd landed.

Before leaving the 'old country' I had written for permission to attempt Everest during the post-monsoon period. Whilst still in New Zealand, I heard that we had been refused on the grounds that we had no Himalayan experience, though how the hell we were supposed to gain it if we weren't allowed to go in the first place was a mystery to us. Mr. Leyden, the Himalayan Climbing Club representative in Bombay, had heard of our imminent arrival and assumed that we would be going to the Central Himalayas where permission was not required. He met us as we stepped off the gangplank. Once introductions had been made, he announced in a gutteral German accent:

"I have the baggage coolies ready for the expedition equipment, gentlemen." When we modestly explained that we were carrying it, he stared in astonishment. He had already lined up thirty baggage porters. Visualising the catastrophic drain on our resources, we hastily assured him that all we needed were two rail tickets to Patna for that night's Calcutta Mail. Mr. Leyden rapidly came to the conclusion that we were mad – an expedition which arrived with two rucksacks and asked for rail tickets in the wrong direction! Finally he had to give in and took this couple of 'verruckt' Scots to the station.

Our journey through India, travelling the cheapest possible way, was a revelation to us; here was poverty we hadn't known existed. From Patna we crossed the Ganges, the Holy River, and took the narrow gauge railway to the Nepalese border at Bergunje. The road to Kathmandu had not been completed so from here on it was to be Shank's Pony.

Bergunje was then a dirty, dusty village with men lounging in doorways, aimlessly swatting flies. We hadn't been questioned on the train and were under the comforting illusion that we must have passed the Nepalese frontier formalities. As a matter of fact, the question of illegal entry into Nepal – now we were finally faced with it – was causing us some concern. Sahibs on foot in those days were objects of considerable interest and so to avoid detection was out of the question. We would have to use our native cunning to overcome official-dom. We also carried a small-calibre rifle with which we hoped to supplement our diet; this would create further problems as we only had an Indian permit for it.

We spent the night in Bergunje in an 'hotel'. An hotel in name only for it would be hard to imagine a more disreputable place; mud floors and walls on which enormous spiders vied with lizards for spare parking space. Outside the door of open wooden slats like the bars of a cage, ran the village sewer, a murky brown stream which doubled as the local water supply. The stream had been diverted through the village to serve the community and the locals even fished it – skilfully employing open umbrellas, ferrule end downwards.

That night we were invaded by rats. One of the more obvious purposes of the cage door was to provide easy access for them. We didn't sleep much. It was a constant battle fending them off. It must have been almost dawn when I fancied I heard a rustling not caused by rats. I reached down to pick up our precious bag of silver Nepalese rupees, and encountered a stranger's hand. I grabbed at it but, with a twist and a scurry, the hopeful thief was away. Later we became quite adept at dealing with all types of nocturnal visitors.

In the morning we staggered out, bleary-eyed, to face the furnace-like heat of another day. Our packs grew heavier by the hour. At one point we gratefully eased them off onto a mysterious stone pedestal at the junction of two dirt tracks, but immediately a policeman came running out of a nearby shack, jumped up beside the packs, which didn't leave him much standing room, and waved us on as if he were controlling traffic on a busy arterial route. Presently we had left even this outpost of humanity behind as the path rose through jungle country. We had tried to find a couple of porters to help carry our belongings but, after timidly testing the weight of our packs, they had decided to remain unemployed! Yet, at that same time, 1953, cars (minus their engines) were carried on long bamboo poles to Kathmandu by coolies.

After a while we decided that we must be safely over the border and were congratulating each other on an achievement as simple as crossing at Gretna, when we turned a corner of the path. Straight ahead of us under a tree stood a man in uniform holding a rifle. He appeared to be guarding a small shack. Unfortunately, we soon discovered that he was guarding the few hundred square miles to the north as well, and that one of the more overworked words in his limited English vocabulary was the word 'pass'. We offered him our passports and sat down resignedly on our rucksacks in the gloaming, trying to fend off the hornets and imagining Nepalese prisons, while he disappeared behind his hut. He returned presently:

"Yoos Hinglish?" he asked . . . insulting, we thought.

"Scottish," I corrected him, mindful of Nationalist friends back home. He surveyed us quizzically:

"Pass, please." We flourished a smallpox vaccination in front of him and I took from my pocket an airmail letter from my mother. After prolonged scrutiny of them – upside down – he finally pronounced:

"All light; you go," pointing along the dark tunnel of the path to Kathmandu. We were very aware that it had been a narrow squeak, and decided to work out some strategy for future encounters with the law. Next time we might not be so fortunate as to be stopped by an illiterate policeman.

There were a few fellow travellers on the Kathmandu trail and numerous tea shops where hot, syrupy tea was decanted into tumblers. This was most welcome and cheap fuel for load carrying. A well-dressed Nepali, flourishing an elegant brolly, offered us tea at one of these stops. We accepted with alacrity whilst he knocked back glass after glass of chang – the local beer made from rice or barley, and strained through a wicker basket. In Nepal then the umbrella was the status symbol, as the transistor radio became later. (In India now, since transistors have been being presented to volunteer vasectomy patients they have started taking on a rather different significance!)

"Ve go together to Kathmandu," our patron beamed, giving a loud belch. "I vill buy you char . . . Boy! Two char for my friends." Our glasses were refilled. Later, as we sweated along the mountainous track, our drunken friend, well shaded by his umbrella, would inform passers-by that we were his white coolies. They must have thought us good value from the size of our loads!

For the last stage of our journey a bus operated along the flat floor of the Kathmandu valley to which we had descended. Thankfully, we bundled our packs onto this archaic vehicle and endeavoured, once inside, to find something to hang onto, for the bus was grossly overloaded.

"Ten rupees, sahib," the pock-faced driver yelled at us above the din, his mouth awash with betel. Since we had been told by our Nepalese friend that the correct fare was one rupee, we were determined to pay no more. The driver was equally determined not to lose face, and insisted on his overheads. We discovered, however, that it wasn't very easy to conduct an argument in a language which you don't understand so, rather than continue a fruitless conversation, and to avoid a fracas, we tried to get off the bus. It was quite a struggle. Once outside, I reached up to grab my rucksack as the driver also caught hold of it to prevent us leaving and thereby ensure his backsheesh.

25

Since he was quite light he didn't make a great deal of difference to the weight of the pack so he left the bus too! This had a sobering effect on him and he immediately agreed to take us for the normal fare. Near the door, beside us, a man lay moaning. He had apparently been bitten by a snake and was later simply dumped off the bus by the roadside on the outskirts of Kathmandu; no one made any attempt to help. Equipped only with a five shilling Boy Scout first-aid kit bought in Melbourne, we couldn't offer much help either.

We realised that our passage through the Nepalese capital would be a critical time in our enterprise; it was essential to escape detection at this stage. We hoped therefore to avoid meeting the police or any sahib who might be connected with the British Embassy. With this in mind, the expense of hiring a taxi seemed fully justified for two white men who would otherwise have to carry conspicuous packs through the streets of the city. There was, besides, a curfew in operation. But we committed the folly of chartering the oldest (we assumed it would also be the cheapest) available taxi: an Essex of unknown vintage.

"Rupees for gas, sahib," the driver flourished an empty petrol can. "I go for gas, sahib." We didn't seem to be having much luck with transport in Nepal, but I presented the man with two rupees and he dashed off down a side street, leaving us wondering if we'd ever see him again, and grieving over our already dwindling bank roll.

He came back, however, and with the assistance of ten curious natives who had been pressed into push-starting the vehicle, we were under way.

"Hotel!" I shouted to the driver above the din; we were careering through the bazaar in a dangerous fashion.

"Les, les, sahib . . . Elmbassy, I know. . . ."

"Not the bloody Embassy. A H-O-T-E-L, understand?"

"Les, les, I know. I dlive tourists . . ." Fortunately it was getting late when we drew up in front of the locked gates of what I realised was in fact the British Embassy.

"Here, sahib . . . Two more rupees."

26

"Look here, Jimmy, it's a hotel we want, not this place," I bellowed, pointing at the gates. "A hotel, and jildi!"

The hotel which we eventually arrived at was literally a palatial establishment; it had been a palace in its youth. The manager was sympathetic and offered us cut rates. There was only one other sahib staying there: Earl Riddiford from New Zealand, a friend of Ed Hillary. He had just returned from an expedition and was much amused by our venture, offering useful advice on among other things how to deal with the packs of pariah dogs who charged en masse at every village. Earl told us that they would scatter to the four winds if one pretended to pick up a stone. For the first time (and the last for several months) since leaving the ship, we slept between sheets, in king-sized beds draped with mosquito nets.

The hotel manager had arranged more reliable transport for us the next day and long before dawn a jeep arrived to collect us, taking us east as far as the roadhead at Badgaon, famous for its temple and carved doorway. At that time it was the end of the road. We had learnt from Earl that there were police check-posts on the trail to Namche Bazar and we would have no option but to pass through them. Earl also had a Sherpa with him called Nima: a gaunt man with a constantly worried expression who spoke in a whining voice, surprising for a Sherpa as generally they are laugh-happy people. He wore the ubiquitous balaclava and Clive of India shorts which accentuated his matchstick legs. We decided that if Nima accompanied us to Namche (where he was already bound), his presence might assist our passage through the police posts. Though he refused to carry anything other than his own small pack, on the credit side he would cost us very little and he did speak a bit of English.

It was on our trek to the east of Kathmandu that we first encountered leeches. I found the creatures nauseating then, and I still do. One night I woke up with a start to find a large leech firmly attached to the back of my throat, waving in ecstasy at its succulent meal. Later on, we had cause to regret that we had chosen to travel through Nepal during the monsoon; it is one of the worst leech-infested regions in the world, and they are most plentiful between 4000 and 6000 feet.

Occasionally we found a couple of porters to help us, but for the greater part of the journey we had to carry our swag ourselves. This became a leg-bending task. Nima unfortunately proved to be more of a hindrance than a help at the police posts.

"Sahib, le permit?" he would whine like a petulant child while the police looked on. "At le last post you say other sahib has this, but when he come he no have this . . ." I could willingly have strangled him; heaven knows what he told the police.

We had by now developed several techniques for dealing with the police. John and I sometimes travelled about a quarter of a mile apart when we knew a post lurked on the horizon. The first one to reach a checkpoint would greet the police affably:

"Hello, Jimmy" – the all purpose Glaswegian greeting – "Fine weather this – for ducks and leeches," and wave airily behind to where the other was struggling along, adding, "Friend has pass." The 'friend' would then turn up, obligingly drop his rucksack and unpack it – belongings scattered all over the path – before declaring:

"Terribly sorry about this, Jimmy, but it looks as if my pal must have the pass after all . . . But we'll show it at the next post. Where is that, by the way?" Being somewhat lackadaisical, the police generally allowed the last one through, rather than pursue the first offender, often volunteering the welcome intelligence of the whereabouts of the next checkpoint. If we came across a post unawares, we adopted the 'laughing' technique: we would begin to laugh immoderately and slap each other on the back. This act usually caused considerable amusement and in the end they would let us continue, often laughing themselves.

One day we were carrying over some very arid country where it had been dry for several days. We had previously avoided drinking the water because of a cholera epidemic but were soon regretting it; by then there was no water to be found anyway. In the late afternoon we staggered exhausted into a pleasant-looking village on a watershed and dropped our packs under a great mango tree whose rustling leaves sounded like running water. Wiping my face with the bottom of my shirt, I observed that there weren't many people about; no doubt they were having a snooze and avoiding the sweltering heat. We drank our fill from the village water supply, an evil-looking pool, but nevertheless we savoured each mouthful. Then Nima arrived – he inevitably brought up the rear insisting on his 'union' rights for countless 'smokos', or rather tea breaks since he didn't smoke; he had learnt this from the New Zealanders.

"Vely bad place, sahib," he pronounced. "Many die – cholera."

"No wonder there's nobody about," I observed. "They're dead . . . !" During the next few days our imaginations ran riot, inventing umpteen cholera symptoms.

One day Nima told us of a short cut over a series of passes known as the Dudh Khunde which could save us three days' march. Only one white man had ever been that way before; an old colleague, Raymond Lambert, a Swiss guide who was on the same expedition as André Roche. He and Lionel Terray had rescued me from the Grand Charmoz six years before. But it was essential to find a couple of very able porters for this detour was a strenuous one, we were warned.

We managed to get hold of two coolies: Tundro Badro and Niram Chrissar. They were real professionals who moved with effortless ease like well-oiled engines even when carrying heavy loads. Tundro and Niram proved to us just how tough Himalayan hill-men could be. The Dudh Khunde by-pass was also frequented by coolies carrying ghee to Tibet. There were huge boulders to sleep under at night, one of which must have been capable of sheltering over a hundred men. The climb seemed endless and we rose steadily to the monsoon snows. I remember particularly one deep gorge which took a full day simply to descend and then go up the far side.

Finally, late one evening, we dropped down to the Dudh

29

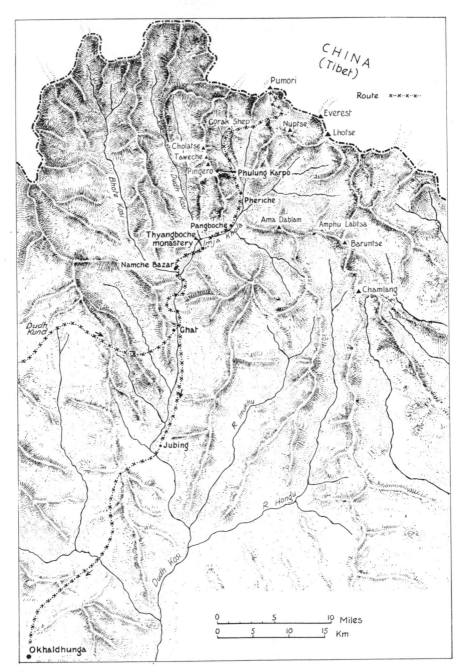

*High Nepal, the area of our peregrinations.*

Kosi river and joined up with the main path to Namche Bazar. Nima knew one of the villagers at Ghat, a small township strewn along the edge of the river as if deposited there by floodwater, its tiered fields rising like a giant's staircase up the slopes.

"We have good party tonight," he promised. "Much raksi and chang!"

I succumbed, for at that time my sleeping bag wasn't attractive enough to tempt me to an early night. Indeed, I generally looked forward to the hours of darkness, and the associated discomfort, with trepidation. The bag was a hideous shade of green and stuffed with large feathers. As it was too short for my lanky frame I had opened the bottom, thus converting it into a sleeve. In its early days it earned the title, 'the reciprocating sleeve'. I had subsequently discovered and perfected the technique of moving up and down inside it to warm the frozen parts of my anatomy. It was one 'bargain' bought at the Glasgow Barrows that I constantly regretted. It must have been a good party at Ghat as I can't remember much about it! Certainly both chang and raksi flowed freely and my final slumber was interspersed with a Saturday night vision of large intoxicated leeches carrying ex-W.D. rucksacks . . .

The walk up the side of the Sun Kosi was pleasant; only a day and a half later we were climbing the final steep zig-zagging path to the Sherpa village of Namche Bazar. We were slightly uneasy by now, in case word of our illegal travels had reached Namche for Nima had maliciously informed us that the police there had a two-way radio. We arrived at the neat whitewashed houses of the village which seemed glued to the mountainside. Nima took us to the house of a friend where we had our first taste of buttered tea. Even in my ravenous state, I disliked it, but he warned us that it would insult our host if we refused, so I gulped it down rapidly as if it was a quinine cock-tail. My discomfort was complete when the cup was instantly refilled!

It was the next day that we received an invitation to have tea with the police. But this time it was to be Indian tea! 'The condemned men made a hearty meal', I thought wryly as we made our way along the narrow street to their abode.

"Come in, come in," we were greeted effusively as we stooped to enter the Sherpa house where they lived. "I hope you both slept well?" A Brahmin was sitting cross-legged on a rug; beside him stood a tall well-built Indian with high cheek-bones, his head nearly touching the roof. We murmured something appropriate for the occasion and were invited to sit down.

"I am so sorry that we didn't know you were coming," the Brahmin apologised. "Our two-way radio is out of action, so we don't get much news these days . . ."!

The Brahmin officer and his assistant were both keen on athletics and a games afternoon was proposed the next day. We had putting the stone and jumping, in which, despite our lack of acclimatisation (Namche is at 10,000 feet), we managed to hold our own.

"I see that you Scotsmen are very fit," our stolid Brahmin friend observed. "But I think my friend will beat you at wrestling, for he has done much . . .", he pointed at his tall compatriot.

"An excellent idea," I applauded enthusiastically, and hurriedly measured out an arena for the contest, placing a large stone at each corner of the improvised ring. John seemed impressed by my alacrity until I pointed out that, as an ex-wrestling champion, he was more fitted for the contest than I, a mere novice at the game! The contest proved to be fast and fierce, with John pinning the Indian who looked twice his size, in the second round.

The police took their defeat in good spirit and the next day we set off once more on our travels. Before we departed I had a look at their transceiver (professing some knowledge of the equipment) and ensured that its faults would not be easily remedied! The primary function of the police post at Namche was to watch movements from Chinese-controlled Tibet; in any case, they were probably not too concerned about the peregrinations of two wayward Scots.

We were glad to leave Nima behind at Namche.

"You vely strange sahibs," he told us as we said goodbye. "You have my knife and fork for backsheesh!" It must have been one of the very few occasions that a Sherpa offered back-sheesh to a sahib when being paid off! We accepted them gladly; there was no snobbery in our code of conduct, besides, until then pitons had been our only eating utensils.

March by march I puzzled through 'em, turning flanks and dodging shoulders,
  Hurried on in hope of water, headed back for lack of grass;
Till I camped above the tree-line – drifted snow and naked boulders –
Felt free air astir to windward – knew I'd stumbled on the Pass.

[from 'The Explorer']

The walk from Namche Bazar up to Thyangboche mon-astery, then on up to Everest Base Camp, must be one of the finest in the world. We were awestruck by the imposing tombstone of Ama Dablam. Here were peaks beyond our wildest dreams. So far the trek had taken us ten days from Kathmandu; for a good part of the way we had carried packs weighing over 100-lbs. We were certainly fit now, having recovered from an early bout of dysentery.

It would be difficult to imagine a more ideal place for worship and contemplation than Thyangboche. Located on a spur, this high meadow surrounded by rhododendrons and birch commands an unsurpassed view of Everest. The mon-astery or gompa is an important one in the area now that Rongbuk, on the far side of Everest, is under Chinese control. Thyangboche is presided over by the Nwang Gurmi Lama, a reincarnation personified by a local youth who was finally tracked down by astrologers after many years' search. Naturally, we were not considered important guests, but were treated with courtesy nonetheless. A small, tumbledown shack in the slum quarters of the monastery was put at our disposal. During the next few days, spent within the precincts, we very nearly disposed of it – at least the slat roof of the building –

33

since there was no other firewood and it was cold and damp.

That first night at the gompa was a memorable one. It must have been about midnight when I heard a terrific din. At first I thought it must be an avalanche. But no, merely the gompa night shift commencing; the avalanche sound–effects were created by large horns, backed with drums and cymbals. It was worse than Hogmanay, was my verdict as I turned restlessly over in my sleeping bag. Just then, in the light shed by spluttering pine splinters, I saw that someone was trying to enter the shack. An old bench which we had propped against the door to deter nocturnal visitors, crashed to the floor. I grabbed the Message and leapt up, my feet automatically shooting out of the bottom of the reciprocating sleeve. Dressed in my green quilted kilt, I bounded across the room drastically restricted by my 'hobble skirt'. My action, intended to be purposeful, came woefully short of that as I fell in a heap. But it was only a monk who had spent the early part of that day bargaining with us. He had been trying to sell us a tin of pâté de fois gras and two tins of boot polish. Our offer then of a few coppers had been too low; now, with gestures, he indicated that he was willing to re-negotiate.

I don't think that 'unwinding' would be the correct description for our stay at Thyangboche; more exactly, it was re-winding for the rigours ahead. We gorged ourselves on chips cooked in yak butter – a favourite dish. One day, when I asked a monk for some 'alu' (potatoes), he replied quite naturally: "Golden Wonders, or Arran Pilots, sahib?" Our shack smelt like a Glaswegian chip shop.

We were perhaps feeling malicious when we composed a ditty to the Nwang Gurmi Lama, set to the tune, 'The Rich Maharaja' . . .

> The rich Red Lama of Thyangboche-e,
> He has 300 prayer wheels to turn all day,
> He has Ata [flour] and Rice at an exorbitant price,
> But he just cannot swindle the Creagh Dhu . . .
> Ta-di-da, ta-di-da, da-di-da-da-da . . .

34

Chorus:
See him beating his great big drum,
Chanting 'Om mani padme hum',
In the setting sun, with a big salaam
We'll chuck him off the top of Ama Dablam . . .

We had only had one hot spell since leaving Kathmandu.
Here, at the higher altitude of Thyangboche (13,000 feet), it
was cloudy most days. We were obviously going to encounter
a lot of snow higher up. In our original plan we had hoped to
reach the Swiss food dump below the South Col, and wait
there, acclimatising, until the weather cleared. Now, since we
had to buy and carry our own food, our stay at higher
altitudes would be limited.

We remained a week at the monastery; then it was time to
move on. We managed to obtain the services of a stout local
who was so hard-up that he agreed to carry an enormous load
for us. We had bought a sheep so our unfortunate employee
staggered down the picturesque trail behind us through the
rhoddies and pines, with one reluctant sheep on tow and a sack
of potatoes on top of his load.

"I'm glad I didn't volunteer to lead that bloody sheep!" I
spoke fervently, glancing behind me. "It's causing more
trouble than his pack!" The coolie was dragging the poor beast
along, its hoofmarks leaving furrows in the track as evidence of
its obstinacy. The monks had forbidden us to kill the sheep at
the monastery, and at the time, it seemed more sensible to
persuade the animal to transport itself to our base camp on the
Khumbu glacier.

The walk from Thyangboche to the Khumbu glacier is like a
walk through fairyland: then carpeted with edelweiss. You
make your way up a valley between giants with magical
names, Taweche, Ama Dablam, Nuptse, Cholatse, and
Pumori. The path is a good one; at intervals, as is customary in
Nepal, there are 'om mani' stones inscribed with the Tibetan
prayer 'Om Mani Padme Hum'. These are often fashioned at a
gompa where a stonemason is employed. Indeed, while

35

following the path which rises above Pangboche, a hamlet and site of a small nunnery, we met an old man dressed in rags, carrying an enormous slab of rock suspended from a headband.

"Do you think he's on his way to post a letter?" I suggested. The coolie, who had probably never seen a white man before, was utterly bewildered by the sight of us, and hurriedly tried to lower his load. But it was so heavy that, as he attempted to sit down, the weight of the stone – which must have been over 140-lbs – catapulted him backwards over the top of it and he crashed heavily on the ground . . .

That same day, as we neared the cluster of stone huts at Pheriche, we met our first yaks. These ungainly-looking creatures are actually very sure-footed and we were told that sometimes, when negotiating ice on a glacier, their herders cut steps for the yaks with their ordinary firewood axes. The 'pasture' which we were entering consisted of a barren rocky valley where there were hundreds of yaks, picking diligently at the sporadic clumps of coarse grass. Here were the summer shielings of the Sherpas who spent the monsoon months with their herds: a similar pattern to the summer common grazings of crofters back home. From the versatile yak the Sherpas obtain milk, fine hair is combed from their shaggy coats for spinning and even their dung is used for fuel. But they are primarily beasts of burden, and only really thrive at an altitude above 10,000 feet.

We spent the night at Pheriche, pitching our tent within the sheltering walls of a yak pen. Here we were given yak milk and bought some butter. A snell wind was blowing down from the Tibetan border and for a few moments it lifted the tenacious cloud cover. As we were peeling our Golden Wonders, we saw a rock pinnacle – an outrider of Taweche – shake off its monsoon coat. It looked worth climbing, so I turned to a yak herder:

"Hey, Jimmy, what's the name of that peak?" I pointed up at the rocky fang.

"Atcha, sahib, boat crappe."

"We know the weather's shitty, Jimmy . . . but the name?" I pointed more specifically.

"Pingero, sahib," the Sherpa replied, holding up a finger. "Pingero." We decided to keep the 'finger' in mind for a rainy day.

Our exhausted porter had staggered into Pheriche long after darkness and refused point-blank to go any further. His natural stoop, which we had observed at the initial interview, seemed more pronounced. He left next morning, slightly straighter, and his parting gesture was a vengeful kick aimed at the sheep.

However, at Pheriche we enlisted the help of one Sadi Khali who, it was reputed, would never let us down. 'The fastest man in the Khumbu', he was billed, and could carry an enormous load. Our plan was that I should stay at Pheriche, or rather move up a couple of miles, to a cluster of yak huts called Phulung Karpo and sort out our gear. I would also try and shoot some fresh meat whilst Johnny and Sadi Khali set out to Everest Base Camp, planning to return the same day. They each took a load of about thirty-five pounds and set off at a fast trot. Meanwhile I ferried the remainder of the gear up the valley to our new camp site; later I went hunting but didn't see a thing to shoot. All the large wild turkeys which we had seen daily lower down, had vanished, apparently having got wind of my intentions. Anyhow I discovered later in the day that our ammunition was useless, having fallen victim of the monsoon.

It was after dusk and I had a brew ready when John arrived back, ahead of Sadi. He was tired, having been all the way to Gorak Shep and back. He had only caught the briefest glimpse of Pumori in the cloud. Gorak Shep was the site of the 1953 Everest Expedition Base Camp and at that time there was no specific trail to follow through the glacier moraine. Nowadays expeditions take three days to travel from Pheriche to Base Camp, a wise precaution since the danger of developing pulmonary oedema is well illustrated by the numerous cairns en route, each marking the place of a death. We didn't know anything about pulmonary oedema then but, fortunately we hadn't rushed things earlier. We must have been feeling fairly fit to even contemplate carrying 90-lb loads up to Gorak Shep!

As we felt unequal to dragging the sheep all the way up, we

decided to dispatch it. We approached Sadi and asked him to perform the slaughter. I drew a hand across my throat express-ively and pointed to the sheep which was tethered by a nylon line to a large boulder.

"No, sahib!" He raised his hands in horror. "Buddhist, sahib; gompa . . ."

"Well, I suppose we'll have to kill it ourselves," I said resignedly. "May as well do it now and get Sadi to butcher it. I imagine his conscience will allow that, anyway!"

I picked up Nima's knife dubiously; it seemed unlikely it would cut slush, let alone a lump of bone and sinew. Neverthe-less I strode purposefully towards our stubborn captive. The knife proved so blunt that it didn't even mark the skin. I let go of the sheep in disgust. It gave a bleat which sounded like a laugh. Sadi had been eyeing the proceedings in amazement.

"You have good kukri, Sadi?" I held up the knife and pointed to his kukri stuck in his belt. "This one boat crappe."

"No, sahib, no give kukri. After kill, yes . . ."

"That's no bloody good now. We've got to eat . . ." I paused, then turned to John. "I tell you what – I'll garrotte it! Give me a bit of that nylon line." With little ceremony I made two slipknots on the two ends of the thin strong cords, each knot running on the opposite piece of line, and slipped the loop this formed over the head of the recalcitrant beast. I can't say it died immediately, but it was as painless as I could make it.

"There's no sense in going further – it's the edge of cultivation,"
[from 'The Explorer']

"You were right, John," I gasped as we staggered into the small depression in the glacier moraine known as Gorak Shep. "What a bloody trip . . ." All day we had been moving up through soaking thick mist. Now it was cold as well. Fresh snow lay just above us. That day for the first time we sported our longjohns, bargains from the Glasgow Barrows; John wore shorts over his.

Sadi Khali spent another night in our tent and left at dawn. We were faced with the unwelcome prospect of ferrying our potatoes and mutton further up the glacier to a camp site beneath our objective: the face of Pumori.

"It's pissing wet again," I spoke gloomily. "Ruddy mist or rain . . . it's worse than the Rannoch Moor!" In those days, before the advent of countless trekkers, the Khumbu valley was a spooky place. The previous night we had heard a crunching noise close to the tent. It was probably just a boulder rolling down a slope, loosened by the damp, but that didn't altogether satisfy my imagination. On the Khumbu glacier I had an unpleasant sensation of being continually watched. This same experience had been mentioned to me by various people who spent time there in the early 1950s.

Throughout the day the weather deteriorated and the temperature fell. It made life uncomfortable but we had the consolation of knowing that the mutton would keep longer.

"Any idea where we are?" John demanded, as dense cloud enveloped us on the glacier. I was supposed to be the expert on local geography, having at one time borrowed a couple of maps from Bill Murray, who was on the Everest Reconnaissance with Eric Shipton in 1951.

"Aye, we're no' far off Tibet," I informed him, wiping large snowflakes off my face.

We spent a cold bivouac on the glacier that night; and awoke to find a fresh covering of snow. Not delaying even for breakfast, we moved on to look for a suitable site for our camp beneath the slopes of Pumori. We couldn't trust the tent, which resembled a sieve, in the full exposure of gale-force winds, but we found a hollow by a pool on the edge of the glacier where we could erect it under an overhanging rock. The following morning we returned to the Base Camp site to collect the rest of our gear and the sack of potatoes.

During the next few days the weather was uncompromisingly foul and we were glad of the security of our small hollow. It was a pleasant spot from which we avidly studied the face of the mountain as best we could during the infrequent clearances in the cloud. During these long hours of waiting for the weather to improve, we discussed a possible route up the peak and decided on a rib on the face, which we felt would offer us some protection from avalanches. These were so frequent that it was like being at a busy railway junction, one deep-throated roar following after another.

I was worried about the cold – though not on my own account. But my suggestion that we should take our precious tatties into our sleeping bags to save them getting frosted met with scant co-operation.

"You can if you want!" John retorted. "It's only a tattie sack you have, anyhow."

After our enforced rest, we began to ferry loads up the slope to where we hoped to establish the next camp. This was on a steep section of the rib where we would have to build a platform for the tent. As the tent was still needed below, the first day's trip consisted of carrying up food and the rope. The climbing was awkward, not the sort of ground where one wanted to carry a heavy rucksack, but there was no alternative. After building a rough ledge, we left a load of mutton and potatoes and could only pray that the cache would not be swept away in an avalanche.

When we set off the next day the weather was little better. We had resorted to headbands for load carrying, worn native fashion, as well as shoulder straps. We could then rest aching shoulders and aching neck muscles alternately. We soon discovered that the exclusive use of the headband gave one a very limited outlook on Nepal, restricted to six feet either side of the path or, as on the mountain, a small section of rock or snow. This was definitely not conducive to route finding.

It was late evening when we reached the platform. Securing our loads to the rocks on one side, we set about enlarging it. Not an easy task since the loose rocks were covered and the snow itself not solid enough to take weight. As darkness was falling we put the tent up. It was bitterly cold and I was glad of my ex-submarine crew mitts, which had cost me two bob.

"It's not that I don't trust our dry-stane dyking," I remarked as we prepared to move inside the tent, "but I'm going to take a belay on that rock face up there. Otherwise we might just tag onto the tail of one of those passing trains," I pointed to a small, hissing slow-moving wet snow avalanche which was passing close by like a large snake.

"A good idea," John agreed. "It'd be a pity to lose height after all our work!"

Later, as we crouched over our fume-belching primus, willing rock-hard potatoes to cook, John complained that the meat wasn't cooked through either, and demonstrated with loud crunching noises. My suggestion that we should save valuable fuel by letting the mutton lollies melt in our mouths was not well received.

Next day we did a recce of the rib in foul weather, returning to our camp early; the climbing rope was frozen like a steel hawser. The conditions were even worse than we had anticipated. Also the primus was as temperamental as a ballerina and the tent was filled with even more noxious fumes than normal.

"Up along the hostile mountains, where the hair-poised snow slide shivers"
[from 'The Explorer']

The following morning we roped up inside the tent and, clad in longjohns under camouflaged army overtrousers and matching anoraks, we set off on what was to be our summit bid and planned to bivouac high on the mountain that night. We wore crampons despite the deep soft snow for there was ice beneath which made the snow very unstable. Keeping to the rock rib as much as possible, we made slow progress, moving together – roped up alpine fashion – except on more difficult sections where we belayed.

We had climbed to a point just under 22,000 feet when the conditions became so dangerous that we realised we would have to retreat or run a high risk of being killed. There were avalanches all around us, fortunately mostly the small, slow-moving wet snow variety which we could dodge, but it was only a matter of time before we would be caught in a bigger one from which there would be no escape. Reluctantly, we decided to retreat and made our way down the unstable rib. Even the rock was loose under the snow. Below us spread the floor of the Khumbu glacier and across the valley we could look into the Western Cwm. I wondered whether there was still some food up there, left by John Hunt's party and I had thoughts of succulent bars of Swiss chocolate.

When we arrived back at our platform, we found our tent had been ruptured. The elements had been just too much for it.

"It looks as if the flea pit hasn't come off as lightly as us," I observed as we started to dig our way into it. "I can see we're going to have an uncomfortable night." There was a large rent down one wall and I reasoned that as John had the best sleeping bag, he should sleep on that side. He muttered something about making capital out of my reciprocating sleeve, but beyond this made no protest. It says much for our early weekends, roughing it in Scotland, that we endured our numerous hardships without complaint and never once quarrelled.

That night was one of the worst I have spent in the Himalayas. Drifting snow came in through the holes in the tent and the rotten fabric began to rip as the weather deteriorated. I had little hope of sleep in the 'sleeve' and spent the night trying the 'internal heat' yoga exercise, without success. I reluctantly came to the conclusion that it is more practical to buy a decent sleeping bag, than to measure the amount of snow melted by faith through the course of a night!

During a frozen mutton breakfast, we talked over our situation. The weather was as bad as ever and the mountain patently in hopeless condition. There was really no alternative but to go down.

We spent the next night back under the rock in our hollow and listened to the wind racing round the mountain. I wasn't exactly snug, but I did manage to generate a bit of a fug in my damp bag and the primus had kindly abandoned its high-altitude 'go slow'.

"That's the queerest high-altitude stove I ever saw," I remarked as we fried one of the last chops over it. "It works better lower down. It'd go like a bomb on the banks of the Dead Sea."

We now had about a pound left for our future ploys in Nepal – above our train fares back to Bombay, so beneath our rock we discussed other possible inexpensive excursions. There was that smart peak we'd seen on the way down from the Dudh Khunde, and the one across the valley from Ghat looked fabulous – straight out of a Walt Disney film.

"But the valley leading up to it looks a swine," I pointed out. "Though it's a fine peak . . . Wait a minute, how about that rock spike, the one the shepherd at Pheriche told us was called Pingero? It would make an interesting day's outing." John agreed so we rummaged around to see how much food we had left: the sum total – one tin of pâté de fois gras and a bar of chocolate. The potatoes had suffered from frostbite and the graveyard of mutton bones didn't look exactly appetising. Next day we jettisoned our useless gear and headed down the glacier to Phulung Karpo, the cluster of yak huts which crouched at the base of Pingero.

Though Pingero is only a subsidiary peak of Taweche, we decided it should afford considerable entertainment if we went directly up the face from the valley floor; hopefully this could be accomplished in one day. That night we pitched the damaged tent beside a yak hut, but it was more as a final gesture against the elements, than as a shelter. The night stayed dry and we awoke before dawn to what promised to be reasonable day. Stealing two turnips from the owner of the hut and feeling slightly guilty, we set off with high spirits and easy strides.

We were travelling light, minus rucksacks, just with the rope and a few rock pegs. We felt like fairies (the proper variety) and climbed fast, mostly unroped except for a few dangerous sections. At one point I was above John and travelling too quickly up steep rock with snow covered holds; I slipped, but was 'fielded' by my companion, literally by the scruff of my neck as he grabbed my anorak hood.

"That was close!" I remarked mildly, regaining my breath. "You might have suffered some discomfort if I'd landed on you with my crampons."

We reached the crest of a ridge, thinking we must be at the top, but still the rock rose above. The cloud had clamped down again and visibility was as bad as a Clydebank fog. Eventually we ran out of mountain on a tiny platform and collapsed thankfully. It was already late evening and we hadn't stopped since dawn. Despite the lateness of the hour, we devoted a few minutes to a repast of turnips and pâté de fois gras.

We then descended by the same route, climbing difficult sections and only using the rope for abseils. Darkness dropped on us like a black sponge before we were even halfway down, but we kept going and, after what seemed a life's span, stumbled down the last boulder-strewn slope to the valley floor. At 2 a.m. we collapsed, exhausted, into our ventilated tent. There was nothing to eat.

In the morning we acquired a few potatoes from a Sherpa and fried them for breakfast. It was a fine meal. Chips and fried tatties are a great invention! Feeling better now, our thoughts turned to the other peak that looked like the Weisshorn which we had seen above the village of Ghat. We decided to move down and have a spy on it.

After ripping a couple of strips of canvas from the tent for handkerchiefs, we decided to donate what remained to the chap who owned the wee hut beside which we had camped.

"After all, we did pinch his turnips, and he can always make a skirt for his missus out of it," I suggested. "Though it would be gae chilly," I added reflectively. "The wind blows right through it."

The Sherpa was overjoyed at the present of our tent and a few rusty pegs made out of sheet steel from the hull of a Clydebank ship. As we headed down the trail with lighter packs, I wondered how annoyed the Mank would be if he knew we'd given away his products to be used for tethering yaks.

As we descended the weather improved and when we reached Thyangboche in the late afternoon the sun was shining, sailing warmly through the clouds. It was good to be alive. There were fried potatoes for tea!

The next two days we spent recuperating at the monastery. We were more tired than we'd realised; the strain of heavy load carrying had taken its toll. On our way back through Namche we called on our police friends and were welcomed like prodigal sons. We had a good meal and loosening our belts set off down the steep hillside to the Dudh Kosi river, heading for our new snow peak. We had been warned by the police of heavy flooding to the south; bridges had been swept away and they told us there was a dire shortage of food, many people were dying.

Late one evening at a small hamlet above the banks of Dudh Kosi, I went outside the tumbledown shack in which we were lodged for the night. I was suffering from toothache and I felt I must also get away from the constant smoke; besides, I was beginning to itch: a sure sign that I'd picked up more 'billie-willies' as Nima sweepingly called bed bugs, fleas, lice and things that go nip in the night. As I stood gazing at the seething river, I heard the sound of approaching music. Presently, a procession of monks dressed in rich robes passed by carrying a lama on a sedan chair. He wore a tall lamistic hat like the Wizard of Oz. I asked a native standing nearby who this dude was.

"Burra Lama, sahib; Rongbuk," he pointed up the valley towards Tibet. It appeared that he was indeed the lama from Rongbuk Monastery in Tibet, on the far side of Mount Everest. The locals gathered round like flies when his entourage stopped outside a substantial house. Presently he installed himself inside on a dais, with his entourage seated cross-legged on the floor in front of him. In a surprisingly short space of time there was a queue of locals with offerings of money and food. In return he placed a white scarf round each of their bowed heads.

Huge urns filled with raksi and chang were produced and

soon there was an undercurrent of subdued but purposeful merriment. I was handed a mug of fiery raksi and motioned to drink. I didn't care for the attitude of the 'waiter' who sported several kukris from his belt; he was obviously the senior dobber of the lama and he stooped over me in a threatening manner, making impatient gestures to me to drink quickly. I achieved this bacchanalian feat, not wishing to cause offence or spoil sport, but was then mortified to see that the mug was instantly recharged with another pint of the foul liquid. I was permitted to drink this in a more leisurely fashion which only prolonged the agony; fortunately I was rapidly becoming anaesthetised.

The noise in the low-ceilinged room was deafening. The lama's band was now swinging and drums competed with long nashangi horns and cymbals. It was like being in a corrugated shed witnessing a competition between sheet-metal workers and blacksmiths. My toothache had disappeared. Then an even nastier bodyguard came over, a one-kukri man, but that kukri was menacingly large. Grabbing me by the hand, he pulled me along through the seated throng. I gave an intoxicated belch as I tried to straighten up. Sitting cross-legged doesn't come naturally to me! Nor does 'walking' with the flat of a kukri pressed down on my scalp as bodyguard two motioned me in no uncertain manner to keep lower than his reverence. The lama was a short man who also appeared to have a short back. As his dais was only the thickness of a couple of Bibles, keeping my six feet lower than him required all the assistance of number two's kukri.

I had observed with some trepidation that when the local people were presented to the lama each in turn offered presents. Coming from such poor people, some of them were substantial: baskets of potatoes and handfuls of rupees which they could obviously ill afford. As I crawled along the floor, I endeavoured to rummage through my pockets to see what I could find. There was nothing but a roll of 16mm cine film which I had picked up at the Everest Base Camp site and which, by some strange chance, was still in my pocket. Taking my weight on one hand, not so easy after a pint and a half of raksi, I placed the roll of film on the dais. I knew that the lama was too well-mannered to inspect it right away and that I would be safely back in our shack before the useless item was examined too closely. 'After all,' I consoled myself, 'it's only etiquette!' The lama then placed a silk scarf round my neck and I wove my way like a drunken crab back to my portion of floor at the back of the room.

As the night wore on the raksi improved and I found myself reciting to a Sherpa some lines from the Rubaiyat:

> "As much as wine has play'd the Infidel,
> and robbed me of my Robe of Honour – well,
> I wonder often what the Vintners buy
> one half so precious as the stuff they sell."

Chang agreed with me better than raksi and it must have been long after the witching hour when I crawled back to our shack. John lay sound asleep.

"Hey, MacInnes, wake up, you great slob!"

I was served with several variations on this theme before I stirred. The faint light inside the hut was painful to my eyes. John was unaware that I'd had an all-night booze-up, having retired to his 20 Below sleeping bag at a respectable hour.

"I had a late night," I pleaded, my throat felt as if I'd been gargling with turps. "I went to a lama party!"

I don't think John ever quite believed me, as the lama and his entourage had already departed; he quietly assumed that I had invented the whole incident to explain the loss of the film which we'd hoped to flog for a few rupees in an Indian bazaar!

At the entrance to the steep valley leading up to our virgin peak stands a small mill driven by the turbulent stream emanating from the gorge. Here we made a hard bargain for a few eggs and more potatoes. Keeping quality office hours now, we set off at 10 a.m. on a fine morning. It wasn't long before we were climbing up the mountain stream reminiscent

47

of a Scottish gully. There were boulders of immense size jammed between rock walls.

Jimmy Roberts, who accompanied John Hunt's Everest Expedition as transport officer, had also noticed this fine peak on his way to Base Camp that year, and had succumbed to the temptation of having a closer look. Instead of making up our valley he sensibly went further down the Dudh Kosi and crossed the watershed to the east, reaching the peak from the Hinku on the far side.

We spent an arduous day, forcing our way up the valley. The climbing was often technically difficult, though the rock, washed by melt water, was good. On either side, green-clad walls rose thousands of feet. The rock problems increased, long, tricky pitches following one after another. Dusk came quickly and suddenly and so we stopped at the foot of one such barrier and decided to spend the night. We lit a fire as there was plenty of fallen timber, and by its warm glow debated how far we had come.

"We must be about a quarter of the way up," I said, watching John as he skilfully turned an egg in our small dixy which seemed to manufacture its own brand of adhesive fat. "And this is the easiest section. It could take about two weeks to get to that ruddy peak this way." I reached over for my share of eggs and chips before continuing, "We don't have a hope – that last section, which we saw from the Dudh Khunde on our way up to Namche, looked desperate: far worse than anything down here."

We had finally decided to review our position in the morning, when John gave a yell, complaining that something was burrowing into his armpit. I had a quick look, using a blazing log as a torch. There were three tick-like insects firmly embedded in his flesh, each about the size of a marble. When I tried to pull them off, I found they had a hard shell which I couldn't grip as my nails were soft from climbing up waterfalls all day. So I tried instead to burn them off with a glowing ember. This manoeuvre only succeeded in raising an oath from my companion.

48

"You know something?" I observed intently. "They're almost out of sight now. But wait a minute! I've got Nima's knife somewhere in my pack; I'll have a go with that." John gave an anguished moan, recalling the saga of the sheep. Although he didn't prove quite as tough as our unfortunate sheep, the knife didn't make a very elegant job of the incisions, but I had thoughtfully taken the precaution of sterilising it in the fire before I began the operation.

The following day, as we had suspected, the difficulties increased, and we knew we didn't have a sinner's chance in heaven of getting up the valley with only four eggs left to our name.

"Let's go to Bombay!" I put forward the motion in exasperation as we arrived at the foot of yet another slimy, vertical wall, with only the occasional small bamboo shoot for a hold. "This is no place for white men!" John seconded the proposal and, without more ado, we started to descend.

We realised that to return through Kathmandu would probably lead to arrest, so I suggested that we should head due south to Jaynagar, on the Indian border. At that time it was a route which had only rarely been taken by white men. It meant traversing part of the Terai, then one of the wildest regions in the world, with tigers, rhinos, bandits, and a superb selection of snakes which would satisfy the most fussy herpatologist.

Soon we were back amongst the leeches. They lurked everywhere; it had been an unusually bad monsoon and in consequence they seemed exceedingly prolific. We had to stop from time to time and wring blood from our socks. The blighters even sneaked through the eyelets of our boots, and got into our hair at the other extremity. We ripped them off in disgust. We were approaching the Dudh Kosi river at Jubing when I complained of a pain in my back.

"Rheumatics," John diagnosed. "You get it after dossing for years under boulders!" I put my pack down and pulled my shirt up, only to discover that the 'bloody' rheumatism had its origin in a large cattle leech.

We stopped on the banks of the Dudh Kosi, well-named

Milk River, by the remnants of a bridge. Floods had removed it recently, so we repaired to a nearby village and sought out the headman. In a halting mixture of Urdu and Nepali, we asked how we could cross the river.

"Tigh high, sahib," was his response. "Tigh high." He then took us into his hut and offered us fried corn on the cob which tasted delicious.

"He doesn't seem to be doing a great deal about getting us over that bloody water," I observed, gratefully stuffing my mouth full of sweet corn. "But I can't say that I mind roughing it here for a bit – at least we'll have something to eat!"

"No doubt it'll go on our bill," my friend observed dryly. But, as we had only ten rupees left to our name, it was doubtful if he could overcharge us.

The headman had meanwhile despatched one of his men, carrying a long horn, down to a promontory beside the river; the instrument was used to signal a village on the opposite bank, situated on a spur about a mile away. Contact with the inhabitants was established and they stretched a thin line across the river – we never found out how – followed by a heavy bamboo rope. This operation took up the remainder of that day and we realised we would have to spend the night in the village. This suited us fine as we were constantly plied with food and chang. Later, the inevitable party got under way. It was apparent that there wasn't much work, and we seemed to be providing them with a contract worth celebrating, though by this time we had convinced the headman that our rucksacks weren't bulging with rupees. We fervently hoped that the villagers would be sober enough in the morning to get us across the river.

The entire village turned out the next morning and we proceeded to the river bank. There was almost a carnival atmosphere. Even our rucksacks were carried for us.

"We're certainly getting the red carpet treatment here, John," I commented, ripping a large leech off my arm. "It's probably the inauguration of a new service . . . in the name of the wee man, look at that rope!" I pointed, horrified.

"Definitely a one-way trip – no wonder we've been fêted like gladiators!"

A taut bamboo rope, about an inch thick, was stretched across the river, forty feet above the white water, and I, for one, didn't fancy crossing it. So I suggested to John that we should test it first with the lightest member. Naturally, he disagreed, pointing out that the argument worked both ways. In the end the fact that I had the camera to record our epic won the day; the sun was just right for photography from the near bank.

Accordingly, John resigned himself to the testing of the apparatus. The villagers provided a U-shaped bit of wood and hung it over the bamboo rope to act as a pulley, whilst a thinner rope was tied to the two legs of the 'U' to form a loop in which John could sit. Another light cord, from the far bank, would be used to pull him across, whilst a rear line enabled the men on our side to bring the 'bosun's chair' back again. There was an air of expectancy amongst the villagers.

"Good luck!" I yelled encouragingly as he was launched from the platform and went swooshing down to the middle of the rope. It sagged ominously, just above the foam. His feet were submerged but the rope held and he was slowly pulled up out of the water onto the far bank. The natives gave a drunken cheer as he was grabbed by welcoming hands. They were obviously pleasantly surprised – so was I!

"Very good," I said to the headman. "I go now . . . kinni paesi?"

"Char rupees, sahib," he beamed, well pleased with his efforts, and emitted an alcoholic belch. "Char rupees," he repeated, holding up four grubby fingers.

"Tigh high," I replied, handing him four rupees. For about 20p we had secured the employment of over a dozen men and received free accommodation, food and drink. Then I shot across the river with much trepidation, whilst John looked on with amusement. From high on the southern bank we looked back to see a queue now waiting to be ferried across. Apparently quite a few people had been wanting to cross the river for some

time, but were unwilling to risk this method of travel before
our safe passage.

We had now reached the point where we had decided to
travel south, rather than west to Kathmandu. Soon we were
traversing narrow footpaths which were the turf walls of
paddy fields. There was much cloud about, quite usual for the
season, but at first there didn't seem to be any great shortage of
food. The people didn't seem any worse off than elsewhere on
our travels. They were at least fatter than we were! I was pure
skin and bone – perforated by leechbites. Gradually food did
become scarcer though, and as the temperature rose it became
increasingly humid. Eventually we neared the Sun Kosi river,
one of the great waterways of Nepal which, like all the rivers in
this part of the world flows ultimately into the Ganges. We
knew we would have to cross this expanse of water and didn't
know if there was a bridge.

One morning, when the sun was frying us from a cloud-free
sky, we suddenly came across the river. We had been journey-
ing through jungle terrain and it lay hidden in a deep cleft
between the hills. There we met a Ghurka soldier going home
on leave who conjured up a bottle of chang like a white rabbit,
which we shared. From his few halting words of English, we
gathered there was a boat; this information was followed by
drunken gestures which we took to represent the paddling of a
canoe; either that or he was practising using a cross-cut saw.

We were right. There were three unpromising dug-outs on
the rocky margin of the river.

"Oh, no!" I groaned, "we haven't got to cross in one of
those?" But we had, and together this time, John gleefully
pointed out.

"How much?" I inquired of a native. One of four ferrymen,
he was dressed in a loincloth, the width of a bandage. He eyed
me shrewdly. His alarm at being confronted with what was
probably the first white man he had seen was swiftly overcome
by his instinct to make a quick chip.

"Das rupee, sahib."

"Come off it, Jimmy! We don't want to buy it, just to go

across – tigh high?" I pointed to the distant bank. Then we dumped our packs on the bank and lay down in the sun. "We'll wear the bastard down, John," I continued, "we've all the time in the world, and four pounds of potatoes!"

There were a couple of other natives close by and I asked them the cost of the ferry before the wily 'Bandage' could intervene. We learned that the charge was one rupee. Without consulting the 'Boss' further, we loaded our packs into the craft and motioned him to be off. Deferred payment terms . . .

I can't say if that trip was worse than crossing the bamboo rope, but it was certainly more prolonged and very frightening. After being launched from the boulder-strewn bank we were in white water in a trice, being swept along like the proverbial water-logged cork. There was virtually no freeboard and the four paddlers forced the craft diagonally across into the main current. Though they were headed for the far bank and paddling furiously, we were travelling downstream at a far greater speed. I wondered where the first waterfall was, but we made it, albeit several hundred yards below from where we had started, and I gave the man his two rupees. He took them with a resigned shrug. Imagine making a living doing that! I thought, you wouldn't have to worry about superannuation!

But the thickets dwined to thorn-scrub and the water drained to shallows,
And I dropped again on desert – blasted earth, and blasting sky . . .
[from 'The Explorer']

We now found ourselves in a country which seemed devoid of food. For the past three years there had been drastic crop failures and now many people were dying from starvation. A new drawback was that the natives were most reluctant to let us sleep in their houses at night. Westerners being an unknown quantity, there was none of the open hospitality we had encountered in the north from the hill people. We developed a

53

technique of moving into a house before its owner could bar the door; once inside, they seldom tried to remove us. One evening our 'host' drew a knife as we were sitting round his fire, and we had to restrain him hastily. However, he was quiet for the rest of the evening and we left in the morning without trouble.

I always slept with a thin cord tied to the rifle attached round my waist, as there had been several attempts to steal it, generally in the depth of night. Two days after the knife incident, at about 3 a.m., I felt a gentle tug like the tentative bite of a timid trout; then a sudden jerk as the weapon was whipped out the bottom of the reciprocating sleeve. I was instantly wide awake, of course, and very nearly minus one arm. I reached down quickly with my unfettered hand and grabbed a bare leg. But the rifle was hurriedly dropped and the leg torn from my grip before I could take a fresh hold.

Okaldunga is a garrison town about halfway on the track south to the Indian border. We thought we might run into trouble there, but the soldiers on duty let us past without question. Once outside the town we were joined by a small bandy-legged man who had obviously skirted round it for some reason. He seemed friendly enough and offered to share some rice with us.

We soon discovered that 'Sandy' was a smuggler. He took drugs to Tibet and usually arranged for coolies to take other items south; on this trip he was travelling alone. He was afraid of dacoits and the wild life of the Terai. It was evident he wished to accompany us as he thought our dishevelled appearance plus rifle – without ammunition – would prove a powerful deterrent to would-be bandits. So he travelled with us for several days.

We came across a village by the name of Dibidab, a cluster of straw huts in the floor of a sun-baked valley. The natives were dressed in loincloths. Here there was food and we were overjoyed when we saw an enormous goose! We would eat it if we could afford to buy it. So we asked Sandy to negotiate.

"Kinni paesi big kukra, Sandy?" I pointed at the proud bird

standing beside a water channel with a smaller version – obviously an offspring – alongside. "The 'burra kukra'," (the big bird), I added quickly.

Our drug smuggling companion obviously pulled a few important strings in this outpost of civilisation and, some time later, inside the goose-owner's hut, a price of two rupees was finally agreed upon. The smiling owner who was a light-skinned man, more like a Tahitan than a Nepali, brought the burra kukra struggling indoors for our approval, displaying it with a flourish as if it was a bottle of vintage wine, before it was led to the slaughter.

"Aye, that's it, Jimmy. I remember the pattern on its chest exactly!" I spoke with true Scots regard to detail, adding in an aside to John, "I didn't want to be caught out." Privately I was thinking my Aberdonian friends would be proud of me.

It seemed an age before the bird was cooked, by which time I had exhausted the supply of saliva which had been flowing freely in anticipation. But in due course we dined sumptuously and afterwards lay back replete on the mud verandah of the hut, idly swatting flies. Suddenly I sat bolt upright.

"Good God – look! I don't believe it!"

"It's impossible," John agreed. "We've eaten it!"

"No we haven't," I answered grimly. "We had the wee bird after all." Just then the owner of the goose came round the corner.

"Kukra tigh high, sahib?" he was still smiling.

"Tigh high – everything O.K.," I confirmed resignedly, sinking down again on the mud floor. I suffered from indigestion that night . . . and dreamt I was an ostrich with my head in the sand. I always seemed to experience these exotic dreams when I ate or drank too much in Nepal. That same night, Sandy tried to steal our rifle. John was up in a flash and put a vicious ankle lock on him; though nothing was said the next day, Sandy limped badly.

We carried on down through the forest and dried-up river beds of the Terai, sometimes forcing our way through tall elephant grass. Water was scarce and we drank from filthy waterholes which, even in our desperate state, sickened us. There were no after-effects: I think we were immune to everything by this time. Sandy still tagged along, dressed in his dirty rags. One day, some ten days south from Ghat, he announced:

"Jaynagar, sahib, do kos [four miles]. Many po-lice." Pressing his hands together, and with a swift salaam, he took a narrow trail across the paddy fields. We never saw him again.

We walked into the dusty streets of this frontier town in the early afternoon, heading for the station, we knew a narrow-gauge railway linked with the main Indian railways. The station-master was most courteous and offered us cold baths. Two large tin tubs were quickly brought into the waiting room which was cooled by a punka wallah's fan, a long blanket-type fan hinged to the ceiling and activated by a cord which passed outside the building. The punka wallah's occupation bore a marked similarity to that of sitting on a toilet seat and continuously pulling the chain – without the familiar noise of gushing water.

We were conveniently immersed in the tubs, flea-ridden clothing piled nearby, and vainly trying to produce a lather from bars of soap which resembled marble, when several formidable Indians in civilian clothes walked in.

"Are you Chinese?" the fattest one (always the boss in the East) demanded truculently.

"Scottish," I murmured apologetically, realising that the authorities had finally caught up with us.

"You come from Tibet?"

"Er, Nepal," John ventured. "We've been on a mountaineering expedition."

"You have passports?"

"Yes, in our anoraks," I pointed to the pile of clothing.

"You must come to the police station. Get dressed, please."

We were marched to the police station between two plain-clothed constables, both armed with the ubiquitous umbrella.

"I think we're being arrested as communist spies," I muttered under my breath to John. At the police station, a tumbledown house plagued by flies, we were subjected to a friendly but thorough interrogation. There was a large fan attached to the centre of the ceiling which revolved so slowly that it hardly succeeded in disturbing the air, let alone the flies who enjoyed a free ride on the merry-go-round.

Our passports were examined in detail and we were questioned closely about our movements. It so happened, however, that one of the police knew John's wrestling partner at Namche Bazar, having attended the same police training course. From that moment on, it was plain sailing. Instead of being thrown into jail, a hospitable programme was planned for us. That day we were introduced to all the smugglers in the town, who greatly enhanced the meagre salary of the police. They were described as first, second and third class smugglers, depending on their contributions. Our new friends were eager to offer us all the amenities of the main street. On either side were stalls, half open and half screened by a bamboo curtain. Within the screened portion the only furnishing was a charpoi, and seated on a small stool in each 'window' section was a gorgeous girl.

"You must take your pick," the inspector urged us. "You play, we pay," he gave a lecherous laugh.

"I don't think I'll bother," I said hurriedly. "I'm tired enough as it is, but I could do with a good meal . . ."

"Certainly, certainly," our newly acquired friend beamed. "You must excuse me – first things first. One must get the priorities right, as you say in England . . . er . . . Scotland. We will have a banquet. Anyhow, you are right about the girls, my friend," he said, taking me by the shoulder. "You know," he added confidentially, "You can buy a rifle here for the same price as a woman, £25, but it's difficult to know which is the most dangerous!" And he doubled up with laughter at his own observation.

We stopped further up the road and the owner of a filthy shop was summoned. There was a scurry of swarthy bodies and a table and several chairs appeared out in the middle of the street. It seemed we were to have our meal there.

"Isn't there a chance of being run down?" John asked apprehensively. Though there wasn't much motor traffic, there were plenty of rickshaws and noisy horse-drawn buggies, their progress heralded by an alarming hooting of horns and ringing of bells.

"I run this town," the inspector beamed again. "If I want my guests to dine in the main street, they dine in the main street!" He leaned over to me, spitting a mouthful of betal nut to the side; "Anyway, the restaurant is smelly, it's better here."

Our plates were large leaves and we ate with our fingers. I don't know when I have enjoyed such a good meal; course after course, ending with Indian sweetmeats. The curried 'chicken' which we ate was probably crow – I learnt later that it was quite a common dish there, but it tasted delicious anyway.

We weren't allowed to leave Jaynagar until we had given a lecture at the local school. The main classroom was packed and as steamy as a Chinese laundry. We were amazed to find that none of the pupils, all of whom could speak a reasonable amount of English, knew where Mount Everest was situated. In the afternoon we boarded the narrow gauge train en route for Bombay. It seemed that the entire populace had turned out to see us off. Even the smugglers were there – probably on police orders.

# 2

# Callery Gold

There are strange things done in the midnight sun,
By the men who moil for gold . . .
        [Robert Service, from 'The Cremation of Sam McGee']

"YOU JUST SUCK IT up into the mouth of this enormous kind of vacuum cleaner and it goes straight into a big sack."

"What goes into a big sack?" inquired Dave Dawe, knocking back a large glass of vodka as though it was water.

"Sheep-shit," the man replied emphatically in a loud voice. "There's a fortune to be made reconstituting it. We just mix in a few of our chemicals once it's forced dried and we've got a fantastic fertiliser."

"You'd be better inventing special crap catchers to attach to the sheep," I suggested, thinking of an easier way to do the job.

"We should stick to our gold-prospecting plans, Hamish," Dave muttered. "It's dirty money. Imagine, earning your bread collecting crap!"

We were at a party in Christchurch, New Zealand, given in our honour prior to a winter's gold-hunting trip to the West Coast of the South Island. As such parties can last a week, the present one at ten hours old was in its infancy. So far I hadn't noticed any signs of fatigue, although three guests had accidentally refreshed themselves in the fish pool; another had almost committed arson by igniting a 'fuse' to a bottle of high octane gut-rot rejoicing in the name of 'Hokitika Fire'. A trail of this liquor substituting for a fuse led across the lounge carpet to where the remains of the upturned bottle reposed under a bureau. The owner of the establishment had fortunately repaired to the kitchen where he was fully occupied mixing a large cocktail in the washing machine and so failed to witness the pyrotechnics.

It was a few months since I had returned from Nepal to Christchurch; solvent once again, I had agreed to join Dave in his gold venture.

Dave had a perpetual mistrust of life, taking everything with a pinch of salt and always ready to pounce on a careless remark and tear it to shreds. He was a brilliant conversationalist and it was stimulating simply to be in his company. I had met him shortly after returning from the Himalayas and we struck up an immediate friendship.

Tom Paul and Bill Smith of the Creagh Dhu had arrived in New Zealand whilst John Cunningham and I were in the Himalayas. They had brought a car (a present from my father to me) on board ship with them. But upon arrival they were faced with an exorbitant duty payable on the vehicle which they were totally unable to meet. By pleading poverty and explaining that the 'owner' was somewhere in the Mount Everest region (thus appealing to nationalism in the light of Ed Hillary's recent success), they were granted temporary possession of it, pending my return. Both had come over as 'assisted emigrants'; but when they were directed to jobs in the North Island, away from the mountains and their Creagh Dhu friends, they simply moved south. Their stay in Christchurch was short however, as the authorities soon caught up with them. Taking advantage of my car for midnight flits, they made a forced but interesting working tour of the South Island. I took possession of the car when I returned to Christchurch, by which time both Tommy and Bill were heartily glad to see the last of it.

"It's worse than a bloody millstone, MacInnes," Bill complained bitterly.

"Aye," added Tommy, "at least you don't get punctures in millstones!" The long sea voyage, during which the car was lashed on deck, had evidently had an adverse effect on the tyres! What was worse, it appeared to be suffering from internal disorders, difficult to diagnose, so I part-exchanged it without regret for an early racing motor cycle, a CS1 Norton, a vintage thoroughbred, then still capable of over 100 m.p.h. The cash difference enabled me to repay my brother who had lent me the money to get back to New Zealand from Bombay, and still left enough loot for me to invest in the gold venture.

I never did return to my health-food landlady in Christchurch. I had had quite enough of raw food by that time, so I leased a rather colourless flat instead. Typical of furnished accommodation, despite the fact that the house was situated in a respectable part of the city, the flat was nothing more than a suburban slum. The front door hadn't been used for years and my rooms couldn't be reached if anyone was using the bathroom-cum-toilet, since the only usable door was the back one. Part of the central hall had been inexpertly converted to form the bathroom and the original bathroom was now the communal kitchen. Unfortunately, I had a neighbour who suffered from constipation so, at times, my patience was sorely tried! I must have contributed to the general discord as one day, after a rather noisy party, I was given an eviction order by the landlady, a woman with eyes like the points of knitting needles. "And I thought you were such a quiet chap," she whined as she pronounced me homeless.

As far as gold prospecting was concerned, I was a greenhorn or 'new chump', as they are called. However, I made a point of finding out all I could about it before we departed. There were many people about, even in Christchurch, who had prospected at some time and I gleaned some useful hints. Two old prospectors, Donald the Dag and Thomas the Turd, told me about gold found in the moss thirty feet above the water level in the area we were going to. This was flood gold which was removed by burning the moss and mixing the remains with mercury in a retort. The mercury is then vaporised to separate the metals. It was amusing to see the old timers' faces light up at the mention of panning and soon I found that I, too, had become smitten by the gold-fever bug. I suppose we are all gamblers at heart, and the thought of making a quick legal buck is irresistible.

Our objective was the Callery Gorge which is situated in dense bush country close to the Franz Josef glacier. Clearly we would need to travel light, so I set about designing and manufacturing a special lightweight sluice box in the short time before departure. A sluice box is normally a wooden channel with battens fixed transversely across its floor at intervals, and with something like coconut matting in between them. When the box is put in a tailrace and shingle is shovelled in one end, the force of the water carries the shingle over the battens, while heavier particles – such as gold – are trapped on the matting floor behind the battens. My lightweight version was eight feet long and made of aluminium but it separated into three sections for ease of transport.

Loaded with piles of swag we left Christchurch by train, crossing Arthur's Pass, the rail and road route over the divide of the Southern Alps. At Hokitika the payment of 5/– obtained us 'Miners' Rights' which permitted one to prospect on Crown land and to stake claims if necessary. Miners' Rights included many fringe benefits such as being able to build a house on a claim. Even in 1955 'Hoki' as it is affectionately known, still had the air of a gold-rush town, albeit without the gold! There was an incredible number of pubs, each sporting a large frontage which obviously once rejoiced in fresh paintwork, but was now in a sad state of repair. Behind each grand façade were concealed small corrugated huts.

The West Coast of New Zealand is in many ways similar to the west of Scotland. It is a land unto itself. The climate, differing from the rest of the country is, also like the west of Scotland, extremely damp. When we arrived in May it was cold and wet since it was the beginning of winter. The glaciers of the West Coast, principally the Franz Josef and the Fox, are unusual for New Zealand in that they extend right down to the fringe of the sub-tropical forest with its native trees, rimu and rata, and the many umbrella-like tree ferns. I caught my first glimpse of the ice as the ancient bus, now our mode of transport, panted through a tunnel of greenery and found every pothole on the shingle road from 'Hoki' to Waiho. By good luck Dave recognised a friend in the shape of a mountain guide based at the nearby Glacier Hotel: Peter McCormack was, I discovered, a warm-hearted West Coaster who had inherited much of his Celtic ancestors' sense of hospitality.

"What are you doing over here, Dave?" he inquired genially.

"Going on a wee trip up the Callery. This is my cobber, Hamish MacInnes."

"The Callery now, well, well . . . I suppose it's gold you're after?" He glanced at us knowingly.

"Well, we thought of taking a short holiday," Dave answered evasively.

"Queer place for a holiday, Dave!" he laughed and added, "where are you staying?"

"We're looking," Dave replied. "Any ideas?"

"Sure – stay in my shack," he pointed down the road in the direction we had just come. "The Stork Club, a hundred yards down on the left. It's the place to hold parties, well out of earshot of the hotel."

After we'd had a meal we went up to the hotel to have a word with Peter or Alec Graham, two well-known figures on the Coast. We were interested to know more about that gold which prospectors had found in moss, high above the normal water level.

In his day Peter Graham had been one of the great pioneer guides in the New Zealand Alps. His record over two decades was astounding and most of his climbs had been made without the use of crampons. He was still an erect figure, but had to use a stick to get about. When we met him that evening, he was slightly surprised to see Dave.

"Hello, Peter," Dave began – there isn't much formality in the Antipodes – "we've come to try our luck in the Callery."

"Well, it's cleaned out, you know," Peter replied, a little disconcerted, no doubt regretting the enthusiasm which he had displayed the previous summer when Dave had sounded him out as to the possibility of working the creek again. Peter had said then that there must be a worthwhile reef in the upper reaches, though possibly still under the ice.

"Hamish and I thought we'd have a go, anyhow," Dave continued unabashed. "We've got some new gear for the job."

"If there is an exposed reef," Peter answered cautiously, now a gleam in his eyes, "there should be traces lower down. It's not worth your while forcing a route to the upper reaches if you don't find colours at Long Beach." Long Beach was a comparatively open section of the gorge which had yielded a large quantity of gold in the past.

That evening and over the next few days we heard many of Peter Graham's tales of the early days at Waiho. It was Peter and his brother Alec, also a guide, making new routes and taking such good care of their clients, who laid the foundation for other great mountain guides to build upon: men such as Mick Bowie and Harry Ayres had the example set by 'Mr. Peter' and 'Mr. Alec' to follow. As a young man Peter had investigated the upper section of the Callery in the hopes of making his fortune. And both Peter and Alec had struck it rich working the Waiho river, close to the mouth of the Callery. There had been other rich claims made at the confluence of the Callery and Waiho rivers. One miner called 'German Harry' after a hard climb of 5000 feet followed by a precipitous descent into the Gorge then forced a route over Mount Mueller and Mount Burster, no mean mountaineering feat in those days, and reached the head of the Callery. He collected several ounces of gold and saw "many nuggets lying in crevices". Upon his return to Waiho for fresh supplies, his information was so enthusiastically received that several men sat up all night, sewing canvas bags in which to carry the gold out! But the weather had the last word then as it does now in the New Zealand Alps and the three men who returned with Harry were beaten by a severe June flood which washed away the gold.

Originally, it was considered impossible to enter the Callery from below. But in the late 1800s several determined attempts were made to get up the gorge. A hardy miner called Jim Nesbit reached the snout of the Spencer glacier, and George Park repeated the route in over Mount Burster; he managed to collect 5-lb of gold in as many minutes, prising the nuggets out of crevices with the aid of his penknife. In 1891 he made his last trip, accompanied by his brother and Charles Reeves. They explored the head of the Callery glacier and looked over into Whataroa from its crest.

The rich strikes at Waiho which the early miners made were all due to gold being washed down from the Callery. The best claims had been made at one of two 'beaches', Little Beach, a rough boulder-strewn section of the gorge adjoining a bigger brother, Long Beach. There is undoubtedly a reef in the upper regions which will eventually become exposed – but when? Our plans were based on this hope. Three decades before, Peter had worked on the same hypothesis, but neither he nor any other miner had ever located the reef.

Early one morning, while the tree ferns were still decorated with frost, we left the Stork Club and made our way along the footpath to the mouth of the Callery.

"The birds make a hell of a racket in this part of the world, Dave," I complained breathlessly, for our packs seemed to weigh a ton.

"They've probably heard on the bush telegraph that we're headed for the Callery and are pissing themselves laughing!"

"I just hope it isn't as bad as I rather fear. Who was last up there?"

"I'm not sure," he replied casually, peering down into the waters; we had halted for a breather. "It must have been some time ago, possibly it was Harry Ayres, the guide."

Four hours later we were making snail-like progress when we came upon a solid wall of Supple Jack, a sinewy serpent-like vine. The sluice box parts which were piled on top of my pack frame were constantly being ensnared, I felt as if I was dragging a clothes drying rack through a barbed-wire entanglement. I suggested to Dave that it would be politic to dump most of the gear, cut a trail through the undergrowth, and return later for our equipment. This plan was approved and duly accomplished.

Towards the turn of last century, the County Council had paid £50 to have a trail cut up the south side of the Callery. Even then, it wasn't an easy path; the terrain is incredibly steep. The track had hugged the edge of the gorge for the first three miles and along this stretch there had been about a dozen ladders, made from long lancewood poles, to overcome awkward bluffs. This trail no longer existed for the voracious bush had enveloped it again. Only occasionally did we come across the remains of a rotted ladder or an old blaze mark. I made my Hansel and Gretel contributions with new blaze marks using my short axe. But we used slashers to cut the vines and as I worked I remembered hearing from some friends who had patiently worked their way through Supple Jack in Fiordland using secateurs.

Despite the fact that the bush was very dense in the gorge, the occasional promontory offered glimpses of the glaciers far ahead. Another landmark on this 'Midas trail' was Nesbit's Slide on the far bank of the river. Here a miner called Nesbit was reputed to have put his shovel down for an instant, whereupon it shot 1500 feet straight into the river. A few months before our trip friends of ours had descended the ridge opposite – the Burster – and found the going so fraught with difficulty that they had to climb from the top of one tree to the next in order to make any progress; but they didn't make it into the Callery. One of these climbers was called Marty Tessab whose several claims to fame included a unique talent of belching the National Anthem and the more enviable ability to retain his water for up to thirty hours during the often protracted bad weather in the Southern Alps.

"The Burster certainly looks rough," I said to Dave as we stopped for a breather on top of a moss covered bluff. "Those old timers must have been tough bastards to come over there!"

"And mad," Dave observed dryly. "But probably not as mad as us; at least there was the chance of making a lot of bread then!" As this was the first doubt Dave had voiced, I was slightly amused and couldn't resist teasing:

"So you think we're wasting our time?"

"Not at all," he replied hastily. "There must be a reef somewhere." Picking up my axe, I made a long blaze on a rata tree, muttering determinedly: "Just making sure we'll find our way back out of this hole. I've no intention of spending my last days lost in a green grave!"

Bush-whacking is a depressing occupation at the best of times. Continual damp, lack of light and the sheer timelessness of it makes it frustrating and exhausting.

"At least we don't have any sandflies at this time of year," Dave commented breathlessly, slashing viciously at yet another wall of Supple Jack. "You don't know how bad they can be!"

"I'm well enough acquainted with the Scottish midge though," I reminded him. With them you get more punctures to the square inch, only the bite isn't so bad.

It was late evening before we arrived, shattered, at Little Beach. Our dripping clothes were just beginning to stiffen for the evening promised to be frosty.. Through gaps in the canopy we caught glimpses of the precipitous bush-clad face across the river which climbed in a curtain of foliage to merge with the blue at a neck-craning angle. I started to put up a tarpaulin we had brought as a fly and revised what I had read of the Callery. Burster camp lay upstream across the river; it was an eight-hour trek from Waiho. It was there that most of the gold was winkled from crevices; small nuggets jammed tight in cracks, nature's gold fillings! The prospectors had cut and blazed the trail for two and a half miles beyond Burster to within a mile of the Spencer glacier. Four men were employed in making this trail and they had to provide their own food and equipment. One of them, Arthur Woodham, had set up a tailrace here at Little Beach. He thought it might be worth investigating for he found some traces but, running out of supplies, was forced to return to Waiho. When he told his fellow trail-makers about the colours he'd found, they came up and with his permission set to work, obtaining 75-lb of gold within two weeks! It was tough luck on Arthur. There are plenty of similar tales about the 1870 gold rush, but few of them have been recorded.

The following morning we returned for the gear we had cached and made good progress back to camp. In the evening we had time for a quick look round the beaches. Dave found one small gold nugget the size of a matchhead. Next morning everything was frozen solid. But, wearing gloves and duvets, we climbed down to the beach, determinedly clutching our gold pans to prospect for colours. If there are colours, that is traces of gold particles, then a tailrace can be set up with the sluice box. The river itself was not frozen, being fast-flowing, but the shingle was, so it was with some difficulty that we washed the gravel thoroughly until only the heaviest and smallest particles were left in the pan. It was cold, back-breaking labour. Colours were few and far between.

"Doesn't look as if we'll make a fortune here, Dave," I said gloomily. "More profitable sucking up sheep-shit!"

"No, not many traces," he agreed, gazing at the narrow cleft of the gorge. "How about climbing along the rock walls? No prospector could have managed to get in there, surely?" He pointed to the almost vertical rock faces through which poured the waters of the Callery.

It was midday before we had rigged the ropes for our descent of the walls. The gorge was so narrow that even at that time of day there was little light. Here at twelve noon one could see the planet Venus. It reminded me of being in a mine, though evidently not a goldmine!

"Hey, Dave!" I yelled presently above the roar of the river. "I've found a good nugget." It wasn't a big one, only a few pennyweights, but I got a tremendous kick from the find. As I prized it from a crack with the tang of a file, I almost dropped it in my excitement. This would have been disastrous since I was hanging 70 feet down the face on the end of a rope which was anchored to a tree at the time!

"I've got one as well," he shouted. "But I'll have no trouble carrying it!"

So intent were we on our quest that it seemed no time before darkness came down like a pot lid. We had found a number of nuggets during the day but their total value was peanuts.

"How did you fare?" I asked Dave as we pulled ourselves over the cliff face.

"About enough to pay for our dinner, if we have bread and jam," he answered wryly.

"Well, I don't suppose I've made a fortune either," I looked down at the small collection of irregular nuggets which felt surprisingly heavy. "But it's encouraging." I thought wistfully of those two prospectors, Friend and Watson, with their three helpers, here at Little Beach. Between them they washed up an average of one pound weight of gold per day. "You know, Dave," I said as we coiled up the ropes, "we were born into the wrong century. Imagine being here back in 1871 . . ."

"I've often felt like that, I must admit – but at least we've still got plenty of mountains to climb!"

We were both sitting round the fire; I served up the meal on two tin plates. Dave chose what appeared to be the larger portion of dinner; but as I had carefully hollowed out the potato mash he was soon looking daggers at me, having discovered the trick. When climbing together we had adopted a policy of one dividing, the other choosing; obviously there were certain drawbacks, as Dave had found out!

During the next week we worked the cliffs in the vicinity of the Beaches but with little further success. After we had squeezed the last small nugget from its crack, a cold and exhausting business whilst hanging on ropes, we decided to call it a day. Like German Harry's bag-makers, we didn't have any trouble carrying our gold! We left our mining equipment and even the flysheet, lying on the tiny patch of level ground where we had camped, the only flat area we had seen in the whole region. Now we had finally decided to pull out, we were overjoyed at the prospect of leaving this gloomy hole; it had a depressing effect and we were looking sallow from lack of sunlight.

We finally emerged from the shadow of the 4000-foot high

walls of the Callery in the late evening. It was a joy to walk on a proper path again, to be able to move without wrestling ceaselessly with vines, or being constantly dripped upon.

"A schooner of beer and one of cider!" We had dumped our packs inside the bar door of the Glacier Hotel. Heavy rain bounced on the corrugated iron roof. It was only when I had drained my glass and ordered refills that I noticed an old man sitting at the end of the bar.

"Who's that old bloke?" I nudged Dave who was apparently hypnotised by his beer.

"Oh, that's Old Jim," Dave answered. "I didn't see him."

Jim was bent over a large glass and appeared to be almost asleep, though his eyes were open. He looked up as Dave went over and silently held out his nuggets for inspection. A high falsetto laugh was emitted by the sourdough, for he had prospected in the Yukon way back before coming over for the New Zealand goldrush.

"Hee-he-he . . . Where've you been, lads?" he demanded with a twinkle in his faded eyes. Dave scrawled his reply on the back of a cigarette packet, for Jim was stone deaf.

"Someone can't have liked you!" Jim chortled with glee. "That place is only fit for rats and bush baptists, hee-he-he . . . I remember being holed up there with a big Maori in 1890." As he recalled the incident, Jim's drooping tea-stained moustache quivered. "After three weeks we'd no tucker left, ho-ho . . . I had to run for my life; the big bastard was going to eat me!"

Jim was in a reminiscent mood that night so we listened spellbound to stories of the old days on the Coast. He told us of a particular party down the coast, a place where the giant moths were unusually plentiful and these had provided the raw material for an unusual competition. Here he paused to wipe some droplets of rum from his chin, before concluding triumphantly:

"I beat them all! I ate thirty-four. I was ill for weeks afterwards though . . . It wasn't the moths, they tasted fine. But the drunken so-and-so's gave me mothballs; they said the moths would perforate my stomach!"

Another time Jim was down a mine, preparing to blast gold-bearing quartz, when the charge accidentally went off and he was buried alive. His dog escaped the fall and went yelping for help to Jim's partner who was panning a short distance away. The dog led him to where his master lay buried and thus saved Jim's life. But ever since that day Old Jim has been stone deaf, and he's always had a dog.

"Sometimes I had little more than the clothes I stood up in, and a few blankets," he told us. "But the whole West Coast of New Zealand's South Island was swindled from the Maori for about the same amount. Twelve rums is usually my limit," he continued confidentially, taking an enormous gulp, "but to-night I've had fourteen. Last June I didn't make it back to my shack; I woke up blooming cold in the morning – hee-he-he . . . I'd been lying in the stream bed all bloomin' night!"

Later, Peter McCormack came in with Harry Ayres, the Chief Guide. After hearing of our adventures, Peter suggested we should move back into the Stork Club until we had decided what to do.

"You chaps looking for a job?" queried Harry.

"Could be," I answered non-committally, "we haven't had much luck in the Callery."

"Come and see me in the morning. There's bound to be something doing. I've been in the same boat myself; I know what it's like to strike a bad patch."

So Dave and I spent an enjoyable two months trail-cutting at the Glacier Hotel and got to know Harry well; like Peter Graham before him, Harry Ayres was one of the great New Zealand guides, and we became good friends. That winter we also did a fair bit of climbing, probably the first serious climbing to be done in the winter months in New Zealand. On the first ascent of the West Face of Mount Rudolf, a peak on the Main Divide, Dave had his fingers badly frostbitten whilst bivouacking near the summit. When spring came along we got itchy feet and decided to return to Christchurch en route for a summer's climbing in the Hermitage region.

But we returned to Franz Josef later that same year. The

hotel had been burned down shortly after we left and, after inspecting the ruins briefly, we caught sight of a solitary figure sitting on an upturned box, a dog at his feet. It was Old Jim. He didn't recognise us; an old man wrapped up in his thoughts. He looked incredibly lonely and we didn't disturb him. The lines of an anonymous poem flitted through my mind as we walked away:

> Change was his mistress, Chance his councillor,
> Love could not hold him, Duty forged no chain:
> The wide seas and the mountains called to him.
> And grey dawns saw his camp-fire in the rain.

# 3

# The Prospect
# of Christmas

All thing which that schineth as the gold
Nis not gold as that I have heard it told.
[Chaucer, *Canon's Yeoman's Tale*]

MY STAY IN NEW ZEALAND was a series of adventures; I did
everything from lumberjacking to prospecting, but I spent
most of my time mountaineering and got to know the Central
Alps as well as some of the lesser ranges. I climbed mostly with
Dave Dawe and another New Zealander, Ken Hamilton, and
two Americans, Peter Robinson and Dick Irvin.

It was Dick who accompanied me on another fortune-
making ploy in search of paua shells. When polished, these
large blueish, translucent shells are used for ornaments and
jewellery. I had been told about them by Maori fishermen, and
of how one of their friends made £600 in one week (a lot of
money in 1956), just picking the shells up from the high tide
mark where they are washed up from time to time by storms
of the Tasman Sea. It seemed easy pickings to me.

"If you need a quick buck for your next Himalayan trip,
Hamish," one of them had remarked, "this is it! We can drop
you off on that coast anytime."

I had kept this offer in the back of my mind and so one day
Dick and I turned up at the port of Bluff in the south of South
Island, to hitch a lift from my friends, the cray fishermen, to

the Fiordland coastline. We had also arranged for an amphibian aircraft to pick us up from a remote inland lake, close to the area we were going to work, in ten days' time for there was to be no guarantee that the fishermen could get us back – they could be anywhere on the coast when we needed them. It was strictly a one-way passage.

We were rowed ashore in a dingy from the crayfisher early in a coppery dawn amidst cries of good luck from the remainder of the crew. The Maori who rowed us to the deserted rocky beach, Andrew by name, was an expert oarsman and took us through the surf like a taxi driver going through rush-hour traffic, taking us right into a steeply shelving beach where we jumped out smartly and scrambled up the debris-littered shingle. Giant baulks of timber lay everywhere.

We pitched camp nearby for we were impatient to start working. An hour later we were methodically working our way along the shore like a couple of industrious oyster-catchers, Dick slightly nearer the water than I, each wearing an empty rucksack for collecting shells on the return journey. There was an encouraging abundance of pauas so we built small colourful cairns with them as we moved south.

During the next few days we combed those intriguing beaches, often climbing headlands of sheer rock, and with little leisure for eating during the day – working all the daylight hours; anyway, we didn't have much food. We had hoped to shoot a deer or, more optimistically, a wapiti. Needless to say, we saw little game except seals which we didn't like to kill. It was too much like shooting your pet dog. Leviathan bones, bleached by sun and sea, lent the beach an aura of an extended graveyard. This was a famous whaling coastline in the early 1800s and for a time there was a thriving industry. Ghost towns can still be found south of where we were working.

"I guess we've enough shells now, MacInnes. What do you think?" Dick leant on the rifle as he swatted sandflies.

"Yes, but how in the name o' the wee man are we to carry them to the lake?" I asked, dismayed at the prospect of abandoning any wealth. We broke up the shells, keeping only

74

the thicker section of each, and so managed to reduce an enormous pile of them down to two very heavy loads. We then had to find our way inland to the lake where we'd arranged our amphibious pick up.

"It was your ruddy idea." Dick pointed an accusing finger. "I'm beginning to suspect that you're a super optimist. Has anyone ever reached this lake before? I know it's marked on the map, but that's from an aerial survey."

"Well, I don't know exactly," I confessed lamely. "But it's not very far! The pilot seemed quite confident of landing there."

"The aeroplane doesn't have to go through that bush! I've been thinking about it for the past few days," continued my companion, warming to his task, "you'd need to have the head and body of a ferret to make a passage . . ."

Dick was right, of course. When we tried to ferry our first load, following a compass bearing towards the lake, we were confronted by dense bush. There was, however, the odd game trail, and it was on one of these that we shot a deer.

"Aye, this'll fill a hole in my stomach, Dick," I said gleefully, as I put down the rifle.

"True enough, but we're going to have a job butchering it without a knife – I've lost mine and it was the only one we have."

"We'll use the tang of this file," I replied, always ready to improvise. So we cut – or rather, hacked – two haunches from the still warm carcass and pressed on.

"These bloody game trails never seem to run in the right direction, Dick!" I spoke despairingly as I fought a wall of impenetrable bush. It was late evening already and we hadn't covered a mile.

"Yes, it looks pretty hopeless," he agreed. "What the hell are we to do then? That god-damned plane will be coming the day after tomorrow." He sat down on his pack which emitted a dull clank from the shell shrapnel, sounding as if he was a traveller in broken pottery.

"Let's go back to the beach," I suggested. "It's our only

75

hope. I feel like an overgrown flea doing a slalom through a hairbrush!"

"Starving or not, I'm leaving this bloody venison," said Dick in disgust. "Just look at me! You'd think I worked in an abattoir." He did in fact look as if he had just despatched Mary Queen of Scots. I watched him hurl the haunch away into the undergrowth.

Following our blaze marks, we reached the shore long after darkness had fallen and immediately built a real white man's fire – one which you had to stand twenty feet from. The night was speckled with stars and the Southern Cross hung magnificently in the heavens. We were utterly bushed, and recognised a new meaning to the word.

A boat was going to be our only chance, but it was the following evening, as we were again sitting by our fire, dozing and wondering what we could eat since we had finished the venison and there was no further sign of game, when we heard a shout out to sea. It was a fishing boat whose crew had spotted our signal fire. They had been keeping a weather eye on this part of the coast as our friends had warned other boats by radio of our whereabouts and it is probably due to their forethought and no doubt their more accurate appraisal of our enterprise that we were picked up at all.

It was difficult boarding the cockleshell dinghy which was sent in for us through the heavy surf, but the truculent craft was eased in with uncanny skill, stern first, close to a large rock. At the appropriate moment we each in turn jumped down into it. All Maoris are fantastically hospitable, so I was dismayed when we were each handed a plate containing just four fried cod livers. I reckoned I could have eaten the several tons of crayfish in the hold. But the cook laughed at me when he saw my expression:

"You just eat those, fellah," he urged. "There are plenty more . . . and if you gobble them all it will be my shout at the bar in Invercargill when we get back."

Sure enough, they proved to be so rich that I even had to leave one, though they tasted delicious. Ice cream and tinned fruit followed, washed down with a mug of scalding coffee.

"Well, thanks lads," Dick drawled finally, in his strong Californian accent, "I was just wondering how MacInnes would taste when you saw our fire. It was either him or a big bull seal which lived in a cave near our camp: an aggressive bugger."

"You know something, Dick? The Scotsman's reputation for being tough is based on the taste of headhunters and cannibals, not on his strength and powers of endurance. The seal would have been a better bet!"

"I dunno," mused a huge grinning Maori, propped up against a bunk. "My grandfather used to say that the *pakiha* tasted really good, provided he didn't smoke." This sally brought a roar of laughter from the rest of the crew.

The shells didn't make us much cash; we had apparently kept the wrong pieces when we broke them up!

My climbing days in New Zealand were more successful than my money-making ploys, and I managed to do some enjoyable routes. I climbed Mount Cook, the highest peak in the Dominion, several times. On one such solo climb of the mountain I ascended Zurbriggen's Route, ostensibly to leave a cache of food on the summit for use when I attempted another route, a new one, later that year. On the way down the Linda glacier, the normal descent, I had to jump a large crevasse and unwittingly dropped my gloves on the edge of the uphill side of it. Two friends descending, having climbed the mountain by another route that day, saw the gloves lying on the brink of this gaping chasm (probably about 100 feet deep) and assumed that their owner had met with an early, though not – when they found that it was me. – an unexpected death. They seemed distinctly put out when they found me installed in the hut, hale and hearty and drinking tea!

"Do you realise, MacInnes, that we spent ages trying to climb down to your body in that crevasse . . . ?"

I was fortunate enough to spend several months at Milford

Sound in the heart of Fiordland. This is now a tourist jampot but it is still one of the finest areas of natural beauty in the world. A great attraction is the Milford Track which is close to the Sutherland Falls, one of the highest waterfalls in the world. The Track leads over the MacKinnon Pass which was discovered by Quintin MacKinnon in 1888. Close to the bottom of the Falls is the Quintin Hut.

During my stay at Milford I did some flying with a bush pilot; one of our jobs was to airdrop supplies at the Quintin Hut. Our target this time, we were informed over the radio, was some sheets of corrugated iron. We left the then hummocky and rather abbreviated airstrip hacked from the bush close by the hotel, where I was warned by the pilot: "Keep two bags of coal on the wing beside the cabin, Hamish, ready to chuck off in case we can't clear the trees at the far end of the runway!" Fortunately, I didn't have to perform the emergency drill and in due course the coal hit the centre of the corrugated sheets beside the Quintin Hut, bang on target. Imagine our surprise when, as we flew round in a self-congratulatory circuit after the fourth direct hit, two horses emerged from underneath – we had demolished the stable! Our other drops were equally accurate but none so misdirected; we even succeeded in sending a supply of newspapers through the open door of the Hut. It certainly gave one a kick, banking round in the narrow valley under the great Falls which cascade in three tremendous leaps, almost 2000 feet from Lake Quill to the valley floor.

Another interesting excursion I took in Fiordland was sparked off by a visit to Hollyford Valley. This valley runs in south-eastwards from Martins Bay – which lies up the coast from Milford Sound – following the Hollyford River to join up with the Milford road at the southern end of the Darran Range. The Darran mountains are rugged, precipitous peaks, the highest of which is the snow-cowled Mount Tutoko, 9042 feet. My companion this time was Ken Hamilton, a tall, dark, quietly spoken man – an expert skier as well as a formidable climber. We had been attempting to climb a virgin peak known

78

as the 'Barrier Virgin', now called Mount Sabre, but had been thwarted by a strong party from Invercargill who, upon hearing of our plans, had jumped in ahead of us and beaten us by a day to the first ascent. We consoled ourselves by making the first ascent of the West Twin, a fine peak though not in the same elegant class as the Virgin.

At the remote hut on the shores of Lake Adelaide, in the heart of the Darran Range, we had spoken to its sole occupant, an Englishman, who had told us of the Invercargill party's triumph.

"You're Hamish MacInnes?" he then continued.

"That's right," I looked at him, astonished that anyone should recognise me in this remote place.

"We did some climbing back home together in Glencoe. Remember? Raven's Gully and Agag's Groove in the winter with Chris Bonington?"

"Of course," I shouted, "John Hammond! Imagine meeting you here . . . What are you doing?"

I gathered that John had just come over for a holiday from Canberra, where he was engaged in government work; he was returning to the United Kingdom that autumn. He had come in with our friendly rivals from Invercargill but, due to a slight injury, had not accompanied them on the route. I left some climbing gear with him as he was short of equipment and arranged that Ken and I should meet him in the Mount Cook area in two weeks' time. However, I never saw him again; he was killed whilst descending from Mount Cook and his body still lies in a crevasse within the glacier.

As we swung down the Hollyford trail, dog tired after a long day, Davie Gunn's homestead loomed ahead in the mist. Ken knew Davie a great old man, one of the last genuine outback pioneers. Besides running a herd of almost wild cattle, he operated a tourist walk – made partway on horseback in easy stages to Martins Bay. Once inside the house, the rigours of climbing in that rough country seemed pleasant enough in retrospect as we sat around a blazing log fire drinking mugs of tea.

"You once mentioned to me," Ken began, "that you thought there might be gold down on the John o' Groats river?"

"Ah well, I'm not so sure about that," replied Davie with a grin. "There is a rumour that an old prospector died somewhere up the river who was said to hoard his gold in a jam-jar! Whether that's right or not I wouldn't like to say, but there's often a grain of truth in these legends – a few colours, so to speak."

"Where is this John o' Groats?" I asked, my interest aroused. "The only one I know is in the north of Scotland; there's supposed to be gold near there, too," I added reflectively.

"Between Milford and Martins Bay," Davie replied. "A bloody rough place by all accounts."

Next day Ken and I started back along the path to reach the Homer Tunnel, through which the main road runs to Milford. It is a superb example of alpine engineering. Ken's father owned a hut close by it which would be our base for the next few days, or so we intended . . .

"I'm interested in John o' Groats, Ken," I remarked, adjusting my pack as we walked along. "How about a trip there?"

"I was just thinking the same thing," he admitted. "I know the chap in charge of the tunnel who has a geiger counter; we could borrow that. I heard from a pilot mate that there are interesting outcrops further up-river."

I conjured up a vivid mental picture of a skeleton which was once found near Glencoe, clutching an empty whisky bottle. Could a similar one, lying in the John o' Groats region, hold a jam-jar within its final grasp?

"We'd better get down to Milford pretty smartish," Ken suggested. "Bill Bragg, a friend of mine, might be up with his boat just now; he'd give us a lift right to the river mouth."

Equipped with Ken's rifle, enough food for five days and the geiger counter as well as our usual climbing gear, we hitched a lift down to the hotel at Milford the following morning from the tunnel foreman; a descent from the tunnel of 3000 feet in eleven miles. As he dropped us off and turned his pick-up

Hamish MacInnes on Pumori, 1953, with Everest behind.

Village folk of the Everest region.

Dave Dawe, Hamish MacInnes, Dick Irvin, right, at Malte Brun Hut on the Tasman Glacier, New Zealand.

Milford Sound, with Mitre Peak behind.

round, he shouted: "Don't forget I'm to get fifty per cent share in uranium finds, you buggers!"

"We won't forget," laughed Ken, 'but you sure drive a hard bargain!"

"I think that's Bill's boat – look – second from the jetty," Ken pointed as we walked down the track. "Maybe we're in luck."

On the south of the Sound, rising out of the inky water of the fiord, stood Mitre Peak, as shapely as the Matterhorn and over 5000 feet high; a wedge of granite. The North Face drops in a smooth sweep of bare rock straight into the 1300 feet deep Sound. It was quite a wall, climbable, but the problem would be approaching to land. I had recently climbed Mitre Peak by the normal route before teaming up with Ken. Old 'Cussie' Berndtson had ferried me across in the hotel launch in the morning. The weather had been fabulous but I was slightly worried as to whether I could make the top and back down again in a day. The fastest previous time had been nine hours, though actually the peak had only been climbed three times before. The first part of my ascent had been Tarzan stuff up vertical vegetation; then the bush thinned and I reached a narrow ridge with a game path snaking along it. That path, with the thick moss, felt like foam rubber as I ran along it. Below, near the head of the Sound, I could see the Bowen Falls diving 530 feet in a graceful curve, a mere white ribbon from my high vantage point. I had also watched a fishing boat head for the mouth of the Sound – and felt I could almost spit on it. The last part of the climb was a piece of cake, so I had left my rope on a horizontal section of ridge just before the last steep step to the summit. It had taken four and a half hours from the shore. The rock was excellent – just like the granite of Arran, and not difficult, if exposed in places. On the summit I had found a bottle under the cairn with the details of J. R. Dennison's first ascent in 1912, as well as his handkerchief!

When Ken and I reached the jetty he soon found his Maori fisherman friend, Bill Bragg, and over a coffee we explained our problem to Bill and his two crewmen, Cessie and Leo.

"You see, we want to get round to the John o' Groats river," explained Ken, sipping the hot coffee. "Do you know it?"

"Oh, we know it," Bill answered, him, "we know it well – but we'd have to land you south of the mouth as the rocks there have teeth – like sharks. What's this about a fortune?"

"Gold!" Ken replied. "At least, there may be, we're going to take a look. We've brought a geiger counter along as well – to sort of diversify the prospects!"

"So that's what it is!" commented Leo. "I was wondering why there were wires on Hamish's pack."

"The wires are for an auxiliary power supply," I explained.

"I thought it must be a new device for electrocuting sand-flies!" laughed Bill.

"I've never heard of any gold around there," Cessie, the quiet member of the crew remarked thoughtfully. He'd been around a lot and had done some prospecting himself. So we told him the story we'd heard from Davie Gunn.

"Well, there could be something in it," he admitted grudgingly. "But how do you mean to get back?"

"We've been thinking about that," replied Ken, rolling himself a cigarette. "We hope to cut over to Harrison's Cove, or follow up the coast to Martins Bay."

"It's a pretty slim chance," said Leo. "The bush is a bastard up there."

"A jam-jar of gold!" muttered Bill under his breath and spat with great accuracy at a floating tin, expressing better than mere words his contempt for the fishing industry. "Yes, fellas," he continued, "the bush is a bastard there; takes a bush rat to get through it!"

"Oh, we'll have a go," Ken shrugged. "But perhaps you'd keep an indulgent eye open for us after you drop us off. It may be the sandflies which will screw up the trip."

"Well, we're heading out tonight," Bill concluded. "We'll drop you off in the morning. Come on down and have some tucker. Chops and roast potatoes didn't you say, Leo?"

"That's right, and plenty for everybody!"

With a freshening breeze sweeping in from the Tasman Sea,

and twelve shopping days to Christmas, we headed down the Sound under the great face of Mitre Peak. Across the Sound, Mount Pembroke's broad forehead was white with snow; to starboard echoed the Stirling Falls. Both the Stirling and the Bowen Falls are over 500 feet, but the scale of the great sea-cliffs of Milford is so gigantic that they are dwarfed by comparison.

It is thought that Milford was given its name by a Welsh whaling captain, John Grono, who sailed these waters up to 1823. But it is the name Sutherland which is synonymous with Milford Sound. Donald Sutherland, a dour hard Scotsman, settled there in 1887 and lived the life of a hermit with his dog Groatie. He had a boat and a few tools and thought nothing of rowing up to Martins Bay to see friends! He prospected for gold and other minerals and discovered the Falls and the Sound which now bear his name. With his own hands he built two small cottages which he named the 'John o' Groats' Hotel, Milford City. However, he soon found he needed other companionship besides Groatie and in 1890 married a widow in Dunedin. She was an enterprising lady who planned, built and conducted a boarding house there; in this way the Sound gained popularity. Sutherland himself died in 1919.

The Sound now narrowed and we could distinguish ahead the white horses of the Tasman Sea; on the hazy horizon bad-tempered-looking clouds were brewing.

"Look at that bloody weather," commented Bill from the wheelhouse. "We'll have to lift the crayfish pots before we drop you off, lads."

"Okay by us," I said. "We'll give you a hand."

We headed down the rocky coast for a few miles to where yellow marker floats were riding the swell. It was all hands on deck. Two hours of backbreaking work later, some twenty-five pots had been accounted for, while Ken, much the worse for the weather by this time, lay wrapped in a tarpaulin on deck.

"Crayfish bait," Bill shouted, nodding at Ken.

"Not yet," I observed. "He must be still alive – I see bubbles when the deck's awash!"

Six days of foul weather made us perforce the guests of the fishermen. We sheltered in a small cove off one of the fiords, amusing ourselves line fishing and occasionally, during rare lulls, venturing out to the fishing grounds. Torrential rain fell, over an inch an hour, and waterlogged cloud shrouded the peaks. Bird calls still reached us from the bush and in our comparatively sheltered cove the *Kotahi* swung contentedly at her anchor. Outside the sea was a heaving desert of foam and spray.

At last the weather lifted and we rounded the point of the Sound, heading up the coast a short way. Bill studied the shoreline, examining the pattern of breaking waves with his binoculars, searching for a suitable place to put us ashore in the swell, and switched on the echo sounder.

"I think I'll drop you on that rock in there," he pointed. "Doesn't look too bad."

"Great," I replied with as much courage as I could muster, thinking to myself that this was ruddy ludicrous. "Sorry to be such a bother, Bill."

"Come back in time for Christmas dinner," invited Leo, wiping his large hands with an oily rag. "We'll have a fair dinkum meal back at Milford."

"That's a date then," Ken agreed as he dropped some gear down into the dinghy which Cessie had lowered.

Bill rowed us ashore. All seemed well to begin with. It was a long rolling sea; then suddenly we were in the surf and the small dinghy felt more like a cocktail mixer than a boat.

"Keep baling with that milk tin," Bill bellowed, "or we'll go to the bottom!" He was fully absorbed as he took the dinghy in, stern first, easing it towards the large rock. Every few minutes it appeared through the foam and Ken, poised at the stern, waited for a chance to jump, clutching his rifle in his right hand. With one energetic bound he was on to the rock and danced through the spray over the inner rocks to the shore.

I stood upright balancing at the stern and after what seemed ages, leapt, just as a large wave was subsiding and the black mass of rock emerging. The dinghy had been rising and falling about six feet with the swell.

"Christ, that was close, Ken!" I gasped as I joined him.

"Not the sort of thing you'd want to try after a binge, or when seasick," he agreed with a grin, "but it's great to feel Mother Earth beneath our feet!"

We waved farewell to Bill, a tiny scuttling blob in the waves as he pulled back to the *Kotahi*.

We moved up the coast staggering slightly, not due to the weight of our packs, though they were heavy enough, but because of our enforced confinement aboard the *Kotahi*.

"It's great to get going again."

"Terrific," Ken agreed, "though I feel a bit like a clockwork doll."

A strong breeze was blowing in from the sea; the sky was now clear and the surf made a fine healthy roar. Hopefully I had switched on the geiger counter. This was another beachcomber's paradise, reminding me of my paua shell expedition. Mountainous banks of shingle were heaped by past storms; on top were immense whale bones like leftovers from a cyclops dinner, bleached by sun and salt. A couple of Fiordland crested penguins looked curiously at us as we passed and a bush robin landed on my packframe, a wonderfully friendly bird, although no relation to the English robin redbreast. On the horizon a tramper could be seen, belching smoke like a smouldering branch of wood on the edge of a campfire.

It was two very tired aspirant prospectors that finally downed their packs at the mouth of the John o' Groats river. We had to do some strenuous climbing on the way for at frequent intervals bluffs jutted out into the sea; these barriers just had to be climbed.

"It's a pissy little stream, Ken, despite all that rain," I observed with disgust as I dropped my pack.

We fixed our flysheet between two cabbage trees growing conveniently close together, and soon had a comfortable camp on the bank of the river.

Not a great deal of gold had been found in Fiordland. There

had been workings at Martins Bay and Big Bay and Preservation Inlet, but as it was all alluvial the returns didn't add up to an El Dorado. There had also been one or two quartz reefs discovered at Wilson's river and near Te Oneroa, but they were badly faulted and by 1900 most of the prospectors had gone, according to Ken.

"Doesn't seem much hope in this deal," I mumbled as I finished my soup. "I bet if there is a skeleton up there its bones are rattling with laughter."

"Mind you," Ken went on, recalling some old gossip, "Sutherland was supposed to have found diamonds in the Milford area and he used to row up the coast here quite a bit."

"Aye," I mused. "We'll bear it in mind. He must have been a tough old blighter!"

We were awakened in the morning by a wonderful chorus of birdlife and bites: with the sandflies even the most slothful prospector becomes an early riser. The air was astir with the crystal notes of the bell bird and the tui. A kaka, a large greenish bush parrot, greeted us from the bush nearby; it has a fascinating call, unequalled in New Zealand. But we didn't see or hear any keas here: those superb mischievous parrots claimed to be the reincarnations of dead climbers. They are, however, very common in the Central Alps and I have idled hours away watching their comical antics. They have a wicked sense of humour: a friend of mine took a photograph of one rolling up a mattress. And they can tear the lead washers from roofing nails or rip the hood of a car with equal ease and enjoyment. One of their favourite ploys, while one tries to get some sleep in a mountain bothy, is to glissade down the corrugated iron roof, shrieking with delight. I must confess that on another trip when, to risk a pun, we were feeling peckish, we fed some keas our last remaining slice of bread soaked in meths, no charitable gesture on our part, and they were even funnier drunk than sober. Some became truculent and assaulted their mates whilst the more placid simply went to sleep. These were the unfortunate for we snaffled a couple for dinner. Later from the depths of my stomach I felt cannibalistic guilt!

The John o' Groats is only about fifty feet wide and now it was only five feet deep. Next day we started to prospect the riverbed, looking for traces. We spent the whole of that day panning, moving slowly up river. Progress was only possible up the bed itself, because of the dense bush. My back felt as if it had been massaged by the tracks of a crawler tractor. The only creatures getting anything out of the exercise were the sandflies and we celebrated them in an exasperated adaptation of 'The Blue-tailed Fly':

> Down the coast near Martins Bay,
> There lives a miner old and grey,
> And to his hut so warm and dry,
> There came each night a big sandfly.
>
> Chorus:
> Tucker's all gone but I don't care,
> Tucker's all gone but I don't care,
> Tucker's all gone but I don't care,
> Goodbye, big sandfly.
>
> Then one day the old man said,
> Far too long on me you've fed:
> I shall starve and you will die –
> I'll get rid of you, you big sandfly.
>
> Then one day the old man died,
> They placed his billies by his side
> And on his tombstone plainly wrote:
> 'Victim of the big Sandfly'.

We slept that night with the sonorous beating of the surf somewhat muffled since we actually had our heads inside our sleeping bags in an endeavour to outwit the sandflies.

Next day, as we tried to move up river taking bivouac gear with us, we found the remnants of an old hut which had been made from the trunks of the large fern trees.

"Looks as if this has been used, Ken," I observed, kicking at the remains of the rotten walls with my climbing boot.

"Yes. Might be worth trying this stretch of river for colours."

"No sign of any jam-jars?"

"No bones either," Ken laughed.

We spent the next day prospecting, but didn't find a colour at all.

"It's clean as a whistle," Ken pronounced in disgust. "What the hell are we going to do now?"

"Blazes if I know. We'll never get up the river with our swags; these vines are too dense. How about up the coast to Martins Bay?"

"She's a cow, that coast," Ken answered vehemently. "But let's go back and take a look. I think there are too many bluffs, some would take a whole day to turn, I reckon."

We returned to the coast. A short walk up the shoreline confirmed our worst fears.

"No use this, fella," I said. "We can't get round to the south; the walls on the north side of Milford are vertical for miles. Not only that, but they're thousands of feet high."

"I guess we'd better go south of John o' Groats," said Ken, with resignation, "and trust to luck that we'll be spotted. At least a fishing boat can get a dinghy in where Bill dropped us off."

The following day we prospected the creeks as we moved south. Ken was panning alongside me. Suddenly there was a rapid clicking from the geiger counter.

"Hey, Ken, something radio-active here! Getting some counts!" He turned away from me to put his gold pan down and I lost the counts; when he turned round they began again.

"Sorry," I apologised. "It must be your watch. I'm picking up a signal from the luminous dial!"

That afternoon, after great difficulty, I caught a penguin and decided to carry it with me to a point where I remembered a particularly fine view of the coast.

"It will make a super foreground, Ken," I enthused. "The

photograph could be worth pounds." My companion shook his head sorrowfully, obviously putting it down to my artistic temperament. The bird, however, was heavier than I had bargained for, and after a short space of time I bitterly regretted the plan, but I didn't admit this.

"You're bloody well mad, MacInnes," Ken observed as the furious bird, tied inside my rucksack with only its head protruding, the drawcord holding it securely pinioned, it persistently pecked the back of my neck as if it were a woodpecker and I a block of wood. My regrets were further justified when, after five miles of very rough going, I took the bird out, camera in hand, ready to create my masterpiece. I then observed that it had registered its disapproval by leaving ample evidence of its confinement; my sleeping bag never recovered from the encounter! To add insult to injury, when I placed the bird on the rock at the precise point I had in mind with, I may add, no great display of gentleness, it promptly jumped into the sea with an indignant squawk. Ken, convulsed with laughter, watched this spectacle from a comfortable seat on a nearby rock and my subsequent ungainly and abortive attempts at recapture; it took him about half an hour to recover.

"You know, Hamish, that's about the funniest thing I ever saw! I thought you were going to follow it to Antarctica.

Our trip along the shoreline was mercifully easier, as it was low tide and we could by-pass many of the difficult cliffs which we'd been forced to climb when we had first travelled northwards. Eventually, Ken pointed to a small bluff at the edge of the greenery: "There's an overhanging rock up there; should make a good bivvy."

That evening, listening to the cheerful strains of Ken's mouth organ, I had my second brainwave:

"Hey, Ken, let's build a raft!"

"Fantastic!" he whooped, throwing the harmonica down. "We've got all the gear; we can unravel the climbing rope for lashings." Ideas flowed freely amidst wild enthusiasm.

"Great," I agreed. "And we can use the big flysheet for a sail."

"We might have to wait here for a week before we're picked up, anyhow," he remarked. "God knows where Bill Bragg is now; probably fishing down by Dusky Sound."

It was a raft-maker's Paradise! Huge logs dry and white littered the beach and in no time next morning we were guiding them through the now placid surf towards the big rock. By the evening we had constructed the framework of the raft. At dawn the next day we decked it with smaller timber using my axe from lumberjacking days for trimming the ends. A mast shaped like goalposts was made from lancewood and the heavy flysheet was to be attached between these uprights. Two large sweeps were manufactured from split sections of a large rata log.

"She looks great, Ken," I observed, feeling justifiably proud of our work. "I think those two wrens want to sail with us!" I added. The birds were sitting on the sweeps, being gently rocked by the sea.

"My only worry," remarked Ken, "is that we haven't much water."

"Oh, don't fret about that," I returned airily. "There's the empty whisky bottle I found; we'll fill it up, then we'll just wait for a good westerly breeze, launch her and sail up Milford Sound."

We lazed happily round the big camp fire that night, half dozing as it seemed to be the sandflies' night off. A breeze was now testing its lungs from the south-west.

"What the bloody hell are you new chumps doing here," a voice crackled across the water like breaking glass. We jumped as if we'd been addressed by the Archangel Gabriel. It was the *Kotahi*; her dim outline could be seen, nodding peacefully a short way off. Bill was using the loud-hailer.

"Come on in, Bragg and get us to hell out of here!" shouted Ken.

"She'll be right lads, I'll be with you in a couple of shakes."

In the dim light we could see a boat being launched over the side, so Ken and I quickly gathered our belongings and went down to the raft. It served admirably as a jetty and Bill had no trouble bringing the dinghy in to join us.

In the galley we told them our tale over tea.

"You know something, you blokes may know a bit about climbing and perhaps even a bit about prospecting . . . but you know bloody well nothing of the sea!" said Bill emphatically. "Do you realise that if you'd launched that contraption from there, you'd have been out in the Tasman like a dose of salts." We stared at him incredulously.

"Next stop Australia," added Cessie.

"That's right," confirmed Leo who was serving up some bacon and eggs. "There's strong currents sweeping out from Milford."

"And another thing," added Cessie. "There's a Force 9 gale forecast for tomorrow. That's why we're heading back to Harrison's Cove. At least there in Milford we'll have shelter."

"Oh well, we're always learning," I observed, tucking into my meal. "I must say you blokes always seem to come along on cue!"

The next day was rough, even sheltered as we were in the cove; waterspouts whirled across the fiord as if they were doing a tarantella.

"Do you know," Bill observed as we sat on deck, both wrapped up in oilskins, "those willy-willies once tore the oars from my grasp when I was rowing back to the boat down at Bligh Sound. They can be real scarey."

During the next few days we helped with the maintenance of the boat. Ken did some splicing and I helped replace a bearing in the propshaft.

"It's Christmas tomorrow," observed Cessie, handing me a spanner. "Any ideas?"

My thoughts roamed towards two enormous geese, kept as a tourist attraction at the local hotel. Ken was of the opinion it was a job for a man descended from a long line of Border reivers, and stuck to his splicing.

A nocturnal trip, with an oar as a long-handled shillelagh, a few muffled protestations from our prospective dinners and I was back on board once again, lavishly laden. I was obviously more successful as an assassin of geese than as a prospector!

The sun struggled through the next day, the deck dried off and cloud rolled up like blinds to display those naked peaks freshly washed. In the bows Ken and Cessie played a Maori tune in duet on their mouth organs. Bill lay by the winch, a bottle of beer in one hand and a novel in the other. I sat on some crayfish pots, gazing around at the great circe of rock. A wonderful smell stole from the galley.

# 4

# Gods and Monsters

STRANGE CREATURES HAVE ALWAYS held an irresistible fascination for man, be they of the mythical variety such as hobgoblins and leprechauns, or borderline cases in this realm of belief, in the form of Loch Ness monsters, gigantic squids or yeti. Having access to the happy hunting ground of at least two of these animals, I naturally take more than an academic interest in both Nessie and yeti.

The Loch Ness monster creates considerable controversy, even in its own backyard, whilst tourists flock to the shores of the loch with cameras optimistically at the ready, often contrary to their professed beliefs. Year after year Nessie is spotted; evidence has been amassed from thousands of eye-witness accounts. Records of sightings go back 1400 years: St. Columba himself, en route for the palace of King Brude, saw a certain water monster – an 'aquatilis bestia' – in the River Ness in the year A.D. 565.

Anyone who studies this surfeit of evidence must be impressed by the consistency in the reports. For example, over the centuries no one has mentioned the monster giving any call or making any noise other than that caused by its natural movements. The most scathing sceptic must surely admit that it is within the bounds of possibility that the 975-foot deep loch can hold a secret, even a monstrous one! Loch Morar too, the deepest freshwater loch in Europe, possesses its own particular brand of aquatilis bestia, and there are many reports from contemporary witnesses concerning this monster, affectionately known as Morag.

An unbeliever may well ask: why are there no good photographs of these creatures? Well, there certainly are, of Nessie at least – as good as one could expect in the circumstances. One cannot expect professional photographers to spend years of their career awaiting the rare opportunity of a sighting. After all, there are about twenty-five miles of Nessie-frequented loch and she doesn't often risk her elegant neck by displaying it to the public; it is generally only a small part of her anatomy which breaks the surface of the water.

The reason for this digression into more aquatic pastimes is to illustrate the kind of problems encountered in a search for that elusive beast, the yeti. Imagine hundreds of square miles of dense forest, much of it unexplored, where one's range of vision can often be measured by an arm's length and where gorges funnel white rivers from glaciers whose source lies in the highest mountain range in the world. If they exist at all, there may easily be more yeti than Nessies, but the difficulty of coming across them is a hundredfold greater. Searching high in the wilds of Spitti, or the headwaters of the Choyang, is a far cry from sitting in a car on the A82 overlooking Loch Ness with the heater full on and a pair of binoculars. Also, there are far fewer reliable reports of yeti or abominable snowman sightings than of Nessie sightings, and many of the yeti reports appear to be figments of extremely fertile imagination.

An early account of the *Bun manosh* or wild men came from B. H. Hudson in 1832 when he was British Resident at the court of Nepal. Though his movements were curtailed in that then forbidden land, he sent natives out to collect botanical specimens for him. Some of these natives were frightened by the 'wild men'.

In 1889 Major L. A. Waddell first reported mysterious footprints in the snow. He was told that they were the tracks of yeti, but he himself thought that they belonged to red bear, *Ursus arctos isabellinus*. I suppose that as Westerners we have been conditioned to accept footprints as valid evidence: a tangible proof, unlike the mere sighting of a great beast in the loch.

More than fifty naturalists and mountaineers have described

yeti spoor but, if one delves deeply into the evidence, there is always a lingering doubt. Only one or two sets of photographs provide a watertight case for a large biped frequenting the high Himalayas; of these, Eric Shipton's shots are the most convincing. Strange spoor with no adequate explanation, were photographed by Shipton's party in 1951 whilst they were crossing the Min Lung glacier close to the Nepal/Tibet border. These photographs of individual prints clearly show an unusual off-set big toe with an imprint slightly larger than that made from a large Alpine climbing boot and twice as broad. The tracks had been made only a short time before the photos were taken, possibly only a few hours previously, so there was little likelihood of distortion by radiation.

There have been reports, if not photographic evidence of unexplained footprints through the thousand miles of the Himalaya chain from Sikkim to the Western Karakoram, and even from the Karen of Northern Thailand and Burma. Descriptions based on supposed sightings or bones appear to be fairly consistent. There are two types: a small yeti, and a larger, more powerful model. The vital statistics of the smaller version are suggested as being in the region of four to five feet tall, greyish-brown in colour, with a coat of short coarse hair. It is tailless. The head is pointed with a marked sagittal crest and it has a flat, hairless face, as if someone had bashed in its features. The yeti is reputed to have exceptionally long arms (though other creatures – including the author and Rob Roy Mac-Gregor, that notorious Scottish outlaw – share this affliction!). It is bipedal, but can revert to four-leg drive when in a hurry. The feet, as already described, are large, and the toes prehensile. Dr. Wladimir Tschernesky, a lecturer in zoology whom I have known for many years, is an expert sifter of yeti evidence and has reconstructed the foot of a yeti. He concludes that it corresponds in many features to human and gorilla feet, and with the Neanderthaloid foot from the Kuk Koba. The yeti is certainly no lightweight; Wladimir calculated that its prints have a surface area one and half times as great as the sole of a mountain gorilla, 6' 4" in height. The weight of such a gorilla

*A reconstruction of a yeti, drawn from available evidence in 1957 by zoologist, Dr. Wladimir Tschernesky.*

The Cursing Oracle, in striped blanket, gets on with the god business.

*Above* Jeff Douglas leads off on the yeti hunt.

*Left* The bridegroom was 29, the bride 9. A wife cost about £20, but a second-hand one sold for as little as £10.

*Below* These, we decided, were the prints of a large brown bear.

would be in the region of 500 lbs. The yeti must therefore be
one and a half times heavier and not less than seven feet tall: a
formidable creature indeed!

Apart from the footprints, various yeti scalps have been
produced, ostensibly from monasteries in the Everest region.
These have proved 'bones of contention' over the years. The
Khumjung scalp, for example, thought by sceptics to have
been constructed from the shoulder of a serow, *Capricornis
sumatraensis*, had hairs of a simian character. Parasitic mites
collected from the scalp and a serow sample were found to
differ and this again raised doubts. The scalps from the Everest
region are about 300 years old and all have the characteristic
pointed head.

Just what can the yeti be? Is it a type of mountain gorilla? Dr.
Bernard Heuvelmans put forward a theory that it could be a
relic form of the giant prehistoric ape: *Gigantopithecus*. It
sounds a valid suggestion. The animal appears to have been
neither a hominid nor a typical ape; its teeth and lower jaw
have been found between the Siwalik Hills of India and South
China. *Gigantopithecus* made its debut about ten million years
ago and survived until the middle Pleistocene. The mountain
gorilla may be similar to it though, as far as we can tell, this
great ape is confined to the area round the volcanoes of Birunga
in Central Africa. Could such an animal, either *Gigantopithecus* or mountain gorilla, survive in one of the last retreats
remaining in the world for such beasts – in the vast loneliness
of the Himalaya?

Before the mountain gorilla was discovered, tales of a
ferocious man-like animal which carried off native women
were commonplace. It wasn't until as recently as 1901 that the
animal was finally identified. It was thought to live above 3000
metres, in the upper bamboo forest. It has since been discovered that it actually lives in the lower forest and seldom
ventures higher, unless disturbed by man. This, most naturalists agree, could equally apply to yeti. Though tracks have frequently been found above the snow-line, they could have been
made by commuting yeti, travelling from one valley to

another. In the higher regions of the Himalaya there is little food for such a large animal, whereas in the vast forests of the Arun valley for example, there is ample food and cover to make a yeti's life, if not idyllic, at least possible. Conditions here are adverse to humankind: high rainfall produces forest and rhododendrons so dense as to make progress dead slow and stop. But if the yeti is anything like the Himalayan bear, it will be able to penetrate this jungle like a tank.

To confuse the issue still further, for the embryo yeti hunter, there are also of course the Himalayan bears to take into account: not just one species, but three. These are colour coded – the blue bear (*Ursus arctos pruinosus*), the red bear (*Ursus arctos isabellinus*), and the Himalayan black bear (*Selenarctos thibetanus*). In certain conditions these animals leave tracks which are very misleading, sometimes even appearing to have been made by a biped.

The chain of events and people which led me to the Central Himalaya yeti hunting in the winter of 1958–59 began during the preceding summer when Dick Irvin and I, partly financed by our paua shell collecting jaunt, went climbing in the Karakoram. Our companions were Bob Swift from California, and Mike Banks, then an officer in the Marine Commandos. We attempted and failed to climb Rakaposhi.

When the others returned home, I was lucky enough to obtain permission from the Political Agent in Gilgit to visit the small kingdom of Hunza. I don't think His Highness, the Mir, was too impressed when I arrived, dressed in pyjamas (the only clothes I seemed to possess at the time), walking alongside his white stallion which he had sent for me to ride. The stallion had been relegated to a role of pack-horse, carrying my scruffy rucksack and sleeping bag! This did nothing to foster initial goodwill. However, in time I became very friendly with the Mir and his family and, though I did not receive the at one time traditional gifts from His Highness of a basket of apricots, a pony and a plump woman, the Rani did give me a unique pull-over which she knitted with the inner hair from sixteen ibex.

After a short stay in that tranquil kingdom I eventually

turned up in London at Mike's flat, and there I met Jeff
Douglas, a former fellow officer of Mike's. Jeff had been a major
in the Commandos and I learned that he had also once been the
Admiral of the Jordan Navy or, as he was nicknamed by his
friends, the First Dead Sea Lord of the lowest navy in the
world. He was now Warden of the Ullswater Outward Bound
School, eminently amiable and a natural adventurer. I had
only known him for a few hours before we were already
talking about a trip to the Rio Morte, at the headwaters of the
Amazon, or possibly a region in north-east Bolivia which I had
heard was of great interest, and he promptly invited me up to
Ullswater for further discussions; he had, I gathered, several
schemes up his sleeve.

I duly turned up, begrimed on a motor cycle, a few weeks
later to find out what Jeff had on his mind. It proved to be a
yeti-hunting trip, he had plans to visit the Central Himalaya
the following year.

We had repaired to Jeff's study, well closeted from the noise
of fifty boisterous youths busily outward bounding. Our taste
in music (and other good things in life) proved to be similar:
'Lucia di Lammermuir' played on the turntable, whilst a bottle
of wine stood between us. I soon learnt that a certain Squadron-
Leader, Lester Davies, who was to take over the Wardenship of
the School when Jeff left (he had already sent in his resignation), had returned from an expedition into Lahoul in the
Central Himalaya with interesting photographs of unexplained footprints and backside prints also. Their adventurous
owner obviously enjoyed a glissade and had left unmistakable
proof of this pastime on a snow bank. As Jeff and I studied the
shots, I became more and more fascinated with the idea of
searching for the creature which had made the prints, and Jeff
rapidly convinced me that I should postpone my South American plans and go with him on a yeti quest. In turn I persuaded
him not to wait until the following year, but to set out that
winter. After all, the beast had to get about, unless it hiber-
nated, and it would be a damn sight easier to look for him in
the snow. Since Jeff was committed to the school until his

contract ran out, two months hence, I agreed to go on ahead and establish myself in the Kulu region of the Central Himalaya and recce there for the best operational base. In those days I was almost constantly hard up; it was symptomatic of my way of life. But Jeff generously offered to finance the greater part of the expedition. So all was agreed, and we drank a toast to the trip.

We drank – too much. It was one of those surreptitious evenings that stalks up behind and catches one unawares. More bottles were conjured up from nowhere, and Jeff's stock of opera discs rotated at ever increasing volume. In the words of Rabbie Burns: 'The nicht drave on wi' sangs and clatter; And aye the ale was growing better.' In sober truth, the night came to an abrupt halt at the doors of a linen cupboard at the foot of a flight of stairs, down which we had both fallen.

We made up white suits from parachute silk, painted our skis white, and I designed a collapsible sledge for hauling our gear. From F.I.D.S. – now known as the British Antarctic Survey – we borrowed pyramid tents and parkas, whilst I took the precaution of obtaining a jam-jar full of powerful tranquilliser from an egg-head friend of mine. Our stock of firearms included Jeff's .45 automatic pistol.

Sir Wavell Wakefield, now Lord Wakefield of Kendal, was a frequent visitor to the school and took more than a casual interest in our schemes. He had considerable influence in an airline called Skyways which operated troop-carrying runs for H.M. Forces, besides carrying monkeys for a vaccine programme from the Far East and India. Sir Wavell suggested that he could arrange a free flight by signing us on as 'crew members'.

My arrival in London Airport, complete with a load of equipment and firearms, caused quite a stir. The pilot had been warned about his extra 'crew member' but was somewhat taken aback to see him arrive, armed to the teeth! My equipment was immediately requisitioned and stored in some distant part of the Hermes freighter; the firearms were put in a locker and the pilot pocketed the key.

"Regulations," he explained smilingly.

After take-off I was told that I could get some shut-eye if I could find somewhere to bed down. I had held onto my sleeping bag, anticipating such a possibility, and went aft into the body of the aircraft. I was surprised to find it empty, except for one packing case lashed to the centre of the hold, which had stout 6″ × 2″ wooden battens supporting it. I assumed it contained some heavy item of machinery, but there was no label or marking on it. However, weighing it up as a possible bed – there was nothing else in its class in the hold, only bare metal – I approvingly spread my bag out on top and, with the ease of long practice in the art of dossing, I was soon fast asleep. In fact I didn't wake up until we reached Athens where a good-looking stewardess (she was travelling to Hong Kong, to return in a troop carrier) shook me and asked if I wanted anything to eat. The crew was going into an airport hotel. I yawned and asked where we were; then discovered that I was starving and followed her eagerly out onto the tarmac. There was a short delay whilst the pilot stirred a heavy-eyed soldier to guard the plane. This did not strike me as particularly odd, knowing that the light-fingered gentry are not the monopoly of Western Europe. But at Bahrain I lost my couch; it was removed from the plane with considerable difficulty under an escort of soldiers. I discovered that my 'bed' contained gold bullion, in payment for oil rights! It was surely my most expensive bed-night ever.

We were not the only party interested in yeti at that time. A rival expedition was currently in Nepal, financed by Tom Slick, the Texas oil millionaire. One of his companions was described by the press as 'a shapely Californian heiress'. 'Just my luck to be stuck with Jeff,' I thought enviously. The University of Leningrad was also in the high peaks of the Soviet Union, on the lookout for yeti, whilst the *Daily Mail* Expedition in 1954 had aroused considerable interest. When I arrived in Delhi I was soon approached by *Time/Life* for the first option on yeti material which we might obtain over the winter months. They provided a welcome nest-egg of dollars, besides supplying me with cameras and multitude of yeti evidence in the form of charts of sightings and references. It seems inevitable that the more official an expedition is, the more it becomes bogged down with bureaucracy and equipment which ensures the maximum number of porters and the slowest rate of progress possible. By the time I reached Manali in the Kulu valley, I felt overburdened in my role as intrepid hunter, but I consoled myself that I would soon be free of these encumbrances which included packing cases of food, arsenal, and my poisons cabinet. I was looking forward to getting into the hills.

The hills were white when first glimpsed from the delectable valley of Kulu. Above the orchards they beckoned tantalisingly, in contrast to the arid plains of India. I had had more than my fill of commuting on the sub-continent, having made the train journey to Bombay to collect the gear which had come by sea. Now it was late fall, the persimmons were ripe, and I really felt that I had entered the garden of India.

I enjoyed myself thoroughly during the next six weeks. I studied the country to the north over the Rotang La, crossing it on skis, and accompanied local shikaris on hunting expeditions into the mountains. None of these men, all with a vast experience of the Central Himalayan region, had ever seen or heard of a yeti except at second or third hand. I grew particularly friendly with Renu; he was then forty-five, tall and athletic, with a bronzed face and almost classical Greek features. He wore an elegant sweeping moustache and had, at various times, seventeen wives! He was also the drummer to the local goddess. Each village had its god or goddess, an effigy made from mini masks and elaborate drapery erected on a wooden framework which could be carried on two poles like a stretcher. I used to visit the hunter in his quaint two-storied house; large, thick slates covered the roof. Currently there were only two wives, the others had been sold off, and as soon as my climbing boots were heard echoing on the verandah, the younger of the wives automatically filled a tumbler with sharab, the local hell-fire drink.

The Banan family who owned orchards in Manali were also most helpful. John, the son, was a keen hunter of my own age and often came out with me. His father, well versed in the ways of the hill people, would visit the house they had kindly lent me almost daily with the latest yeti story (or, as it was known locally, *jungli admi* – jungle man). He even unearthed a tale of a *jungli admi* who had been a slave at the old palace of Nagar in Kalu. My sorties into the mountains were punctuated by short but pleasant retreats to the Banans' house. During this time I found plenty of bears and photographed many prints: some measured as much as 12" × 8" with a stride of 39"; often, especially with Black Bear prints, no claw marks were visible. Sometimes, too, the rear prints were superimposed on the fore prints, giving the misleading impression of a biped.

Bear spotting was a potentially dangerous pastime; the Himalayan bear is a mean creature. Whilst in Manali I heard one report of a person dying from mauling, and several others who were badly injured. One day, out on a hunting trip with a few of Renu's friends, we found some unidentifiable spoor. They were 8" × 4½" and appeared to have been made by a biped. However, since there were some sadus living in remote valleys in the area, we regretfuly attributed them to one of these recluses, or possibly friend Bruno or Blackie.

Only someone brought up in a far northern clime could contract sunstroke during the Himalayan winter. I succeeded in doing just that on another hunting trip, and had to recuperate in a cave whilst Renu's friends patiently waited for me to recover.

On our return to Manali, the shikaris proudly bearing their trophies, we were informed by Renu that there was to be a wedding the next day. I was invited to attend.

"Plenty of your favourite drink!" he laughed. But next day, when I saw the bride, I was astounded and turned to Renu:

"What age is she?!"

"Nine years old," he replied with a smile. "The bridegroom is twenty-six, she had property left to her by her father," he explained. The bride was dressed in red, indicating that she was approaching matrimony; this particular doll wore a great deal of hardware. Heavy bangles clanked on her wrists, like out-of-tune cowbells, and a large blak (a ring some 5″ in diameter) was fixed to her nose. 'A lamb to the slaughter', I thought, as I gazed at her.

"A wife costs about £20, and second-hand ones sell for as little as £10," Renu continued. There were simple rules for both marriage and divorce. If someone wanted another man's wife, or if she was willing to go with him, leaving her husband, or was suspected of adultery, the prospective husband had to pay the tune, finally agreed upon after a lot of haggling.

The marriage feast lasted two days. Everyone, with the exception of the bride and groom, got drunk. I was reminded of binges in New Zealand's Westland, and in the Scottish islands. I understood now, fully, why sharab was illegal . . . it had the kick of a piledriver and hung over one like an atomic cloud. As I left the village to return to my house, I stepped over the local law enforcement officer who was lying in a ditch, looking as if he had just died his thousandth death.

Interestingly enough, I kept coming across references to strange lights. At the time I hadn't heard of U.F.O.'s, but the local name for such phenomena is 'jauldrin-a-bauldrin'. I first heard about them when I was staying in a cave with the shikaris. They had built a lively fire at the cave entrance and the shadows of the hunters played on the walls. It was a good setting for the tale. I had just consumed a meal of flying squirrel and was in a receptive mood. One of the hunters who could speak some English translated, whilst a shikari related his story. A few months previously he had been returning to his village when, turning a corner in the trail, he had been confronted by five bright lights, as bright as pressure lanterns, suspended a few feet above the ground. "They rose . . ." he pointed dramatically towards the roof of the cave, "And then they were gone."

There were many such stories, all told without any prompting on my part, when I questioned the natives about the yeti

which they hadn't seen. I remember reading in one of Jim
Corbett's books how he and the Viceroy of India saw such
strange lights moving about a cliff face where there could have
been no *Homo sapiens*. Corbett could offer no explanation;
nor could the Viceroy.

One day, as the sun was struggling over the snow covered
Rotang La, old man Banan called at the house with an interesting piece of information. He had heard of a cave in which there
was a large skeleton. Its whereabouts was known to an ancient
hunter and he concluded that it could not be the skeleton of a
bear since the shikari would be familiar with bear bones. This
certainly sounded more promising than anything to date, so it
was with an element of excitement that I discovered the
location of the village and proposed to visit it the next day.
Banan promised that he would arrange a guide. My ambition
to buy a Mercedes 300SL with the proceeds from yeti evidence,
was once again rekindled: that exotic car had been a dream of
mine for some time – on such flimsy foundations are castles
built or chariots bought. But the dream was cruelly shattered
later when we were told that the shikari had died; no one else
knew the whereabouts of the cave.

Six weeks flashed by, like someone expertly shuffling cards,
and suddenly Jeff was due to arrive. I had meanwhile resolved
that the best area for our search was to the north of the Parbati
Valley. It was suitably remote and desolate and seldom visited
by humans.

The winter snow now lay deep and silent at Manali. Jeff's
arrival coincided with an interesting rite at Renu's village: the
Cursing Oracle. The oracle is the goddess's mouthpiece; we
were assured that the spectacle would be both interesting and
educative; John Banan offered to be our interpreter. The rite
was enacted amidst snow-covered paddy fields some distance
from the village. We joined a crowd of small boys, each armed
with a willow wand. The adults of the village assembled at the
fringe of the houses, a couple of yards away.

Presently the oracle arrived, a dark sullen-looking man with
heavy features; he looked as if he dealt in depressions as well as

magical spells. He was dressed in the usual home-spun suit which, though warm and functional, definitely lacked the Savile Row cut. A bunch of flowers adorned his hat. He was accompanied by two men carrying a bamboo pole and the drummers. Renu, as chief drummer, looked suitably serious now that god-business was pending.

The drums rolled, slowly at first, then the beat quickened and the echo ricocheted from the crags. The boys started to run clockwise round the oracle in a large circle, shouting excitedly and waving their wands. The oracle, sitting astride the pole, was lifted *à cheval* by the two natives and slowly carried in the direction of the village. All this time the boys kept up their leaping circuit, but they stopped shouting as soon as the oracle spoke. He delivered a terrible mouthful of invective which was immediately repeated with great glee by the boys. Each subsequent utterance was worse than the last, the oracle's vocabulary seemingly inexhaustible, and his appetite for the expletive insatiable. The boys took up each new curse at the tops of their voices; many of the four-lettered words were corruptions of English ones (after all, we do have the finest collection of four-lettered words in the world!). John found no difficulty in translating. He had been educated in true colonial tradition in a good English school in India.

No one was spared – what was said about Jeff and me was obviously embarrassing as John refused to translate most of that. We took it in good part! The curses grew more and more rapid; the drums sounding like a continuous throb. The boys ran faster and faster.

Finally we reached the village where the oracle was depoled. No doubt his uncomfortable ride contributed to his abuse of mankind; it certainly ensured that the language of invective was passed on to posterity! He was now joined by two other long-haired oracles; after ritual dancing, they repaired to the temple where they stripped and each appeared to enter a trance. Seated cross-legged in the snow, their eyes rolled alarmingly as each in turn made elaborate contortions with his arms. A couple of villagers playing long narshingi horns competed with the drums. This moving and disturbing mumbo-jumbo continued until nightfall when the oracles broke up segments of clay and predicted the coming year's crops.

Within a week of leaving the Cursing Oracle, we were skiing in the lonely subsidiary valleys of the Parbati. We established camps high above the snow-line so that we could travel between them, searching for spoor. We found plenty of prints; bear again, and those of the skulking snow leopard which enjoyed padding round our tents at night. We travelled on skis – any other mode would have been impossible as the loose powder lay deep. Our ski tracks froze up over night so that our trails resembled miniature 'Cresta Runs' until a fresh fall of snow 'slowed' them again. We were inexpert skiers and dreaded the thought of a broken leg.

We found one set of prints at 14,000 feet amidst high peaks. This seemed odd: it was an unusual place to find them and they numbered only fifteen. I call them prints, but actually they were indentations in the snow, some 8″ × 4″, starting from nowhere and leading nowhere: just a set of fifteen prints in an open snowfield. Whatever – or whoever – made them appeared to have taken a dislike to Mother Earth or the snow when it landed, and didn't extend its visit. A field of blank snow surrounded start and finish. Finally we realised the futility of our quest. It was all very well theorising back home that winter was a good time to yeti hunt, but one must credit the yeti with some degree of commonsense. It probably had a lot more than us, and was even then comfortably installed in the lower forests where there was an adequate food supply, shelter and cover from inquisitive eyes! This theory was later endorsed by other naturalists who also came to the conclusion that the barren region of the Himalaya is no place to support a large animal. After two months' fruitless hunt we moved back down to the Parbati. It was great to see grass again, so startlingly green that it was like dropping into a colourful fairyland. Later, on other Himalayan expeditions, after spending weeks above the snow-line, I have always looked forward to this descent into lusher regions.

There are hot springs at Manikaran in the Parbati. We had a much needed bath there. Later that same day we headed down the broad trail towards civilisation. We had stopped on a level section of path for a rest, when we heard sounds of an approaching band. Our coolies became very excited and shouted:

"Deabta, sahibs!" A god was approaching. Presently, round a corner came a queer procession, men and women in their Sunday best – a riot of colour – carrying cauldrons and tridents. The band of ten men boasted some weird instruments – which would give a plumber nightmares, and was busy churning out an obviously popular number. It was more a case of manufacturing music, than playing it: an endless cacophony of smashing cymbals and trumpet blasts. The god, or goddess (I never could tell the sex of these effigies) was in the centre of the group, the cloth adorned with braid and flowers. It was carried by two men.

This was no ordinary god vacation. We learned it was going for a bath at the holy hot springs at Manikaran. The oracle had relayed the god's wishes to the 'congregation'. One emaciated individual in the group was already in a trance. He was apparently high on a surfeit of godism and his eyes kept rolling as if fixed on a point of the perimeter of a large rotating wheel. The men carrying the litter also seemed to be under some sort of spell. They jostled the poor eye-rolling character, knocking him to the ground several times whilst his face contorted in agony. This condition seemed to be derived from some other influence as the godbearers didn't appear to hurt him physically.

I took some cine film of this incident, fascinated by the way the god swayed to and fro and sometimes leapt up, as if pulled by some force other than that exerted by the two bearers. It was like a puppet animated by invisible strings. The bearers must have been apt at this 'sleight of hand', giving the effect of unknown forces at work, whilst appearing mildy surprised at their own arm movements. But it was a disturbing spectacle; in a few minutes they had moved up the trail and it might all have been just a dream, had it not been for the diminishing sound of the band, tackling the latest scrapyard hit with renewed vigour.

As we walked down that trail towards civilisation I felt sure that the yeti didn't exist, or at least that it was now extinct. But little did I know then that twenty years later I would once again be searching for signs of it in one of the most remote corners of the Himalaya.

# 5

# The Frosty Caucasus

Between with many a captive cloud,
A shapeless dark and rapid crowd,
Each by lightning riven in half:
I heard the thunder hoarsely laugh . . .
[Shelley, 'Prometheus Unbound']

BEFORE I DWELL ON the Russian Caucasus – that icy turmoil of jagged peaks between the Black and Caspian Seas, I must first of all introduce George Ritchie, and to do so takes me back a number of years to the first time I hitch-hiked to the Alps.

It was in the immediate post-war years when one could flog bread coupons on the Continent and when coffee was worth its weight if not in gold, at least in many extra days' pocket money. My six-week holiday cost £10, thanks to the demand for bread coupons and coffee and, being hard up, I walked if I couldn't hitch. No vehicular traffic was then allowed to the village of Zermatt; even now the road may only be used by locals, and I had to walk to obtain my first prospect of the Matterhorn; a policy which I commend to others as one can savour the initial viewing to the full as it grows in stature with each succeeding stride. It is mind blowing by any standard; and the mountain never fails to exact more admiration than is due to such a pile of tottery rock. One can readily appreciate the love-hate relationship which evolved between it and the early pioneers. I had of course read and re-read the accounts of its conquest by Whymper and Guido Rey and as I wearily sought out the Youth Hostel, I resolved to make the ascent. On that holiday I was sporting my well-worn kilt, naïvely believing this garment would be an asset to hitch-hiking. In retrospect I feel it probably merely cast a doubt as to the sex of the wearer. During my stay I did in fact climb the Matterhorn, on the second attempt. To save hut fees I made the ascent from Zermatt and back in a day, an exhausting climb of 10,000 feet.

Some time before this I fell in with some British climbers, mainly of the Welsh school, who had taken up residence in a barn just outside town. Providentially I was not dossing there as it was burnt to the ground. I was later to make friends with some of the scorched inmates who included an old Creagh Dhu member then living in Wales, Scotty Dwyer. There was also Dicky Mosely and Derek Haworth. Derek was a great extrovert and exuded infectious enthusiasm. In an earlier era he might have been a knight errant. He was probably one of the finest rock climbers of his generation, though lacking in snow and ice experience. He had arrived illegally in Zermatt on his four-valved Rudge motor cycle, which he habitually drove at maniacal speed, and had hidden it under a pile of hay. Fortunately, it had escaped the holocaust. Derek was a doctor and his companion was George Ritchie from Edinburgh. George was more of a mountaineer than a rock gymnast, having climbed widely in the Alps and back home. He was small and dark with quick deft movements and had the energy of a terrier.

As soon as I had made acquaintance with these two pundits, Derek decided that we should immediately try the Zmuttgrat, one of the harder routes on the Matterhorn, failing of course to mention that the mountain was hopelessly out of condition and had not been climbed by a British party that season. Full more with enthusiasm than good judgment we set off for the Schönbuhl hut. I had no crampons, they were beyond my means in those days, but I wore a ponderous pair of boots with a mixture of clinker and tricouni nails. I had bought the boots in the Glasgow Barrows complete with steel toecaps and they ensured that I would inevitably descend feet first in any fall.

We reached the hut about 9 p.m. and the guardian, a tough

morose guide, displayed a marked apathy towards our venture. The route, he asserted, was for experienced mountaineers, not for children – he gave me a disparaging look.

"This season," he spoke in German and George translated, "the galleries are iced up and impassable." George's assurance that he would take our party back before anything disastrous happened did not placate him and in desperation, in the small hours of the morning before we set off, he attempted bribery as a last resort.

"Come back while you still live and I'll give you a bottle of brandy."

We bade him adieu and at 2.30 a.m. set off across the glacier picking our way by the dim light of a candle lantern. We didn't have a guide book, only a postcard (indeed I can recall many years later, on the first British attempt of the North Wall of the Eiger with Chris Bonington I was again using a postcard with the route marked on it – the poor man's 'guidebook'). As the postcard of the Matterhorn was taken in winter, it didn't help us greatly on that grey cold dawn. As a result we went too far over on to the Tiefenmatten face, into the jaws of the notorious Penhall couloir. I was glad that I had left my well-ventilated kilt covering Derek's motor cycle in Zermatt for a cold wind was stirring. My lack of crampons must have held up my two companions, but they didn't complain; I was very much the apprentice. I watched them taking turns cutting steps up that steep icy corridor. There was a continuous hail of ice particles from this activity and from time to time snow would peel away in avalanches leaving a black scar of ice. We moved together, there was no time to belay, but the couloir seemed endless like a treadmill, a treadmill which steepened as we ascended. The reason for this became clear when we broke out at the top; we had obviously missed our way and had come out at the top of a knife-edge of snow, which led to rock teeth guarding the lower section of the summit pyramid, instead of gaining the snow ridge at its lower end.

Our arrival was greeted by Nature's double bass orchestra. Turning round we saw thunder clouds rapidly advancing from

The Shkhelda ridge. Camp 7 with a 6,000 ft drop on the right.

Descending the Ushba icefall, a dangerous gauntlet to run at any time.

behind the Dent Blanche. To me especially, a novice at this climbing lark, my instinct was to get to hell out of it. This reaction I was pleased to observe was shared by my companions. We were rushing down that narrow snow arête like tight-rope walkers on pay night, when the storm struck. It didn't come in slowly, tentatively fingering us with a few more flakes; it arrived as a fully fledged instant blizzard. We reached the end of the snow ridge to find that the normal route from the hut which we should have used to ascend was too dangerous for descent, due to unstable snow. Anyhow, the matter was decided for us, the conditions were now too bad to contemplate doing anything but sheltering and attempting to survive. In this white hell, one feature remained, a cluster of rocks. It was like an oasis. Derek stated, or rather, shouted the obvious:

"We'll bivouac here."

Bivouac was a term which I then only associated with reading about military campaigns, but I was to receive a savage initiation in this the first of many bivouacs in my life, as the site chosen was one of the most exposed on the mountain. We didn't contemplate a snow hole, as such shelters were then unfashionable and it was impracticable in terms of time and effort as they mostly are.

There were a couple of cracks in those rocks which Derek and I, with our strong survival instincts, immediately commandeered, while George set to work building a dry stane wall to huddle behind, a difficult task as the raw materials had to be exhumed. I could only get part way into my fissure and when I next looked out at George from my crack a few minutes later he seemed to be bathed in an incandescent light, each drip of water round his anorak hood was highlighted. It was uncanny. He then heard a buzzing noise, he told us later and realised that the halo of light was St. Elmo's fire. He flung himself down behind his wall and the charge transferred to the rock under which I lay. It started as a small spark of light and steadily grew to a broad arc some 18 inches long. Suddenly the cloud above gave up its charge to the rock above me with a brilliant flash, followed by a god-almighty crash as if the world had split open. I could see from my refuge a splinter of rock glowing red with this discharge, a thing I certainly had never seen before or since. We had of course stowed our ironmongery a safe distance away, but I thought my superconducting boots could provide me with something less than cold feet.

As a kid I had witnessed the great Professor Body surviving some fuse-blowing electrical charge when strapped to an electric chair. I had been suitably impressed at the time and at dawn I felt what that oft-shocked music hall artist must have felt the morning after the night before. But we were all glad to be alive and made little of the actual discomforts of the bivouac. We were soon to find fresh hazards. After we had scraped the ice off the rope and rescued our cached ice axes we set off stiff as toy soldiers. George decided that the safest course of action was to head for the Hörnli hut at the bottom of the normal way up the Matterhorn on the ridge of that same name. It is also from this hut that the Zmuttgrat is usually climbed by a much shorter route.

We managed eventually to traverse across a broad step on the lower section of the north face in deep snow to reach a point above a large sérac. There was a drop of about 70 feet with no other way down. The morning was improving and we could see above us the Hörnli hut and the glint of binoculars; we were being watched. At this point my two friends said that we would have to abseil and the rope was promptly taken off, doubled and the ends thrown down the face. A grunt of satisfaction from Derek indicated that it almost reached the easy slopes below. The stretch, he informed us – it was one of the then new-fangled nylon ropes – would ensure that we reached terra firma. He cut an ice bollard for an anchor. I went down first. As Derek had promised, I reached the bottom without difficulty where I was soon joined by the others. Derek then pulled one end of the rope to retrieve it, but it wouldn't budge! Our combined efforts were no better. Derek then attempted to climb up, hand over hand, but since part of the ascent was overhanging he was unsuccessful. Sliding back down, he announced breathlessly that as the youngest and fittest member of the group I'd have to do it! I told him – with due respect – to get lost. So we made our way uphill to the Hörnli hut, minus the rope. Alexander Graven, who happened to be stormbound at the Hörnli hut at the time, had been amazed to see three figures returning from the Zmutt out of the jaws of the storm. Unknown to us, his companions there had been shouting advice whilst we were on the sérac.

My £10 holiday in the Alps made a deep impression on me and from it developed lasting friendships with both Derek and George. However, it wasn't until 1962 that I again climbed with George. During the intervening years we had both gained experience on mountains in various parts of the world.

George dropped in at my cottage in Glencoe one day to tell me that after several years of negotiation the Scottish Mountaineering Club had received an invitation to send a joint party with the Alpine Club to the Soviet Caucasus. Departure was in three weeks' time, was I interested? I was, but felt duty bound to point out that I was not a member of the illustrious club. George felt that he could overcome such a triviality. I was Scots, he pointed out and it was to representatives from Scotland that the invitation was directed. When my next excuse was raised, that of cost, George generously said that we could drive out and he would meet any expenses beyond my current resources. However, at the time I was making TV films for Associated Rediffusion and when John Rhodes, the producer of the series agreed to accept a thirty-minute documentary on the Caucasus, I was in a position to say yes.

A few days later I gave George a ring and told him I could come. He sounded delighted and promptly started to organise the trip in a frenzy of activity – everything associated with George happens at double speed; he is invariably involved in ten different ploys simultaneously. The third member of our party was a Cambridge don: Michael Vyvyan. He was a member of the Alpine Club, spoke Russian, had visited Russia and knew the British Ambassador in Moscow. Michael was going to fly to Moscow, but we were to make the journey in George's Mini. Minis were then still an interesting novelty and every Mini's owner thought he was at the wheel of a scaled-down Ferrari. George and I were no exceptions and after the usual traumas of obtaining visas, etc., we wound up the car on what was virtually a non-stop drive.

Going through the iron curtain really did feel like rolling into another world, where life took on a grey, metallic aspect. Even the false teeth were made from stainless steel. It was disconcerting to drive along the deserted East German autobahn and find bomb craters in the road, old untreated war wounds. We entered Russia at Brest, where a grim-faced soldier guarded the frontier bridge, his scowl suggesting that he'd been deprived of his vodka ration for some weeks. One evening deep in Russia we sought the sanctuary of an official camp site but were told that we didn't possess the necessary visas or vouchers so, exhausted, we snatched a few hours' kip alongside the road, then were on our way again.

Three days after leaving London we saw like a mirage the tall buildings of Moscow rise out of the plain. It was a moving and unforgettable sight.

We didn't get much sleep on the journey and we met with a nightmare within the capital city. Traffic lights were everywhere and within minutes police with loudhailers, directed at us, were obviously imparting useful information – if only we could have understood! We were rescued by a friendly British tourist who took us to the Leningradskaya Hotel where we had been told to report. A good-looking receptionist smiled at us as she dealt with a portly American. He was lamenting the high prices and saying he would only be able to stay for part of his planned vacation due to the cost. I licked my lips and glanced apprehensively at George who, the good Scotsman that he is, was also taking mental note. When it was our turn to be charmed by the budding Venus we did some fast backpedalling and instead of asking for rooms asked where we could obtain vouchers for the official Moscow camp site. We had hurriedly decided that this could save us innumerable roubles. The girl was tactful, appreciating our predicament, since the effect of several thousand miles in a Mini leaves its mark on even those who start immaculate – which we certainly had not! She came from Leningrad and, like everyone exiled from that city, sang of its virtues. We moved to the Moscow camp site.

Camping in Russia is definitely in the luxury class. There was none of that nonsense of putting up a tent or blowing up an air bed. Everything was provided; the tents even had duckboards over the ground sheet; camp beds were supplied and electricity laid on. It wasn't cheap but we consoled ourselves with the thought that we must be saving a bomb by not boarding at the sumptuous Leningradskaya Hotel.

Food was scarce, but we gleaned from a woman at the market that we could have eggs if we went along the following day. Sure enough, she had put aside half a dozen under the counter for us.

One of the things that struck me most about Russia was the complete unselfishness of the people; nothing was too much trouble for them. At home, one of my long-standing hobbies has been visiting auction sales; I had thus become the owner of an English/Russian dictionary, over a hundred years old, bought in a bargain lot of books. As I thumbed hastily through it to find the required word for some transaction, I quickly gathered a crowd of onlookers, for the dictionary was unique. One glance at it and the Russians would be howling with laughter.

In some ways Moscow reminded me of Glasgow, that's probably why I felt at home there. Apart for a shared liking for alcohol there is the same genuine concern for the visitor. We had only to ask someone the direction to some place and he would immediately feel it his bounden duty to guide us there personally. The second day after our arrival we sought out the premises of the Mountaineering Federation of the U.S.S.R. at Skatertnyi Pereulok in a nondescript alleyway. A conscientious citizen not content with taking us three miles to our destination, insisted on accompanying us up the lift to the receptionist and into the very office of Eugene Gippenreiter, our contact in the Federation. Only when we had shaken hands with Eugene did our guide bow and leave.

We now learned that Michael Vyvyan had postponed his departure from the U.K. as he didn't think we could reach Moscow in three days in a Mini. Eugene also told us that they had made arrangements for our accommodation, and our presence in the city without officially registering could have been an embarrassment. After meeting other officials of the Federation we were taken to a spacious suite in the Edwardian splendour of the Hotel Metropol. Oriental carpets, gilt and red plush furnishings, fountains, discreet chambermaids, as if fresh from the pages of an Agatha Christie novel, and all for the same price as the camp site. We had business visas which, we now gathered, gave us very special concessions.

We absorbed the luxury of the hotel like two dry sponges and awaited Michael. When he arrived we didn't waste much time and next day we flew to Mineralnye-Vody by TU-100 jet. Air travel in the Soviet Union is as cheap as train with the result that peasants from farming districts frequently travel to Moscow by plane to sell their products. Leaving Moscow we were given preferential treatment; in this country where – to borrow a phrase – "all pigs are equal", we found ourselves more equal than most and were ushered aboard first and given our choice of seats. A small but important deputation of Masters of Sport travelled with us; they were to spend several months in the mountains, mainly as advisers. There was also a special 'reporter' on mountaineering matters who would be with the party throughout our stay; he gave most of his attention to Michael Vyvyan. He was later christened the 'Wasp', due partly to a bright yellow and black football jersey which he sported, and partly in recognition of the industrious way in which he buzzed around Michael.

From Mineralnye-Vody we had a hundred-mile drive through fields of tobacco, maize, sunflowers and cowboys on horseback, then progressively dustier and bumpier roads took us into the heart of the Caucasus; it felt as if we were travelling over them. I was reminded of Kipling's lines: "where the trails run out and stop"; for us they stopped at Spartak Camp. Feeling more like rusty jack-knives than climbers we straightened and staggered out. Above the trees the mountains rose in an icy dream. This was what we had come for! The air was keen, full of the perfume of pines and wild flowers. This serenity was abruptly shattered by the Tannoy system calling out a parade to give us an official welcome.

Spartak Camp, like others in the Caucasus, is sponsored by the Trade Unions, but colleges and other organisations also use them. The main building is a substantial structure which serves as lecture hall, games centre and canteen, while the majority of the guests or pupils who come for tuition in mountaineering are housed in dormitories, cabins or tents identical to those we used in Moscow. I wondered idly how many millions of these tents had been produced. We were soon shown to our quarters in one of the cabins close to the main building. Michael, appropriately dressed in Empire Building shorts, announced it was time for tea and conjured up a small kettle, primus and packet of tea from his rucksack, proceeding to brew up on the verandah much to the consternation of the Russians in the adjoining cabins. This course of action was obviously outwith normal procedure!

We soon learnt that there was a strict protocol, reminiscent of army days, not that my service career spent in the Austrian Tirol had been particularly onerous. At Spartak, promptly at 6 a.m. each morning, Big Brother's metallic voice echoed from the loudspeakers telling everyone to be joyous and announcing the hour for P.T. Those in camp were expected to tumble out of bed, full of *joie de vivre*, and run about as if they enjoyed it, play volleyball, or disport themselves in an energetic fashion. The first morning I stared malevolently from under heavy eyelids at a boisterous youth, overflowing with health and dressed only in swimming trunks, who charged straight into our room, urging us to join the youth of the Soviet Union in worshipping the equivalent of Aurora.

"Bugger off, Jimmy!" I spoke with as much goodwill as possible in my voice. "We don't go in for this sort of thing where we come from!"

Any Russian wishing to spend a holiday at one of the Union camps in the Caucasus applies through the Trade Union and, if he is selected, each week a small percentage is docked off his pay for the forthcoming holiday. Holidays on the 'never-never'. The camps are in some ways akin to the Sports Council's centres in Britain where the emphasis is on instruction. The tutors in these alpine camps are qualified mountaineers and are usually Masters of Sport. They come from all walks of life, but to attain this grade takes a number of years of hard training and a host of serious climbs. The Masters of Sport attend the Caucasian camps for several months each year, usually at a reduced salary from their normal professions, and they regard their time in the peaks as a paid holiday. There are various grades of courses, ranging from simple glacier work and river crossing to the traverse of the more serious ridges and buttresses of the Caucasus. All equipment is issued from the camp store; by Western standards it is cumbersome and heavy, though functional. Nailed boots are still used and are quite suitable for the type of terrain, though colder to wear than normal rubber-soled climbing boots and crampons.

A discipline has been instilled into Russian mountaineers which is hard for the Westerner to understand, used as he is to the freedom of the hills. Part of the charm of the mountains to the average climber is the complete absence of bureaucracy; the chance to get away from the thraldom of society and city life. In Russia you may only undertake climbs consonant with your previous experience and skill, and a 'control time' is given for any route you intend doing. In other words, when you apply for permission to leave the camp you may have to justify your proposals to a Panel of Honoured Masters of Sport, bureaucracy if you like, indicating how long you anticipate that particular route will take your party, adding on a day or so for the inevitably bad Caucasian weather to be on the safe side. The Honoured Masters of Sport are generally elderly tigers with blunted claws, though still very much with it. If they are satisfied with your plan and the weather report you receive permission and supplies. If you fail to return within your stipulated time a rescue party is sent out at the expiry of the 'control time'. Usually too, your progress on a route is monitored by the use of flares, indicating the position of your party, or by walkie-talkie. These measures may seem far-fetched and alien to Westerners, but even with such precautions there are a great number of accidents. When mountains of the altitude and the severity of the Caucasian peaks are 'popular-ised', it is inevitable that serious accidents occur. Even during our short stay at Spartak, several people lost their lives.

Returning to our first morning, some time after the cries of eager youth had subsided from the playgrounds, we eased out of our pits and staggered somewhat shamefacedly over to the dining hall to see what we could scrounge by way of a late breakfast. This proved to be a meal more resembling lunch with salad, fruit and dessert. That morning a conference was held to decide how our time could most actively be deployed during our stay. I mentioned that in order to pay the expense of my trip I would have to make a 30-minute film. The Honoured Masters of Sport made no objection; possibly taking pity on me as a victim of capitalism. They even promised to help. It was decided that we should first complete a training climb; then move on to one of the more serious routes.

Two young Masters of Sport were introduced to us, Eugene Tur, an engineer from Gorki and Igor Bandurovski, a school teacher from Odessa. Both were quiet-spoken men: Eugene, short and compact; Igor, tall and lithe. Michael Vyvyan had slightly less ambitious plans than either George or I and decided that a visit to the Bezingi region of the Caucasus with a suitable climber would be of greater interest to him. The official reporter, the Wasp, immediately leapt into action and volunteered to accompany him, much to Michael's chagrin. It was suggested that George and I should attempt the relatively easy, low peak of Cubang Bashi for our training climb. Neither Igor nor Eugene who were to accompany us had climbed it and furthermore it was immediately accessible. After all it was acclimatisation we needed at that moment, so this mountain, just a short way up the valley, seemed to fulfil our requirements. We set off next day under a watery sun after saying au revoir to Michael and the Wasp.

The Caucasus seem to be dogged by bad weather and the day we spent high on Cubang Bashi was no exception. The mist stole down to meet us like a clinging poultice and obliterated everything. It was quite possible to go on and we were about three-quarters of the way up, but as George and I both had a surfeit of damp climbs to our credit back home, we decided that the comfortable cabin at Spartak held more attractions. Our Russian colleagues accepted our logic, but as they had been schooled not to give up quite so easily they were at first reluctant to retreat, though we soon broke down their defences by dint of hard reasoning and with the promise of good Ceylon tea and chocolate biscuits. We made fast time back to camp where we found we were definitely out of favour. It wasn't usual to be daunted by mere inclemency in the weather, not even in the teeth of a blizzard, we were informed by an austere Master of Sport who looked old enough to have made the first ascent of Elbrus with Freshfield. No doubt our Russian companions, Eugene and Igor, were told off in a more forthright manner.

After a further conference at which our proposals for new routes were firmly if politely rejected, our hosts decided to take the initiative and sent Eugene to suggest that we should do the traverse of Shkhelda, a barrier of precipitous peaks about 14,000 feet in height. It was, he said, a "very hard tour" of the top grade, 5b category; it hadn't then been done by Westerners. Despite the fact that we had blotted our copybook on the Cubang Bashi expedition, our application to attempt the traverse was approved and we learned from Eugene that the route could take as long as thirteen days if the weather proved unfavourable. Both George and I have the habit of making light of possible difficulties and brashly stated that we should be able to do the climb in three or four days. Why, even some of the greatest alpine routes didn't take that long, we reasoned; later we were to regret our rashness.

In the Caucasian camp a charming custom is observed; parties going on a major climb are cheered away by the camp residents. We couldn't help feeling as we left with all our swag that we were about to engage in mortal combat with a formidable adversary. In fact, we were. There is also a correspondingly pleasant ritual at the finish – should you be successful – of being presented with large bouquets of exotic Caucasian flowers by the many good-looking girls attending the courses. We had stocked up with some chocolate from home and Complan, a powdered food which, the label assures one, is a totally balanced diet all in one packet, but which leaves much to be desired in flavour. Shaking their heads at this restricted diet our hosts insisted that we take two small aluminium containers of Black Sea caviar, one of red and one of black. We estimated that we had enough food for four days.

We walked up through the trees on a carpet of pine needles until we reached the edge of the Shkhelda glacier. That walk to the peaks of the Caucasus, through the idyllic forests and abundant flora of the foothills is my most lingering memory of those cold mountains. Wild bear and wolves still roam there and the trees felt like a haven in dramatic contrast to the frigid peaks above.

It was to be an easy day and we planned to camp on the edge of the moraine below the first peak so we weren't in any great hurry. The Shkhelda glacier flows from the skirt of the magnificent Ushba, one of the finest peaks of the range, with few rivals anywhere. It then tumbles down in a steep icefall between Pik Shchurovskiy (of which more anon) and the far end of the Shkhelda range at East Shkhelda; then brushes the base of Shkhelda for most of its length before veering north towards Spartak Camp. We were using two Russian tents; possibly the best item of equipment they possessed, made of an aluminised fabric both light and waterproof, and we pitched these in a hollow by the south side of the glacier. We had carried up some wood for a fire, so before the shadows had marched across the ice from the peaks, a healthy column of pine smoke was spiralling upwards.

It was difficult for us to grasp the scale of the mountains. We were camped below the face of the first peak. Eugene and Igor told us the route went directly from our glacier to the summit of West Shkhelda. We had refused to take a bulky walkie-talkie with us, but carried a Very pistol and a supply of flares which Eugene had arranged to set off at intervals to indicate our progress to watchers at Spartak Camp. After our meal that night we were surprised when the Russians suggested an 8 a.m. start; we expected to be away before dawn. Though we exhibited a tendency to laze about Spartak, it wasn't our usual policy in the mountains! But we didn't make an issue of it. It was pleasant on the moraine with the flames playing in a boulder hearth. Warm and relaxed with a good meal inside us . . . what more could one desire?

Next morning we set off across the ice at the time when George normally made his way to his Edinburgh office. It was an indifferent day, as if the heavens were debating their policy for the next week. Later, however, they had made up their minds in no uncertain manner! By the time we reached the steeper slopes of First West Shkhelda clouds were down on the mountains as if trying to smother them. Later they did so – with snow. It started to snow heavily before we were ready to set up camp for the night. It had been an uneventful day, toilsome with little technical difficulty. Now lightning frolicked as if playing tag with the surrounding peaks and soon we were soaked to the skin. However, we manufactured a ledge from the frozen scree, levering large boulders aside and in so doing I broke 'the Message', my ice hammer. Later, finding the site too exposed, we moved camp higher and to one side away from imminent avalanche danger, for the snow was amassing above us at an alarming rate.

Shkhelda was obviously making an issue of it. Scotsmen who had the temerity to underrate her and take only four days' food supply for such a climb were indeed an insult. There were three days in which to contemplate this tactical error, the

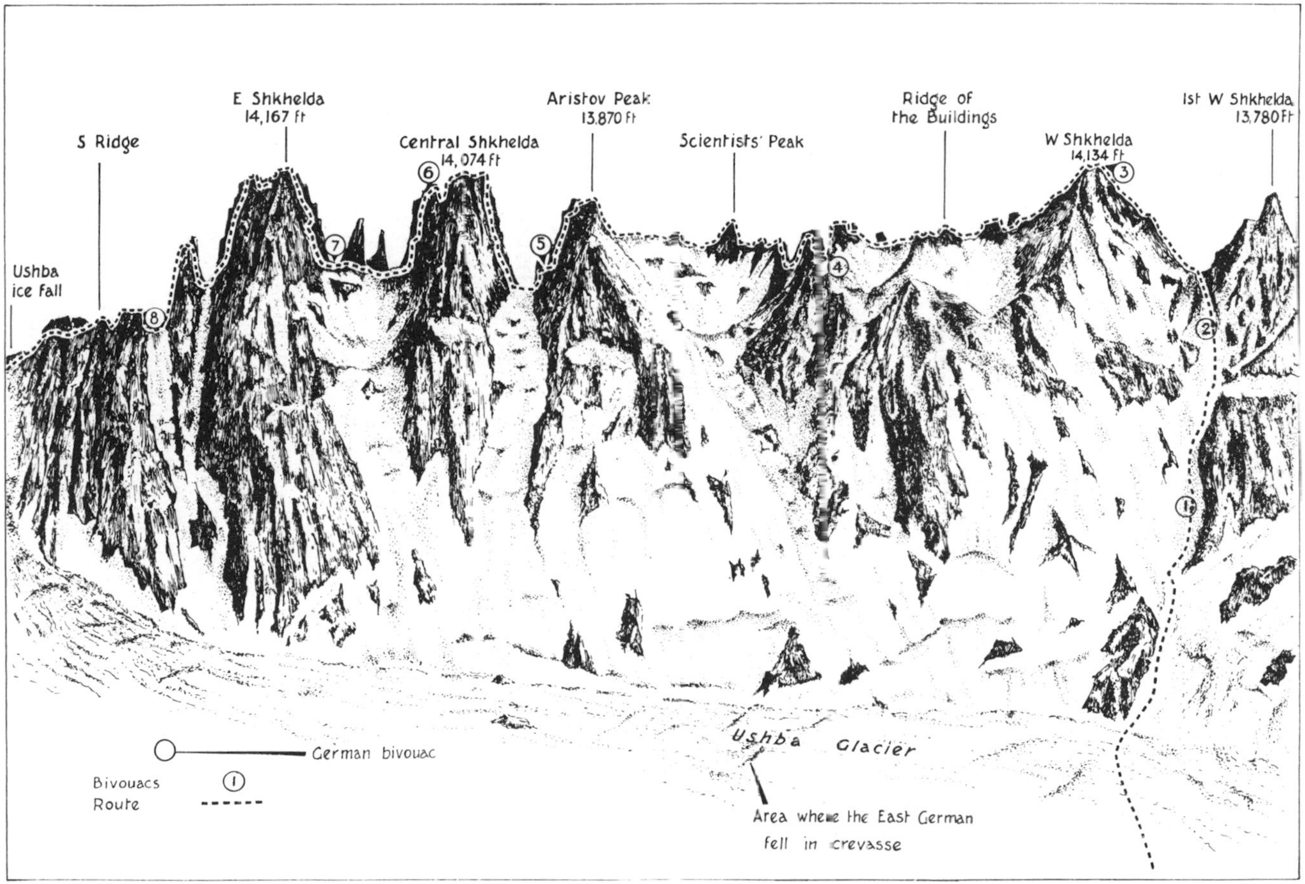
Ushba ice fall
S Ridge
E Shkhelda 14,167 ft
Central Shkhelda 14,074 ft
Aristov Peak 13,870 ft
Scientists' Peak
Ridge of the Buildings
W Shkhelda 14,134 ft
Ist W Shkhelda 13,780 Ft
Ushba Glacier
German bivouac
Bivouacs
Route
Area where the East German fell in crevasse

*The Shkhelda traverse.*

duration of the storm. Avalanches were continuous and there was an appalling fall of snow. One day Eugene was heard to remark wryly:

"The politicians should come up here for their summit conferences and be abandoned until some agreement is reached!"

But all bad things come to an end, and when the weather cleared we headed upwards. There was no going back this time; we were resolved about that. To reach the summit of the first peak necessitated wading of a high standard. We camped on a steep exposed slope, again having to manufacture a ledge and in so doing broke two more ice axes, a serious loss.

Presently George remarked to me, "This place isn't safe, Hamish. Don't you think the whole lot might move during the night?" He was right. The face under the snow was composed of unstable scree. It was like pitching camp on the flank of a steep coal bing.

"I'll run a rope up to those rocks over there." I pointed to an outcrop a short way off. "That should make a good mooring." When I had suited action to words, we ran the end of the rope through the sleeve entrance of the tent and tied on, once safely installed inside our sleeping bags. During the day which had shown a flicker of improvement we had heard distant voices and now, just as we were settling in for the night, a party of Russian alpinists arrived. They had started the climb from a different point and had also been caught in the blizzard; they decided to camp nearby. It appeared that they were members of a Red Army group and, by the easy way they moved they were obviously powerful climbers.

In the morning I took the lead again and the Red Army party fell in behind. It was a glorious morning; everything crystal clear as if the landscape had just been scrubbed white. In fact the fresh snow had frozen hard. Ahead, Ushba reared from its bed of ice like the twin horns of a rhinoceros, whilst in the foreground the serrated edge of Shkhelda snaked out ahead like a giant cross-cut saw. In the immediate foreground was the Ridge of the Buildings – rickety buildings, we were to discover, cemented together to a large extent by the recent snow. Behind us, rising in great obesity like the two ugly sisters, yet elegant in its own way, was Elbrus (18,481 feet) the highest peak in Europe. Elbrus is now a popular ski area and there are chairlifts to the col between its twin summits.

The Ridge of the Buildings was well named: in places it resembled the ridge of a steep cathedral roof, incongruously connected to high-rise blocks. The exposure was guts-turning and in places the edge of the ridge could literally be grasped between forefinger and thumb. We went along such sections *à cheval*, painful to the anatomy but comforting to the peace of mind. There were several towers, or gendarmes, which had to be turned; sometimes left, other times to the right and several direct. There were various abseils en route too, some of over 120 feet. We had become so absorbed in the technical problems of traversing the Ridge of the Buildings that we failed to notice how time was slipping by. Although we had finally convinced the Russians of our capability of early rising and had left our camp at dawn, it was now 3 p.m. and a bulk order of clouds came steaming up from the Caspian, heralded by peals of thunder. We moved more quickly and did a further 120-foot rappel to a minute snow ledge which overhung a breathtaking drop of 6000 feet. We built a platform of stones cemented with ice produced from the only obvious supply of warm water we had readily available and pitched the tents rapidly as the first languid snowflakes fell. Our Red Army friends were not so fortunate. They were caught on an exposed edge by the full fury of this sudden storm. What was worse was the high voltage act. The lightning bounced off the gendarmes as if in a holocaust scene from a space fiction movie. They told us later their pitons and ice axes actually emitted blue flashes and they thought they would be 'cooked' at any second. Eventually they abseiled down to join us, soaked by the driving snow and erected their tent on the only possible place, a minute tongue of snow bordering an unstable cornice which gave me the willies, even looking at it! Their guys hung literally in space as there was nowhere to attach them. We made a weak brew of tea for dinner that night, washing down a spoonful of Complan.

Next day we continued in the now settled weather, settled for the worse in wind and snow, and we made painfully slow progress along the crest. It was still very narrow and our itinerary was similar to the previous day, minus the illuminations. There was a lot of snow now which made that tight-rope crest dangerous, to say the least; we had to be constantly vigilant. A precarious edge of snow gave way once under George, but he managed to stop himself before he launched into space, and just before the rope tightened.

That night we camped on a steep snow slope in thick cloud. Two days later we were still there! The weather had taken a turn for the worse like a chronic invalid, and with virtually no food we were gradually starving to death on minute quantities of Black Sea caviar. I slowly realised that I wasn't enjoying myself any more; we seemed to be concentrating too hard on survival. The others had descended a vertical cliff by rappel; in its lower reaches it curved into a wide chimney. As I went down a rock whistled past, narrowly missing my head. It had more success lower down and hit Igor on the knee. Spiralling down – for the abseil was free the final 60 feet – I could see the Russian doubled up in pain. They were all crouched on a ledge the size of a cupboard door. Many thousands of feet below lay the snows of Svanetia. It was impossible to do anything for him on the sloping ledge but somehow we managed to lower him to a better platform, 70 feet down below a series of overhangs. This was a complicated and time-consuming manoeuvre in such bad weather; we had to arrange a system of piton anchors to enable us to lower him in the right direction so that he arrived direct on target. After what seemed a light year, he landed successfully on a ledge some five feet wide with a clear fall to the abyss below. This we levelled to hold the tents. Once inside, we discovered that the injury appeared to be purely bruising. With luck, we decided, he should be able to continue after a rest. We no longer had to worry about the food running out – it had, except for a sensation of caviar and a trowel full of Complan! It was another night of high winds and snow. We

Alan Chivers and the Old Man of Hoy, the outside broadcast captured the popular imagination.

Rusty Baillie on the East Face of the Old Man, belayed by Syd Wilkinson.

Ian Clough using jumar clamps on the Crux pitch of the Old Man of Hoy.

knew that ahead of us lay the main difficulties: the two high peaks of Shkhelda, either of which would have posed a formidable climb back home or in the Alps.

The Red Army joined us later, but there was little they could do to help us in our predicament. We did consider trying to descend directly down the face to Svanetia which lay to the south, a wild, isolated region with a tradition like that of the Scottish Borders, but the avalanche risk was too great. That night the Red Army climbers gave us two tins of meat, an absolute godsend, though their generosity was embarrassing as they, too, were very short of supplies and would be several days without food before they got off the climb. Next day they passed through, as we had definitely decided to give Igor a day's rest. We watched the Red Army lads climbing through petulant clouds as they made the ascent of Central Shkhelda (14,074 feet). It looked both intimidating and cold.

Later in the day a party from Rostov joined us and built two platforms for their tents. All level space was now covered and every movement of nature and otherwise, required the use of safety ropes. The new arrivals were a cheerful bunch and despite our predicament there was much laughter. That evening they invited us for 'tea' – it must have been one of the weirdest tea parties ever held. Their two tents faced each other on a cat-walk ledge shadowed by a rock overhang above and a blizzard boiling below. I went 'visiting' in socks and almost called in at Svanetia sooner than anticipated as I slipped on the glassy surface where someone had produced a 'hot water' slide. Ten of us crammed into the tiny two-man tent. Over tea we sang . . . George and I chuckled upon discovery that their knowledge of the works of Kipling included a repertoire of his imperialistic songs. I was able to contribute with lesser known songs such as the 'Grand Trunk Road'. And of course Robbie Burns is a passport anywhere in the Soviet Union; the crags of Shkhelda echoed with 'Auld Lang Syne' and 'Scots Wha Hae'. I taught the Russians the 'Caviar Song' which went down well – almost as well as our last mouthful of that delectable food!

Caviar comes from the virgin sturgeon,
Virgin sturgeon's a very fine fish,
Virgin sturgeon needs no urgin',
That's why caviar is my dish.

One of the Rostov climbers was quick on the uptake – he could speak fluent English. After hearing three verses once only he improvised in a fine baritone:

I gave caviar to my grandad,
Grandad's age was ninety-three,
Screams of laughter came from grandma,
As he chased her up a tree.

It was just as well there was no vodka that night, it is very much frowned upon in Russian mountains, or we'd never have made that icy traverse back to our tents safely; it was at least 'severe' in socks!

In the morning, the weather having deteriorated still further, it was decided that I should lead and fix the rope, while the others, including the Rostov party, used it to climb up. The traverse was now taking on a serious aspect; we all knew we couldn't survive such weather conditions for any length of time.

That night snow drifted over our tent and the temperature dropped alarmingly. We were frozen even inside our sleeping bags and the tents were now caked with ice; trying to fold them in the morning was an almost impossible task. Eugene and Igor's tent seemed, if anything, an even more cumbersome parcel than ours.

The next section we approached, the ascent of the Central Tower of Shkhelda, is described by the Russian guide as "A steep couloir on the south of the crest. The rocks in it are frequently ice-covered and piton safeguards are required." Certainly the rocks were ice-covered; I could hardly make contact with them as I inched my way up the steep gully. It was Scottish type ice-climbing on a grand scale and I made 150-foot runouts. I didn't use any pitons for the simple reason that I couldn't find any placings for them. George followed, climbing, but the others made their way to the belay ledges, hand over hand up the 'krepi' or standing rope like a commando assault group. The swirling snow reduced visibility to a few yards and the wind was whipping round the ridge from the north. Eventually I broke out left on to the crest of the ridge and climbed it for about 130 feet before returning to the continuation of the couloir for a further 160 feet. Normally this section is dangerously loose, but at the time everything was well bonded with layers of ice. We made our way erratically up, like a procession of ants on a wedding cake. The climbing in this upper section was of a high standard and when we finally arrived on that hard-gained summit we were shattered.

Eugene started to dig in the snow. At first I thought he was going round the twist – not an unusual occurrence when under stress at altitude on a big route, but was reassured when he explained that there might be goodies buried there. Apparently, on long climbs such as this, students from the camps take food up to individual summits to provide against such emergencies. The first thing Eugene unearthed – or unsnowed – was a great black sausage. We cut it open with glee only to find that it was bad – at least, we thought so. And the *choucas* (alpine birds) which had suddenly appeared with a clearing of the weather, wouldn't eat it either. But there was also a tin of sprats and one of condensed milk. This was good news to us and we pressed along the summit ridge in search of a bivouac site. Going along that edge wasn't easy and we had to keep on the southern side. Once George dropped his ice axe, the only one still intact, but fortunately it landed on a ledge a short way down and I was able to lower him to retrieve it.

We now had to do an abseil of 130 feet, but as there was a narrow rock ledge running across the snow face at this point, we decided to bivouac.

It was a hairy place to put up tents but by now we took such problems as a matter of course. They say you get used to anything except hanging, but we felt that we were almost

131

hanging in those bivouacs! Both the Red Army and the Rostov parties had decided to make a descent now into Svanetia by a subsidiary ridge, thereby shortening the route. But we felt that, having come so far, we would finish the ruddy thing – if it didn't finish us first! We had been unable to send any flare signals to our faithful watchers at Spartak, because of the bad weather, and it was now drawing close to our control time of twelve days. It was our tenth day on the traverse, but we took the precaution of asking the other two parties to tell Spartak we were all right.

The cold, as well as lack of food, was beginning to tell. I was finding the Caucasus as cold as the Himalaya and wondering why the hell I was there. Once allotted the task of leading, I was stuck with it and while George was also climbing, using the rope only as a safeguard and not as a handrail, I had no moral scruples as to our two Russian friends scrambling up the rope. After all, it did save time and when a climb drags on as long as this one had, climbing ethics go by the board.

Sometime during the past few days condensed milk had been spilt over the Russians' sewn-in groundsheet which, subsequently freezing, no doubt added to the insulative properties of the material. In our present state of hunger, this attribute to comfort fell victim to Igor's hunger. That morning, through the blowing snow, I saw him licking with relish this foul mess, now reinforced with bits of wool and dubbin. Its distinctly jaundiced shade also bore witness to his inaccuracy in using his pee tin, a necessary item in such a cold environment.

An abseil next morning brought us down to a col. It was a lung-biting morning with the usual formulae of wind and blinding snow. There were two gendarmes on the crest of the col between Central and Eastern Shkhelda which had to be turned to the south. Normally these pinnacles would have been no problem but, in that weather, it was bivouac time before we reached the East Peak, the last obstacle on our route we dug ledges out of the frozen snow for the night, hacking away like ice-encrusted old age pensioners digging our last niche on the way to heaven. Or perhaps the scene was more like Napoleon's retreat from Moscow than of aspiring mountaineers pitting their resources against a mountain. And one, at least, had boasted less than two weeks previously that he'd knock Shkhelda off in four days!

That night was our coldest on the climb. We were frozen to the marrow and our clothes resembled a collection of oil drums and stove pipes in the morning. Though our boots shared our sleeping bags, they too were solid and, being only single boots, not modern doubles, it was like playing our feet into moulds. The tents folded like hardboard and made a ridiculous-looking burden on top of the rucksacks. I set off, traversing out on small holds on a gigantic slab of daunting exposure, heading for a patch of sun which, though off the route, was as essential to our well-being as drink to an alcoholic. It was a good day at last. Above and to the left, on the steep wall high above the Shkhelda glacier, a small ledge glimmered: it looked like paradise to us. More like a zombie than a climber, I moved up, jerky and unco-ordinated as one often is after a bad bivouac. It is a dangerous time; reactions are slow and hands cannot grip, particularly when the gloves resemble small spades.

The ledge was more akin to a chessboard than a tennis court and sloped slightly downhill to a drop which was still 6000 feet. But the sun blessed it and we were soon all secured and able to take our boots off and massage our feet. Slowly our windproof clothing changed colour from a matt white to a dirty damp hue, then finally steamed. We were all frost-bitten we knew, but not to what extent – it is difficult to tell at such an early stage. The sky was blue and the storybook range of Caucasian mountains lay unfolded before us; it was magnificent. Even in our exhausted state, we felt the exhilaration of just being up there. I led on again; the penalty for such pleasures had now to be paid for and I had to get back on to the route. It proved very hard. First I had to climb an ice-filled overhanging crack on very poor pegs while the ice was continually breaking off. In due course I made it and gained the normal route to the summit of East Shkhelda.

Once on top we took photographs, while just across the

glacier Ushba crouched in her twin-topped splendour. To our right the descent ridge angled down to the south and west to reach the glacier just across from the north-west face of Ushba.

That night we bivouacked at the end of the rock ridge, a pleasant night in relative calm and in the morning descended the Ushba icefall, a dangerous gauntlet to run at any time and then worse than usual. Late that same day we reached Spartak and received a big welcome. The whole camp turned out and flowers were showered upon us. We ate a 'welcome home' dinner under a superb oil painting which an artist had prepared for our arrival, emblazoned across it the Russian words: 'Conquering Heroes'. We were in dire need of that feast, having each lost about one and a half stones during the climb.

Our thirteen-day expedition had put us behind schedule and I still had to make a film to pay for my 'holiday'. The Russians hadn't forgotten, however; Abalakov and Rotentaov, two very senior Masters of Sport, quickly organised things for the following day. The whole camp was put at our disposal and the movie was made on a nearby glacier and round the camp. It was planned to depict the way of life and the training at a Russian Trade Union holiday camp. Later it was shown in the U.K. where I found a Soviet commentator to present it with me – an unusual occurrence at any time, and almost unheard of then.

We made our way back to Moscow where we went to retrieve our dirty Mini. It is an offence to have a dirty car in the city! Needless to say, after being abandoned for so long in Revolution Square, the battery was dry and the Mini was reluctant to start. But Muscovite taxi drivers, I discovered, were every bit as helpful as Muscovite pedestrians. We soon acquired a posse of them, pushing us across the Square while, in high good humour, they chanted some revolutionary or derisive song.

While Michael went by air back to London, we whirled our way along the great straights of the Soviet Union, en route for

Poland. It was harvest time and the land was golden. The barrier at Brest clanged behind us and we had entered the hospitable land of the Poles. It was near Warsaw on a Saturday night that our luck ran out. A cyclist was weaving his way in a manner peculiar to drunks the world over and veered out from the dirt road which runs alongside the main highways in many east European countries. George, who was driving, didn't have a chance; bicycle and cyclist went up in the air. We scuttled back to see if he was alive . . . He was . . . and his invective (recognisable in any language) was wonderful. His concern was all for his bicycle which was suffering from a buckled wheel! Soon a small crowd gathered and divided into two parties: those for and those against the foreigners. It was obvious that the cyclist himself was drunk. One chap stopped in a car and said helpfully to George, in English.

"You pay him £30 and forget about it!"

"Not on your life," George returned, having done his home-work – as a good solicitor should. He'd actually read the small print of the State Insurance which we had taken out at the frontier. So he called for the Police; this move was generally applauded by the pro-Scots.

Half an hour later a police car drew up and out of it tumbled an insurance assessor, a judge, an interpreter and a policeman. Court was held on the public highway.

"How much damage to the car?" George was asked.

"About £3.50," my friend replied, surveying the damage with a critical eye. The damage to the bike was some 70p, apparently. But George then magnaminously declared that as the cyclist was evidently a poor man compared to himself, he would pay for the wheel. Upon hearing this proposal trans-lated, the drunk leapt at George and grabbed him by the shoulders, kissing him on both cheeks. The settlement was obviously favourable! Several horses and carts had drawn up – their occupants in a light-hearted mood. We shook hands all round and got into the Mini to a chorus of farewells. I was sorry to go back through the Iron Curtain, for we had made a lot of friends. Renewing my climbing partnership with George in the Caucasus had brought back many memories of less skilled days on my part at least. I visited George recently at his Edinburgh home and I was surprised to see a familiar sight amid the shrubbery – the Mini. Now a bit rusty and obviously a playpen for George's children.

# 6

# Man o' Hoy

By stack and by skerry, by noup and by voe,
By air and by wick, and by helyer and gio,
And by every wild shore which the northern winds know . . .
[Sir Walter Scott, 'The Pirate']

WE WERE ALL SITTING in the small room of the Rackwick
schoolhouse, long since without the gay laughter of school-
children. Their laughter was replaced with the ribald mirth of
adults. Mac the Telly, alias Ian McNaught-Davis, had us in
fits. He was waxing his most eloquent:

"Here on the remote island of Hoy, providing a phallic foreground to the wide and sombre backcloth of the Atlantic, six
climbers pit their feeble resources against this ravished 450 feet
sandstone column, the Old Man of Hoy." At least his words
went something like that. He was mimicking Chris Brasher's
rehearsal of the Outside Broadcast the previous day, when
Chris got a bit carried away with superlatives. There was a
peatfire burning in the grate and around it were some of the
best climbers in Britain, all crammed into that tiny room. We
agreed that Mac's impromptu recitation was one of the funniest
we had ever heard. Mac with Joe Brown, was attempting a
new route up the east face of the stack, whilst Dougal Haston
and Peter Crew had the task of making a further new line up
the south-east arête, an edge bristling with overhangs on the
landward side. Chris Bonington and Tom Patey were
scheduled to do the 'tourist route', which they had previously
climbed when making the first ascent of the pinnacle.

I don't think I had heard of the Old Man of Hoy until Tom

137

Patey mentioned it to me in 1962. Nothing was done about attempting to climb it then and it wasn't until 1966 that Tom, Chris Bonington and Rusty Baillie, a transplanted Rhodesian, climbed this column of sandstone for the first time, taking three days to do so. Tom Patey was then a G.P. in Ullapool, a fishing port on the West Coast of Scotland, a town saturated with tourists in summer and suffering from the overzealous influence of Christianity in all seasons. Tom, even when wishing to climb on weekdays, let alone the Sabbath would drive out of town respectably suited in black, as befitted his station, whilst in the boot of the car reposed his well-worn crag clothes which he would furtively slip into at some remote lay-by. Tom's talents were numerous: he was a fine musician and his old piano accordion was always with him. As a prolific and satirical song-writer his friends and enemies were never spared as he cut everyone down to size with well-chosen words and musical embellishments. His writing, too, was superbly funny and he had the ability to use his own irrational behaviour to his advantage. For example, he wrote, "Who else but Hamish MacInnes would phone at this hour of the night with such a preposterous suggestion." Whereas it was *he* who used to telephone *me* at all hours of the night, suggesting some apparently hare-brained scheme, though usually they weren't quite so way-out as at first appeared. On another occasion I eavesdropped at one of his lectures and heard him recounting how I had used my longjohns for a sling on a difficult retreat from a climb. "Hamish," he said, amid peals of laughter, "had taken off his longjohns in sub-zero temperatures to use for this abseil sling." In fact they were *his* well-worn longjohns, not mine, which I had used, much to his discomfort on that occasion.

There had been four other live climbing Outside Broadcasts before the Old Man of Hoy: two in Wales and two in France, including the Aiguille de Midi and the ascent of the Eiffel Tower – a somewhat offbeat programme which could hardly be said to have involved the technical problems we were now facing. Tom Patey had prepared a dossier on a possible Old Man of Hoy programme, however, without giving a thought to the almost insurmountable engineering obstacles in the way of such a venture, assuming that repeating the climb itself would be by far the most difficult aspect of such a scheme. Nowadays, when planning an Outside Broadcast, we hardly consider the actual climbing of the cliff for transmission; there are so many competent mountaineers available we don't have to, but rather we concentrate on the technicalities of getting a signal out to civilisation and also on the sheer cost of such an exercise.

Alan Chivers is a name which should go down in television history as the evangelist of outside broadcasting. Though not a climber himself, Chiv, as he is affectionately known, runs many more risks than his climbers. The whole massive investment and his career are balanced on the knife-edge of weather, notoriously unreliable in mountains or on such northern seaboards, and on a jungle of temperamental electronic equipment. But Chiv was the man who had the boldness and foresight to attempt to televise the Old Man of Hoy climb. When Tom Patey's portfolio arrived on Chiv's desk he was duly impressed, but could his engineers attempt such a thing? He passed the query down the pipeline and patiently awaited an answer. This was an unreserved yes. Chiv never questions the capability of his men. They have to be pretty good to work for him in the first place, and he always has their well-being in mind. As a result both climbers and engineers have faith in him and respect for his cool in times of stress. It is said that no man is irreplaceable, but I feel it would be very hard to replace Chiv's dynamic approach and his nerve in taking on a mountain where failure would stir the wrath of millions of viewers.

Our earlier Outside Broadcasts were Micky Mouse ventures compared with Hoy, for at this remote outpost of Britain there were no hotels and the stack was a forty-minute walk from the nearest road. The B.B.C. staff would have to stay at Stromness in the Orkneys and the journey entailed a ferry trip to the island of Hoy, then a car journey to the road end at Rackwick, followed by the aforesaid walk, a daunting itinerary when added to the companion problems of getting a small mountain of equipment up the hill and over the bogs to the headland opposite the stack.

Usually all this electronic gadgetry is housed in a large vehicle called a scanner, which is the nerve centre of an Outside Broadcast. It is to this unit that the cameras feed their signals and within the Director must select from a battery of television monitors which picture to use at any given time. It requires split-second decisions and he has to be a veritable Argus.

It was obviously impossible to take a complete scanner to the cliff-top at the Old Man of Hoy, so everything had to be derigged, packed, and then hauled by two large tractors with a special sledge to the two marquees at the cliff edge. Part of this operation involved hauling the sledge up a steep hillside, using winches, because the ground was too dangerous for the tractors. My particular job was to deliver the cumbersome electronic cameras to their respective positions on the mainland cliff and also to the rock-strewn shore 400 feet vertically below. As well as this I had to operate a minicam on the climb itself during transmission. I had recently perfected a cableway system for mountain rescue work in Glencoe and I put this to good use for the rigging operation. The cableways involved using a long rope angled steeply to the rocky shore below, then tensioned. The cameras and platforms were lowered down this on pulleys using a separate rope. Several hundred pounds of equipment at a time could be quickly and safely dispatched to their positions in this way with great accuracy and delicacy, but getting the equipment up and down the stack itself involved hard brute-strength hauling. The so-called minicam then in use weighed 70-lbs. The whole operation smacked of a military exercise. It was like an offensive against the Old Man rather than a climb; there was no overriding confidence that we could pull it off – the odds seemed to be against us. Somehow or other it reminded me of Alexander's siege of Tyre. A company of Scots Guards acted as caterers to the organisation and their equipment as well as the bulky B.B.C. gear had come to Hoy from the Clyde Estuary by landing craft.

Nature suddenly took a hand in the proceedings; she is always close by in the wings when we do an Outside Broadcast and on this occasion she took the form of a violent storm which flattened tents and left a nightmare of soggy equipment for the engineers to swear over for a whole day. There was also a family of great skua, whose home was on the Rackwick path and they took exception to trespassers and consequently dive-bombed us as we commuted each day.

To us Mac's repartee the evening after the dress rehearsal was light relief. All the climbers and Sherpas, a term given to climbers who do the difficult rigging on these programmes, had a feeling that the whole thing could be a disaster. Everything had gone wrong at the rehearsal: the cameras on the stack, John Cleare's and mine, were in the wrong place at the right time; the radio talk-back equipment which climbers wear and two of the other electronic cameras had gremlins in them as well. It was more like a Goon Show than a serious rock climb.

Rusty Baillie was assisting John Cleare with the other mini-cam and he had brought his dog Puck with him. Puck was trained for search and rescue, that is for finding people buried in avalanches or lying out on open moorland. Rusty had been one of the instructors at my snow and ice climbing school in Glencoe and had as casual an approach to life as to his clothes, which were often unique. I recall, for instance, a long, capacious anorak, modified from a gabardine raincoat. Instead of buttons he had an arrangement of wooden toggles and hemp rope loops. Assisting me and my minicam was Ian Clough, a close friend with whom I had climbed many mountains.

To look after our spiritual needs but on the payroll as a Sherpa was the Reverend Sydney Wilkinson, a minister from Aberdeen. Syd was a strong climber who had lived on Baffin Island where he had made many solo ascents. With the proceeds of his pay he hoped to buy a new washing machine. Syd frowned on the apathy that modern youth presented in an age when climbing and exploration was never so readily available to the working man. One lunchtime he sawed off a section of scaffolding plank about a foot long and placed it between two boxes, then he split it in two with one clean karate chop! I felt there was an implication that we should be doing something more useful with our spare time than singing bawdy songs in the schoolhouse in the evenings. With some misgivings I cut a similar piece of wood and placed it between the boxes. I felt that I would probably be breaking a hand rather than a section of Oregon pine for I had never tried this martial sport in my life. I glanced with trepidation at the edge of my hand, thinking it looked vulnerable compared with his which resembled a blunt blade of an axe. I decided instead to try the wood chopping act using a clenched fist but I didn't deliberate too long otherwise I would have chickened. Wham! I was surprised to see how easily I split the timber without even a trace of pain or injury.

"Have a go, Rusty," I said casually, "it's a piece of piss. I may even dispense with my old hatchet for cutting kindling when I go back home." Rusty will have a go at anything and he repeated our stunts with ease. Syd, somewhat nonplussed at us mere amateurs, rummaged in the pile of planks until he found one that was so knotty that he had trouble sawing it. We all watched in silence, a large group of us now, both climbers and B.B.C. technicians. He placed the wood between the boxes again, but this time with reverence, as if it were a sacred offering. There followed a period of concentration on Syd's part when he seemed to be willing the destruction of the unoffending piece of plank without even touching it. Then, like a streak of light, his hand arched downwards. It seemed to me at least that for that second of crucial contact nothing happened. Just a sickening sharp thud but miraculously in slow motion the timber parted just as I felt sure that his hand was going to disintegrate.

The Old Man of Hoy had captured the public's imagination. Cartoons of it appeared in *Punch*, and other national dailies ran features. It took on the expectancy of an international soccer match. In this age of canned and frozen food and pre-recorded programmes where everything is respectably predictable, an outside broadcast has that dash of adventure about it. It's like motor racing – people expect something to happen, often the worst. I think I was the first person to dub the Hoy Outside Broadcast as a circus. Really that is what it was where gladiators compete on a vertical and overhanging plane rather than on the level, and where the adversary is a mountain or in this case a rotten stack where a hold can come away like an over-ripe apple at any time or a storm can put paid to the whole enterprise.

Hoy and subsequent Outside Broadcasts did much to make the public aware of the art of climbing and also the pleasures and rewards one gets out of it, other than a fat fee.

Being involved in mountain rescue work in various parts of Scotland, I had contacted the helicopter wing of R.A.F. Leuchars in Fife before travelling to Hoy, to find out if a helicopter could be on call for a rescue operation, should this be necessary. At that time they were not so widely used as they are today. I was told that one would be available in an emergency, subject to weather and refuelling facilities on the mainland. This enquiry, plus the wide press coverage of the proposed climb no doubt stirred the imagination of the R.A.F. Buccaneer pilots who were also based at Leuchars and once or twice when we were busy establishing camera positions they buzzed us.

As part of the rigging operation I had spanned a heavy rope between the mainland cliff and a point halfway up the stack for hauling gear across, and for no logical reason took the rope down that night, though in fact it would have been more sensible to have left it up, for we had work to do with it the next day. Just as we arrived at the tents on the cliff-top the following morning there was a roar to the south and we saw a wave-clipping Buccaneer skimming across the sea towards us. The stack is partly sheltered to the south by the arm of a headland, and this had no doubt hampered the style of earlier buzzing Buccaneers. Not this one; he had obviously done his homework for he came in at an angle to the main cliff upon which we stood to avoid the headland, then banked violently so that he was now on a course parallel to the cliff and the sea, reverting the belly of the plane, then with a flick he straightened and before we realised what had happened he had shot through the gap between the cliff top and the Old Man. It was a daring bit of flying which appealed to Chiv who had been a test pilot during the last war. I have often speculated what would have happened if that rope had been left in place. Most likely it would have parted like a strand of cobweb, but on the other hand it could perhaps have created that small disturbance to the flight path which could have been disastrous. Pilots, like climbers, do take risks and after all, the better aspects of life have that spice, that element of risk attached to them.

The great day came at last but we still seemed to be in a state of chaos, though we had managed to get all the cameras in position. Chris Brasher had sharpened up his commentary and Chiv was barking orders from the big marquee as if from the bridge of a destroyer. Large floodlights, appropriately called brutes, had been lowered partway down the cliff face below the marquee for night shots. Ian Clough and I had to cover the 'tourist route' and the south-east arête of Haston and Crew while John Cleare's and Rusty's job was to go up over the top of the stack and descend to a point where they could meet up with the emerging Joe Brown and Mac the Telly. Unfortunately, John's camera never worked on the stack so a greater load went on Ian and myself.

Things went surprisingly well for the first day's transmission, considering the chaos of the rehearsal. The weather was kind and purely for the amusement of the watching millions two of the groups were scheduled to bivouac on the mountain. Joe and Mac had a disturbed night in the Mouth, a gaping hole in the vertical face; I say disturbed, for somehow the contents of a whisky bottle which was being guarded by Mac disappeared overnight. Mac blamed the fulmars who the next morning were puking even more aggressively. Dougal and Pete who had been hammering their way up the arête for two days now in a cacophony reminiscent of the Anvil Chorus, were lodged for the night as planned on a small ledge adjacent to the

*Above* A shifty wait in Warsaw for the man with the zloties. *Right* Svanetian woman spinning wool from the rough Caucasian sheep. *Below* Eugene Tur and Vitali Abalakov.

Ushba, seen from our last peak of Shkhelda. George Ritchie, right.

tourist route. Ian and I had the task of climbing to this ledge and then attaching ourselves to ropes as best we could, for Dougal and Peter fully occupied this haven on the otherwise vertical sandstone. It was a late night show, a sort of "before we close down for the night, let us have a last look at the climbers on the Old Man of Hoy". The illumination came from the battery of brutes on the cliff opposite and a sungun, a portable camera lamp which we had laboriously taken up with us. But the long fingers of trade unionism reached out, even to this remote corner of Ultima Thule.

"Who would switch off the generators?" the electricians asked. They were scheduled to knock off at 11.45 and it would be at least 12.15 before Ian and I could get down from the stack. I talked to Chiv over the walkie-talkie, pointing out that the climbers might be snug in their sleeping bags on the only available ledges, but Ian and I were just clipped to climbing ropes and needed the lights to get off the climb. Alan Chivers is a very independent individual; that is one of his charms and he doesn't brook inefficiency or interference even from his most exalted master or a powerful trade union.

"Don't worry, Hamish," he said, "I'll wait for you both to get off and I'll switch off the gennies myself."

Soon afterwards Ian and I were spiralling down the long free abseil to the base of the Old Man to snatch a few hours' sleep in the marquee, for it wasn't worth returning to Rackwick that night.

Next morning I yawned as I went outside for a pee; the sky was watery and the yellow streaks of dawn reached out into the Atlantic. I thought of how King Hakon sailed down this coastline on his tragic mission to help the people of Skye and how he later returned, a defeated and dying man. In those days the stack was part of the mainland of the island and indeed it is only in recent times that it lost its spare leg, for old prints depicted it as an arch with a lower leg between the existing stack and the mainland. An interesting stack in the making can be seen close to Cape Wrath lighthouse across the Pentland Firth where a narrow gap has formed round a segment of cliff by a constant nibbling of the sea.

The second transmission from the Old Man was not without incident. Ian and I went up ahead of Tom Patey and Chris Bonington who were now climbing the ordinary route in the day, and beyond the Haston crew bivouac ledge we leap-frogged past them when we were off the air. When covering the crack which leads on to a surprisingly spacious summit, a large chunk of sandstone fell, possibly dislodged by a rope or by its own volition, or it may have been the Old Man, like a fulmar, venting its spleen on us rapists. Anyhow, it headed straight towards me and seemed to fill the viewfinder of the camera. By the grace of God it parted just before it reached me so that a piece fell to either side. These chunks disintegrated further on the ledge upon which I stood and, by a freak of Mac-Pherson's or Sod's Law, missed Ian as well. The subsequent pungent smell of brimstone reminded me of my ultimate destination. I gave a shudder and started to climb the crack to join the others on the summit. The O.B. had been an un-precedented success.

Well, it was all over bar the shouting, or perhaps I should say, drinking; a momentous piss-up was arranged at Strom-ness. Chris Brasher promised it was to be the biggest booze-up since the last Berserker wake. It was, and followed a sumptu-ous meal where the unsurpassed seafood of these northern waters featured prominently. I recall quite clearly wrestling with Joe Brown. He always seemed to get to grips with me when he has had his statutory three pints of ale and somehow he fell with me on top of him, his back, which had been a source of trouble for years, received further injury so he had the two following years to reflect on the merits of whooping it up in the Orkneys. Later an enormous Viking bowl of Orkney Cog was produced. It tasted like a mixture of molten lava and nitric acid but Rusty, never to be daunted by taste, quantity or potency, and anyhow by this time his other faculties must have been anaesthetised, swallowed the contents in a long and, for us, breathtaking draught. A roar of approval shook the hotel. That night the citizens of Stromness were tolerant.

I think I was the first to notice that Rusty had disappeared and, being concerned for his well-being, after consuming such a lethal brew, I asked where he had gone. No one knew so we searched the hotel with no success. However, Puck was curled up close to the fire, apparently immune to both the din and the departure of his master and no doubt in a dream paradise of rabbits and buried climbers. As I had helped with Puck's rescue training, I now deployed him.

"Come on, Puck, find your master." His ears pricked up as much as they ever would for he had a pixie look with one ear permanently drooping like a wilting flower. He looked at me as if I was mad but then realised I meant what I said, when he quickly established his master wasn't in the room. Giving a growl, he scampered towards the door. I followed and with nose hovering above the pavement he trotted down the street, followed in turn by the drunken rabble. It must have been a strange procession as we wove our way in revelry behind Puck, a pied piper scene where a sombre and worried dog led the drunks in the general direction of the harbour, like a scene out of *A Midsummer Night's Dream*.

> Up and down, up and down,
> I will lead them up and down,
> I am feared in field and town.

The trail ended at a warehouse, with dog looking up and whining at the corrugated side of the building. On the roof above this spot where Puck had stopped was an open skylight. Somebody climbed up and shouted, "Hey, Rusty's sleeping inside on a pile of fishboxes." His clothes apparently were neatly folded beside him and he was wrapped up in his famous gabardine anorak.

Through the good offices of a kindly Orcadian we later found our hotel but not our rooms; we probably didn't have any. About twelve of us tried to bundle on to Chris Brasher's bed. Chris as yet wasn't in occupation. I vaguely remember something breaking, followed by an avalanche of laughter. About this time most of us ceased to record events and the rest of the night will forever be shrouded in mystery.

The ferryboat to Hoy next morning was filled with climbers who in turn were filled with resolutions to give up drink. The walk across the moorland to the stack, however, had a sobering effect and that morning we didn't even bother avoiding the skuas who divebombed us. Eric Beard, or Beardie, as he was called, had his head cut open by one. This was to be our last day on Hoy as we hoped to complete the de-rigging. Some of the climbers had already left and Mac was due to pass the stack on the *St. Ola* on his way south that morning. Beardie, who was better known for his fell-running records than pyrotechnics, suggested, "Let's give Mac a rocket send-off as the ship passes. You've got all those signal rockets, Hamish." Indeed, I had. These had been purchased in case some form of emergency communication was required should the walkie-talkies fail.

"All right," I agreed, "but no reds. We don't want to stir up a full-scale sea rescue for we've got a good relationship with the lifeboat lads."

This was a reference to the Longhope lifeboat which was later to go down with all hands. We were well under way with the dismantling operation when someone shouted, "There's the *St. Ola*!" There was a mad scurry on the cliff top as a dozen flares, which can soar over a thousand feet, were positioned then fired. They exploded in a canopy of green, high above the stack, giving the Old Man a surreal appearance like an Indian totem pole. There was a hoot from the ship and she veered in towards the Old Man, then hove to. Meantime Mac was enjoying the spectacle on board. That was until he saw the skipper obviously answering what he thought was the most grandiose distress signal of all time. Thinking it would perhaps be better to break the news to this mariner that these were parting but somewhat ostentatious tokens of goodwill from his friends, Mac set foot on the bridge to inform the captain. As one of us Mac realises climbers have an unenviable reputation in some quarters and this was fully substantiated by the opinion of the captain as he hauled the *St. Ola* round and headed south. It was followed by a rousing cheer from our ranks and amplified by a last rocket, a powerful maroon, whose detonation high in the clear heavens morning roused every seabird from its morning contemplation and they took to the heavens in a flurry of feathers.

# 7

# Three Wally Dugs

"The crawling glaciers pierce me with their spears.
Of their moon freezing crystals, the bright chains
Eat with the burning cold into my bones."
[Shelley, 'Prometheus Unbound']

I FIRST BECAME INVOLVED with the British Soviet Caucasus Expedition by default. Denis Gray, a well-known English climber, had originally agreed to lead this trip but due to other commitments and the sheer uncertainty of the undertaking he had to pull out. Trying to obtain permission to climb in the Caucasus was like attempting to win a national lottery. Paul Nunn and Tut Braithwaite, old climbing colleagues, asked if I would care to accept this rather tenuous leadership. They hoped that I could exert my influence, minuscule as it was, with the Russian authorities, for I had enjoyed a good liaison with them since my last visit to the Caucasus with George Ritchie in 1962. Reluctantly, I agreed. The chores had already been done and in Paul Nunn's garage there was a super-market assortment of goods from beer to skittles. Already it had been dubbed Smaug's Cave.

There were six members of the expedition. Paul Nunn, genial, unflappable, Friar Tuck of the climbing world who, with ponderous intent, can float up the most delicate route, is a mine of information, he could for example give an account of the distribution of wheat in Georgia in the sixteenth century. Richard MacHardy is a talented rock climber who enjoys soloing routes of a high standard, he has an exuberant sense of humour and the appetite of a dinosaur. Tut Braithwaite, the

150

superman in the guise of a hunger-striker on his two hundreth day, though built like a hair-spring, has the energy of a nuclear reactor. A decorator by trade and an entertainer by nature, he has an aptitude for alpine climbing which has placed him in the forefront of a generation of alpine hard men. Chris Woodhall was by far the quietest member of the team, an unassuming man, strong and reliable, with the earnest face of a teacher and the temperament of a philosopher; he was then a physical training instructor with a flair for hard climbing. Chris called in to see me just a short time ago in Glencoe when he was up for the weekend. He didn't do much now, he said; but it transpired that in two days he had completed most of the hardest climbs in the glen. Peter Seeds, our assiduous scoop, was a features writer on the *Sunday Mirror* and an old acquaintance of Paul Nunn. He managed to persuade his paper to help subsidise our expedition. Peter, who had done a little climbing before, is a small, gregarious man with a zest for news and a zeal for life. Every expedition should have its Seeds, a born storyteller who sowed throughout the breadth of Russia a little bit of the freedom of Fleet Street.

I had suggested to Chris Brasher who was then working for the B.B.C. that we should make a film of the traverse of Ushba, one of the finest mountains in the world, and the machinery for this had been set in motion, helped by my glowing reports of the co-operation I had received in making the documentary on my last trip, a few days before departure the Russians imposed such a heavy facility fee that reluctantly the film was cancelled. Ned Kelly who had been appointed Director was bitterly disappointed, but later I enjoyed his company in 1975 when he was co-director on the B.B.C. Everest South-West Face film.

Our motley crew met up in London. Fiat of Milan had loaned us two vehicles, a Fiat 125S, a works back-up rally car of considerable pep, but with its compression suitably lowered for the low-octane Russian petrol. The other machine was a Campagnoli, the Italian equivalent of the Land-Rover, a sturdy workhorse. Both vehicles were stuffed with food and equipment and I wondered how we would all fit in. I had taken quite a pile of gear to London myself and was at a loss as to where to stow it. Then, upon lifting the canvas cover on the Campagnoli I saw that the last two feet below the roof were crammed tight with cans of Newcastle Brown. As I don't drink beer, I pointed out that this was an unnecessary luxury and proposed an on-the-spot party to dispose of enough of the cans to make room for at least my rucksack.

We soon settled down to our marathon drive. It was our intention to go to the Caucasus via East Germany and Poland. Within the Iron Curtain I saw many improvements since my last visit. Although I hadn't been to Russia since my Mini drive with George Ritchie, I had been a guest of the Czech Rescue Service, the Horska Sluzba, in 1969 and had been impressed with the new freedom the Czechs were then enjoying. Alas, this was shortlived. Poland to me is a 'come hither' country, a land which immediately takes you to its bosom. When we arrived at a small border village late one evening we were besieged by welcoming Poles, each inviting us to his home and pressing us with drinks. But we resisted the temptation of too much hospitality and that night we slept by the wayside, beneath the fruit-trees and poplars which escorted either side of the high cambered pavé road. Near Warsaw it was too built-up for this sort of nomadic practice and Richard, who asked a passing priest where a suitable camp site could be found, was told in good English "Follow me". We followed, funeral-like, behind the holy man for there was no space in the vehicles and he took us to a seminary where we were welcomed like repentant sinners. Sinners we were of course, but I doubt if any of us had regrets! Beds with clean sheets were provided as was an appetising though simple meal. No doubt our begrimed appearance fostered their suggestion that we might like to use their swimming pool; after the dust of the Polish roads this offer was seized upon with alacrity, and a congregation of aspirant priests beamed benevolently upon us as we descended upon this place of liquid luxury which they had made themselves. Tut, who was the first to dive in, emitted a yell as if he had just tumbled into a snake pit.

"Christ," he shouted, "it's cold." As most of the priests spoke English they no doubt regarded Tut as a devout believer.

We were short of Polish currency; we always seemed to be stopping at banks when they were closed or passing them when open, and we resorted to changing a few illegal profit-making dollars in Warsaw in the shadow of the lofty Palace of Culture, with a shadowy Pole who left us sitting on a seat in a thoroughfare while he went off searching for 'Mr. Big', the brains and the man with the money behind such deals. We soon regretted our imprudence, each of us looking furtively in different directions. Just when we had resolved to revert to the straight and narrow he came back, blatantly clutching a wad of notes which he immediately thrust upon us and he departed with our dollars.

The drive was like being on the road with a music hall act. There were always jokes and laughter with the boys; Paul's great bellowing laugh would rise above the din of the Campagnoli and Tut with the aspirations of a budding Fangio and the ability to steer a collision course with all oncoming traffic, with last-second reprieve, would chuckle and add his own titbit of humour. Our progress across Poland was more of a tourist preamble than a necessary journey to get to our objective as soon as possible. We stopped frequently and not occasionally lost our way.

Close to the Russian border I was travelling with Peter Seeds who invariably drove as if it was close to closing time. It was like motoring in the Australian outback. A cloud of dust erupted as we leapt from one pothole to the next. The road dwindled to a track, then eventually to open ground. Low hills rose ahead with no sign of a highway. We pulled up to be over-taken by our 'smoke screen'.

"I think we've lost the road, Peter," I said. There was nothing like stating the obvious.

"Hey, look up there," he pointed. A short way above we could see a pill-box on stilts. We were obviously right on the Russian border.

"I think it would be wiser to go back," I suggested, "I'm

sure the Russians don't usually have tourists arriving cross-country in a military-type vehicle." We caught up with the others at Shaginia, the official frontier post. Tut shouted across from the other car.

"The trouble with you, Hamish, is that you can't read the signposts. They're in very clear Polish."

Next morning, with a flaxen dawn climbing ahead of us, we took to the long straight Russian roads. There's no way better to appreciate the scale of the Soviet Union than to drive. The horizon seems limitless. It merges in a haze with the skyline, giving an impression of vastness and latent power. It must be hell for someone suffering from agoraphobia.

We now stayed over night at the official camp sites. Making camp by the side of the road was obviously not encouraged. The camp sites, however, were clean and efficient and were frequented by roving Russian students, who made a point of striking up conversation with foreigners. Politics would invariably be discussed and as most of our party was very well-informed in political theory, especially Paul Nunn, who is a lecturer in economics, this often proved an embarrassment to the students, who invariably came off worst in any discussion. They quickly sought more fertile fields to preach Leninism. This was the Centenary Year of Lenin's birth and everywhere there were posters of the great man, some truly enormous.

Kiev, Kharkov and Rostov were soon behind us and we sped along the sun-drenched Georgian highway, a ribbon of melted tarmac lined with poplars. The foothills of the Caucasus rose in shimmering heat. The heat was oppressive. I found it as enervating as India, and even the metal of the vehicles was too hot to touch. The heat, too, seemed to have its effect on the 'snots', as we called the traffic police. There had been one at every road junction all the way from Poland and at Baksan we were told by a posse of them that we couldn't go further. They were quite adamant about that. Four hours later we did, but not without great trouble.

The road up the Baksan river toils through deep gorges and pleasant woodlands; the country is suddenly alpine, the air fresher, even the people seemed more cheerful. The region is a great vacation area of the Soviet Union, frequented by two classes, the dedicated climber and the tourist. Many of the latter are East German holiday makers and they arrive from Moscow with the Germanic determination of those who are going to enjoy themselves. Climbers by force of circumstance, in the mountains at least, are spartan and as we drove up the road approaching Mount Elbrus, we were somewhat daunted by a huge hotel which sparkled into view, ultramodern even by Western standards then. This was the Itkol, the new Intourist hotel which was to be our home for the next few weeks. To us it represented roubles; we would have been happier in an alpine hut. Six filthy climbers caked in the dust of the plains and sprouting anaemic beards creaked from the two vehicles and were ushered into this sybaritic glass palace. The ancient, traditionally dressed Cossack hall porter jerked himself upright as if pulled by invisible strings and gave us a grandiose salute. Later, this man became partial to the Newcastle Brown I had failed to evict in London and received the name of Ivan Beershifsky. He was armed to the teeth, albeit with antique armoury and told us right away that as he was himself a dishonest man we would have to hide all our equipment for he couldn't hold himself responsible.

With the expertise of slum-dwellers we succeeded in lowering the tone of our three luxury rooms in a matter of hours. In London, through Intourist, we had paid for bed and breakfast at the hotel and the other meals, we were told, we could cook for ourselves in our hotel rooms. I viewed the wall to wall carpeting and the finely veneered tables with trepidation and wondered how they would look when we departed.

Close to the hotel, near the bottom of the Mount Elbrus téléférique station, there were several gift shops and to pass the time one wet day we sauntered about window shopping with some Russian climbers with whom we had made a casual acquaintance. Paul innocently mentioned that he liked a certain type of finely embroidered woollen cap, which, he said, would be a nice present for Hilary, his wife. One of the Russians went in and bought it and presented it to Paul. The generosity of the Russians was often embarrassing, yet they obviously derived great pleasure in giving us presents. Money doesn't have the same value in Russia; the State provides everything, everyone gets an adequate pension when they retire, often more than their working wage so money plays but a small part in their everyday lives, luxury goods are scarce and the cancer of advertising is non-existent.

It took us a couple of days to unwind after the long drive, but accommodation at the Hotel Itkol was conducive to easy living and it grew on one like an evening glass of port. We had breakfast in the goldfish bowl dining-room and cooked the other meals in our suites or on the verandah. I met Rotentaov again, the senior Master of Sport who was now acting as adviser to climbing guests at the hotel. He remembered me from my last visit; this was a good omen and we hoped it might help us overcome some of the obstacles which confront 'unknown' climbers in the Soviet Union. Already he had asked what we wished to do. It had been my ambition for some time to visit the valley of Svanetia, that turbulent region we had contemplated trying a direct descent into at a bad moment on our traverse of the Shkhelda ridge eight years before. So without too much hope, I requested permission for a visit. At one time Svanetia was a stronghold of anarchy, where each house had, and reputedly still has, its own protective tower. But it seems the valley is still too independent minded for the Russian powers-that-be to risk encouraging foreign visitors to this remote community in the heart of the Caucasus.

It is a well-known fact that climbers have little respect for either their elders or for bureaucracy. My friend Rotentaov was good-humouredly nicknamed Rotten Tie-off. A tie-off, I should add, is a short section of nylon tape which is used to tie round the neck of a piton which can't be fully driven into a crack. It wasn't convenient to visit Svanetia, he said, but he suggested that we should do the ascent of the north face of Nakra Tau, a 4000-foot wall, first pioneered by that great

Russian climber Abalakov. It had been his first climb after he had lost most of his toes and fingers with frostbite. I don't think either my remark to Rotentaov that it would make a good acclimatisation route or the boys' irreverent reference to it as 'Knackery Tau' were well received, but we got our gear together and awaited the pleasure of the weather gods.

Meantime, we didn't exactly waste the bad weather. We got to know the other guests in the hotel and struck up a friendship with some East German climbers who were staying in a nearby camp, the Adul Suh, a camp similar to Spartak run by the locomotive workers' union. My friend, Eugene Tur, was staying there, acting as instructor for the summer months. It was great to see him again, and he told me that Igor Bandurovski, the other Master of Sport who had done the traverse of Shkhelda with George Ritchie and myself had just left.

Richard MacHardy, always on the lookout for difficult rock to climb, remembered a fearsome cliff which we had admired on the way up from the plains near Tiernauz, and after obtaining permission from Rotentaov, set off to climb on this with Peter Seeds. It lived up to their expectations, Peter had a three star grip on an intimidating overhanging crack. At a crucial point, where our personal correspondent lost contact with the rock, a bionic voice boomed across the valley. It was a group of 'snots' who were speaking over a powerful public-address system, asking them in Russian just what the hell they were doing.

"Hey, you guys," Paul Nunn said, as he joined us one morning after speaking with Rotentaov. "We've got to have a bloody medical before we can go on the climb." He reached out with practised ease, grabbed a can of beer and with a deft flick of his finger took the seal off in one smooth motion. "Perhaps," he added, "they think we've got the clap or something."

"That's no sweat," said Richard, looking up from a primus where he was engaged in his second most popular occupation, that of cooking; eating was his favourite. "I saw the doctor," he continued. "She's a bird and she looks smashing." The fact that it was a female doctor seemed to allay the objection we had to the infringement of our liberty, which was on the tip of our tongues. After our consultations Tut said the doctor didn't believe him when he said that the reason for his racing pulse and high blood pressure was her close proximity; she muttered something to him about "hot-blooded Anglo-saxons!"

Another bird who took an interest in our welfare was one of the hotel staff, a blonde sylph-like creature with the face of a madonna, a modern Ione, whom one could well imagine tending the needs of a needy Prometheus.

We dragged ourselves away from the hotel in the general direction of Nakra Tau and I remember saying to Chris Woodhall as we traversed some grassy knolls, that our trip was degenerating into a nymphs and shepherds picnic, for there ahead of us on a knoll attending a flock of sheep was a good shepherd, a kindly, philosophical man with a wide-brimmed hat and the statutory crook. He was obviously keen to walk with us but none of us spoke Russian. Peter Seeds had been left at the hotel for he didn't have the experience to do a route like the north face of Nakra Tau; he was going exploring, he said. Now we could see our objective across the glacier, a mountain with a rugged north face as furrowed as that of the shepherd.

"It doesn't look too healthy," Tut observed, using his binoculars.

"No," I echoed. "Hell," I pointed, "look at that sérac over-hanging the lower part of the wall. It's got our names on it." The others seemed as apprehensive of this great block of pre-carious ice as I was, but we didn't say any more about it as we made our way across the glacier moraine to find a bivouac from which we could set off the following morning.

Our bivvy proved to be rather an unusual one. We found a crashed helicopter and as there didn't seem to be any bodies lying about we assumed that these had either been removed some time previously or had returned to civilisation under their own power. Here we spent a night, which was like sleeping in a deep freeze with a view.

The next morning was no worse than any other morning I

had been led to expect in the Caucasus and after breakfast of dehydrated food which looked and tasted like nail clippings, we shouldered our packs, switched on our headlamps and were off.

A short time before I had designed a new type of ice climbing tool, the 'terrordactyl', which was later to become popular throughout the climbing world. It was so called by my friend Ian Clough when he first saw the aggressive-looking snout. We had the first 'terror' prototypes with us on the climb and we were itching to use them on steep ice.

First light saw us soloing up a ramp of steep snow. Richard, who suffered from headaches, the legacy of a fall when climbing solo, announced he was going back; he wasn't feeling well. We felt sorry for him but there was nothing much we could do to help. As the difficulties were not great, especially for someone of Richard's ability, it was not even suggested that anyone should return with him. Across the valley on the lower slopes of Mount Elbrus the morning light caught the wires of the téléférique, lighting them like fine strands of gossamer. I remember looking up apprehensively as we went on to the steep ice leading up towards the sérac we were so concerned about the previous day.

The first warning of falling ice was a crunch like two ships colliding, followed by the roar of falling debris. We were directly beneath. So much for those who say unroped climbing is dangerous. Had we been roped we would have been swamped and obliterated in the wake of this fall. As it was we took off, our crampons giving us traction as positive as athletes' running spikes and our performance would have been no disgrace to a sprinter. Though our race track was tilted at an angle of about 50° we stampeded, dignity gone to the winds, in an attempt to gain the top of the snow ramp which we had such a short time previously abandoned.

Though the sérac was probably no bigger than a church steeple, it took down the church with it in the form of more snow and ice, so that a fair-sized airborne avalanche resulted. There was a blast of cold air followed by a cloud of fine snow particles which was reluctant to clear. Once we were safely across, Tut said breathlessly, "Richard!" The awful thought hit us. The avalanche had fallen to the snow ramp below and had swept the snow slope which we had come up; the same slope Richard had returned by.

Meantime, to switch locations, Richard who had fortunately reached the base of the ramp and was on the snowfield below, was thinking, "Christ, the lads." For he had witnessed the whole thing as if it were a horror movie scene in slow motion. He hadn't seen us scuttling like scalded cats to the side.

We may have behaved like scalded cats but we returned to the Itkol like dogs with tails between our legs. Rotentaov was not amused and I could visualise him thinking of the scene in Spartak in 1962 when George Ritchie and I had returned to camp after abandoning our training climb at the first suspicion of bad weather, for the more hospitable Spartak camp and tea and chocolate biscuits. But at least the medicine woman and the Caucasian nymph were glad to see us back in one piece and that night we had a celebratory party. I'm not sure what we had to celebrate but we had plenty of the raw material with which to do it. Peter Seeds had not been idle in his exploring, for he had taken the car back into civilisation, realising that the framework of good copy is based on spirit, and had returned reinforced with an ample supply of vodka. Rudy, the leader of the East German climbers, came along with some of his friends and we had a first-class evening and drank a toast to Lenin. Tut volunteered to drive them back to their camp in the small hours of the morning but he hadn't allowed for the snots who were always on duty outside the hotel. They were friendly but firm: there was to be no driving that night. Rudy and his pals had to walk. The police were of course quite right for we had all had too much to drink, but the only pedestrians about at that time of night on those lonely roads would perhaps have been Caucasian bears.

At that time with the popularity of James Bond sweeping the gullible West we imagined every room from the bog to the dining-room to be bugged, though what interest our drivel

Chris Woodall at the German bivvy, with Shchurovskiy and the Ushba icefall.

Departure ceremony at Spartak Camp, a party being wished well by the camp commandant.

Our Fiat comes off the worse in a confrontation with a Czech farmcart.

would have been to the Russians is hard to imagine. But the thought provided us with humorous diversions.

"Have you that infra-red film well hidden, Paul?" I would ask when we were tucked away in bed.

"Yes, it's in the sealed coffee tin marked 'Caffeine free'."

"Ah, good," I would say, "but ve must get zee signal out." And so it went on, in suitably Peter Lorre accents.

Perhaps it was our imaginations at work but subsequently Peter did have trouble sending copy out to his paper. There was a further amusing sequel to that particular fairytale when upon later opening one of the aforesaid tins of coffee at a high bivouac we came across several dollar bills. Unknown to us, Peter had been using it as a safety deposit.

We were all raring to go, but the weather was forever against us. While hanging about I contrived to contract sunstroke. At various times in seemingly impossible conditions I have fallen foul of this affliction, the previous time, as already mentioned, was in the Himalayas in winter. Though the weather in the high Caucasus was despicable, down in the lush valley of Baksan it was tropical. Dusky maidens bore witness to this as did dusty roads. Eventually, we obtained permission to do a route on Ushba, a possible new line, and we made several sorties to the German bivouac which is first base for this climb and for some others in this area. But we were turned back by storms. Later, however, we did manage to take a supply of food up the Ushba icefall but it was a hazardous business for the icefall was badly crevassed and dangerous.

On one visit to the German bivouac we saw climbers obviously in trouble on the ridge of Ushba, and learned later that it was Rudy's party. One of them had fallen and had to be lowered down the face and two days later a rescue helicopter managed to reach them via Svanetia which is on the other side of Shkhelda and took the East German to hospital in Pyatigorsk. Though mountain rescue is free in Russia, they had to pay for the use of the helicopter which strained their resources.

Time was running out and we kept marching backwards and

forwards to the German bivouac, as Richard said, like the Grand Old Duke of York. When all hopes of doing a route on Ushba were abandoned, I beat a trail to Rotentaov's door with another request, permission to attempt a lower peak, the 14,000-foot high Pik Shchurovskiy, whose North West Face fascinated us. It was the hardest looking wall we had seen in the whole area and as Tut observed, "so bloody steep there's no-where for snow to land". Meantime Tut and Richard had asked for permission to attempt the direct route up the face of West Shkhelda from the Shkhelda glacier, just across from the German bivouac. This is a 6000-foot wall which would obviously afford them plenty of verticality and sport.

With only a few days left of our planned holiday we were champing at the bit and, regardless of weather, Chris, Paul and I set off one morning for the German bivouac, in the fervent hope that we should have a reprieve weather-wise. Tut and Richard resolved to wait a further day at the hotel.

The last stage of the track was up the wide Shkhelda glacier. The glacier looked innocent enough, yet in a few days' time it was to devour one of Rudy's ill-fated party. The bivouac was busy; it was a weekend and there were several Masters of Sport, both men and women, having a busman's holiday in the mountains. We had a pleasant evening with them. The sun came out and chased the snow into the furthest crannies and we swapped both gear and ideas. The Russians make some very good titanium equipment on a personal basis, for many of their climbers are engineers, though the basic gear issued at the climbing centres tends to be heavy.

Our proposed route up Pik Shchurovskiy was a parallel line to one done by Abalakov some years previously. Any climb up the wall was obviously going to be difficult and the more time I spent in the Caucasus the more I respected the ability of the Soviet mountaineers. From my point of view I don't object to their restrictions towards mountaineering and I can't help feeling that some form of priority would be welcome in the Alps where you can get a dozen parties making a beeline for a route as soon as the weather clears, and unless your party is in front you suffer the inevitable penalty of either being held up or having rocks inadvertently dropped on you.

The face of Shkhelda was obviously not on the popular list and the Russian climbers at the German bivouac doubted the feasibility of the climb. They wished us luck, however, and in the morning with a frost adding zest to our hopes we set off the short distance across the ice to come to long overdue grips with a Russian mountain. As usual we didn't rope up until it was almost too late. At least it was difficult to do so by that time, for the snow was at a high angle. Up till now we had been weaving our way through a labyrinth of shallow gullies and steep tongues of snow but higher and quite suddenly we broke out of these at the base of an overhanging section.

"How about heading up to those icicles, Hamish, then breaking right?" That was Chris and, strangely, he seemed optimistic, but I soon gathered that this was because he was expecting me to lead.

"Just like a Scottish gully," Paul added quickly, backing up Chris's opening gambit. "It'll be a good test for the 'terrors'."

"Well," I said with resignation, "I thought when I was asked to come on this trip I was a figurehead; I now see I am the dunderhead."

We had of course known about this pitch before because we had studied the wall on many occasions through binoculars like assiduous generals planning the siege of a fortress, only from where we now stood it looked worse than we had anticipated. Many hours later I was still trying to force my way upwards but at last I overcame the final 'grip' to gain a ledge that any self-respecting eagle would have turned its beak up at as a landing site. Here we all eventually congregated, more or less standing on each other's boots.

"Do you realise the time?" Chris said.

"It must be late," I ventured, "and it's time we got some shelter. It's snowing like Christmas." It was, but under the overhang beneath which we stood we were partly sheltered.

"It's less than an hour to dark," Chris persisted.

"Well, this place won't get three stars for comfort," Paul

commented; by his tone I gathered he didn't think he was sitting in his favourite armchair. I was at that time leaning heavily against him and we were all secured to a peg at knee level.

"How about moving up a short way to see if there's any better lodging, Hamish," he said. "I like you better at a distance."

"That I'll do," I agreed and moved diagonally upwards to a further icy step which in that terrain was all that we were going to find that resembled a ledge, and on this frugal place we settled ourselves for the night. Our legs had two alternatives; they could either overhang the drop, for the ledge, once cleared of ice, was the width of a mantelpiece, or we could adopt the position I've been told that true followers of Islam assume when dead, with knees tucked up to the chin and arms clasped round our shins. Though we weren't facing Mecca it at least alternated the discomfort, and so we spent the night like a row of not very ornamental 'wally dugs' on a mantelpiece.

That night was cold enough to provoke dismay in the legendary brass monkey but in the morning we moved on un-scathed, beyond some mild frostbite. Too late, we regretted not taking sleeping bags with us; the Caucasus is indeed a frosty place to bivouac.

After the barrier section of the previous day we were now on steep mixed ground. It was enjoyable climbing and the weather wasn't worth complaining about, well, not just yet. Though it was apparent that heavy snow had fallen overnight, it hadn't adhered to the face of Shchurovskiy. By early afternoon light coloured clouds steamed in from the Bezingi region like the Golden Horde and swamped the glaciers below us. Then they started to rise. Another cloud which had furtively slipped over the peak descended and presently we were in a sandwich shared by snowflakes. They fell heavily and steadily. Chris had now taken the lead for I had tired myself the previous day and retired to the 'long field' at the tail of the caravan. Our progress got slower and slower. Now heavy snow lay over the old stuff, for we were approaching the summit, and though it was still at a high angle it wasn't as steep as lower down. Just to vary the repertoire it started to hail and as I climbed up to Paul's stance I had to shovel the hail like loose change from the holds. Chris's strength and ability now became apparent and despite this sub-zero inferno he pressed on until suddenly there was no more mountain. We could see about fifteen feet and what we saw was the edge of a cornice snaking away horizontally. We stood on the knife-edge summit like three disillusioned snowmen hoping for an early thaw, relieved by the fact that we were up, but worried by the prospect of getting down. In climbing you just can't win!

"What will we do," Paul shouted, "bivvy?"

"It's a bit early," I shouted back, "it would be more like a siesta. How about going on a compass bearing along the ridge?" I pointed to the only uninviting alternative, which offered positive collapse on one side and possible avalanche conditions on the other. I took up my compass and, racking my glazed brain for an approximate bearing to the plateau of Ushba, the great snowfield at the base of that mountain, we leant against the wind hoping we were going in the right direction. I recollected as we moved at a respectable distance from the cornice Charlie Chaplin in the film *The Gold Rush* taking out his compass, a scrap of paper with north, south, east and west marked on it.

The ridge started to descend and in a short time we could see better. Below us slopes led towards the plateau and soon crevasses appeared. It was almost homely to see good, honest crevasses again, grinning like old friends and we zig-zagged our way through them until it was time once more for 'bed and breakfast'. This time for our overnight stay in the hills we had to contend with the opposite of the steep wall of Shchurovskiy. The gods, just as they had played with friend Prometheus, played a dirty joke on us. Here there was only open space, a wide snowfield. We were without doubt on the Ushba plateau, that we knew, but where on the wide expanse we didn't know. About us the crevasses appeared to have been breeding; there were many more here, making it imprudent to go further that day. To give us that comforting, don't panic feeling like blinkers on a horse, nature pressed cloud down again so that we experienced that sense of detachment that people often describe before succumbing to exposure.

But Paul was already exposed; we had just realised and that was one of the reasons why we had to bed down – and quickly – for he seemed in a bad way, frozen, pale and slightly disorientated. It had happened suddenly, as if someone had pulled a switch, and there was just nowhere to shelter, so we dug pits in the snowcover. I have already observed that I have never gone a bundle on snowholes, thinking them time-wasting conveniences for character-building schools. That night substantiated any doubts I may have had as to their value. Though we were inside our bivvybags the spindrift, blown now by a strong wind, swamped us. It would have been highly dangerous for us all to have gone to sleep, if indeed sleep we could, for we would have been suffocated. But the trouble with oxygen deprivation is that one is not as alert as usual and it is easy to drop into that somnolent state which can precede a real Rip Van Winkle job. From time to time one of us would call out like a muezzin and see if the rest were still awake and watchful, and then remove the accumulation of snow which was engulfing us.

Well, the morning came as it always does. We didn't make a start common to bakers and dairy farmers but awaited the dawn. Above us we heard shouts and it transpired that a party of Russian climbers had also spent the night out, but they, sensible people, had one of their excellent tents. We didn't breakfast that morning. Our nail clippings had finished so we set off down the glacier towards the German bivouac like homing pigeons, but we certainly lacked their ability which was more than apparent when we reached the crevasses of the icefall. We found our food cache, left for the abortive Ushba climb, but we were too shattered to eat. Paul had improved somewhat overnight, though I must admit that the conditions had not been conducive to convalescence and I admired his resilience and powers of recovery.

The Ushba icefall reminds me of those army obstacle courses

which I heard of in the last war, where live ammunition was fired around the participants, sometimes with fatal results. That icefall demands similar initiative with crumbly snow-bridges to be crossed and the valley of death run beneath great séracs which hang over one like a baited trap. On this occasion the icefall also demanded a 150-foot free abseil from the top of a sérac followed by a go-like-hell section.

We reached the German bivvy late that afternoon. Richard had just arrived and he looked worried. He came over.

"One of Rudy's mates has fallen into a crevasse," he said, "down on the Shkhelda glacier." He pointed. "On that long flat easy bit."

"Hell," said Paul, "but there are no crevasses there, they're all blind."

"Not the blighter he fell down," said Richard with vehemence, "it was right on our normal twice-a-week trail up the ice. It's only about eighteen inches wide but he went down seventy feet, and he's waist deep in water as if in a submerged vice. Tut and Rudy and some of the Russians are trying to bail him out now, but there's not much hope. I've come up for blankets from the bivvy here."

We all hot-footed it down the glacier to the small funeral-like party which gathered round the rather insignificant slot. They had him up by this time. It had been a hell of a job apparently and at first glance I thought the man was dead; he had that translucent pallor of a corpse. I felt for a pulse as Paul wrapped the blankets round him.

"Bugger all there," I said, and then decided to risk giving him a cortizone injection, knowing full well the consequences, political not medical, of such an action. At that time we used steroids on severely exposed climbers with considerable success back in Scotland. I felt quite sure he would not recover in the normal course of events for it would be at least six hours before a rescue party reached him and due to the cloud a helicopter wouldn't get in. Anyhow, it was late in the day. After the injection nothing appeared to happen for several minutes, but gradually there was a faint but unmistakable sign of life.

We could detect a slight movement of the chest and within fifteen minutes I felt a weak pulse, but it was still a pulse. There was little more we could do, so leaving him well wrapped up in blankets and duvets with his friends we bade them adieu and took to the glacier once again, now very wary of the faintest suspicion of a crevasse. Next morning a helicopter managed to reach the glacier and he climbed aboard unaided. Down in Itkol I breathed a sigh of relief upon hearing this for I didn't relish the prospect of answering awkward questions to a Russian court of inquiry.

Russians are lavish with their hospitality and our imminent departure was celebrated with a banquet at Itkol, the no-alcohol ban was lifted officially for the evening and we had long and numerous toasts. We were standing up and sitting down like Jacks in a Box as the toasts became more frequent. Paul, who had to hurry over to the Adul Suh to collect some gear from Rudy got involved in a further series of toasts and he later vividly described this 'last Supper' which wouldn't have offended a farewell to Bacchus.

We had had our share of adventures in the Caucasus, but there were still some to come. It was a few miles within the Czech frontier that disaster overtook us, or perhaps I should say, Tut, who was driving, ran into disaster. Tut is a charming in-dividual, as I've already mentioned, and has a disarming sincerity, so that even if the person with whom he is convers-ing happens to be in the back seat of a car he is driving he will turn, as his good manners dictate, to sustain the conversation. He was driving at about 70 m.p.h. in the 125S and it was dusk. The subject of our conversation now eludes me but his attention to the road was punctuated by a swivelling action of his head as if he was watching the finals at Wimbledon. I had a few minutes previously come to the conclusion that Tut's reactions must be far more acute than my own to enable him to perform such a dual role and I dismissed a story I had heard of his demolishing a wall with his car on two separate occasions as

unfair criticism: after all hadn't he rebuilt the wall the last time
for the irate farmer?

Ahead I dimly saw the outline of a cart on our side of the
road and had time to clear my throat to indicate my appre-
hension and to mention as casually as I could the carelessness of
the peasants who took horses and carts without lights on to the
public highways of Czechoslovakia, before the very end of my
sentence was drowned by the crash of our running slap bang
into the rear of this rural contraption. To say that we were
startled would be an understatement, and to say that the horses
and peasants weren't would be a lie. All hell broke loose, as did
the water and antifreeze from the radiator and fragments of hay
floated down in the crepuscular air. We were amazed to find
that we were uninjured. The next thing to establish was what
had happened to the opposition. The peasants were all on the
ground by this time, whether by their own volition or
projected there by Tut's arse-end assault, I didn't enquire, but
they were just beginning to be voluble. Their invective which
rose like an approaching storm seemed uncannily like that used
by the drunken Pole whom George jousted from his bike a few
years previously. It was a case of their not having lights and our
going too fast; at least our speed couldn't be proven. The two
horses, which had been harnessed, one either side of the single
draw shaft, were all right, though no doubt their collars were
strained and their necks permanently askew with a bias to the
right and left respectively when the cart threatened to tear them
asunder in its violent acceleration. It was the Fiat that came off
worst. It was a mess. The front was stove in and though the
engine seemed to suffer little, the radiator and bodywork were
mangled. By the time the police came on the scene and took
statements a large crowd had assembled. The accident
happened on the edge of a village, a village where, we
gathered, the locals had been campaigning for street lighting
for some time and it being Friday night the populace seemed to
have time to spare. After all, it was not every night that a
capitalist car crashes into a cart; moreover it was a car which
had large capitalist posters all over it proclaiming the *Sunday*

*Mirror* Caucasus Expedition. They no doubt thought that this was a new scheme for promoting the circulation of that newspaper in the heart of Russia. Suddenly I had an idea.

"The chewing gum, Chris; where's that case which was left over from the trip?"

"In the back of the Campagnoli."

"Let's have it," I said with enthusiasm, "I've had an idea."

"Oh, not another bloody idea," Tut moaned, "you'll be the death of us yet."

"I think, my friend, that you are leading on points on that score." However, the Wrigleys chewing gum was produced and I opened the case and started handing round the contents like a war-on-want worker, I told the crowd via a young lad, a self-appointed interpreter, that they all had to chew like mad and give the gum back when the sweetness had gone. Thirty chewing Czechs! What had been a babbling mass of humanity a few minutes previously was now a masticating choir with lower jaws going like fiddlers' elbows. The raw material for my plan started to trickle in. First in small isolated well masticated masses of gum and then in quantity. I gave Chris a wad and told him,

"Give me a hand to seal the radiator of the car." Half an hour later there was very little visible of the radiator, it looked like a good plastering job. Alas, when we filled it up with water we discovered that there was a crack in the water pump flange, and the water still poured out on to the ground.

"Well, it was a good try," I said in defence. Tut just shook his head.

"Not only are we without a bloody car now," Chris said, in despair, "but we are also without chewing gum."

Paul, always a mine of information and who radiates a sympathy like a genial Buddha towards foreigners in particular had struck up a conversation with a pretty girl. It transpired that she spoke excellent English and had a sister. She volunteered this last gem of information for she herself was to be married in two days' time. Paul on this brief acquaintance was asked if he would like to be her best man. My mind boggled as to what could have been proposed had their acquaintance been extended to ten minutes. He didn't think that this duty, welcome though it was, would be possible, but seeing some probable advantage to our basic needs suggested that he would require time to consider it and was there somewhere where he and his friends could stay the night whilst he made up his mind? Her house and that of her future husband were immediately put at our disposal and to hers we all repaired, leaving the car, looking rather dejected, beside the road. What to do with this vehicle could be decided another day.

We had a great night. I'm not sure when we got to bed but in the morning we certainly didn't feel refreshed, which is always a good barometer of enjoyment. We realised through quizzing the potential groom that there was no hope of having the Fiat repaired – perhaps in Prague – but certainly not in the eastern part of Czechoslovakia, so by the time we had had breakfast we had resigned ourselves to a long tow, across country to Austria. The Campagnoli was more than capable of this, we knew, and taking out one of our climbing ropes, we 'roped up' and started off, those in the car having a strangely subdued drive with a silent engine.

It wasn't until we arrived at the Austrian border close to Vienna that we managed to have the car repaired, though it still looked a mess.

Our reception at Turin, though not exactly cool, certainly lacked enthusiasm. But Fiat's generosity extended to substituting a pristine model for our crumpled one and we were really treated with a greater courtesy than we deserved. We were grateful to Fiat, for they had done us proud and their vehicle stood all but that ultimate test of Tut's collision, and we were grateful, too, to the Russians who had been so patient with us unruly Westerners. To me it was one of my most memorable holidays for one can't call a journey like that an 'expedition', especially when we enjoyed it: you are not supposed to enjoy an expedition.

# 8

# The Matterhorn Live

"... the rope was taut between us, and the jerk came
on us both as on one man. We held; but the rope
broke midway between Taugwalder and Lord Francis
Douglas ..."

[Edward Whymper, *Scrambles Amongst the Alps*]

ALTHOUGH THE OLD MAN OF HOY Outside Broadcast was a
success beyond our wildest dreams, it did establish a precedent.
New standards in this form of entertainment had been attained
which somehow had to be equalled in any further climbing
spectacular or even bettered. We looked around for a kindred
subject, but each one we considered fell short of the universal
appeal of that unique finger of sandstone. Many ideas were put
forward but we were committed to a maximum cable run of
5000 feet from the scanner to the cameras and the number of
sea-cliffs and crags within this range is sadly limited. A small
survey party evolved by natural selection to look into the
possibilities. This was made up of Joe Brown, Chris Brasher,
Alan Chivers, an engineer and myself. We contemplated other
sea-cliffs, such as the Great Kame of Foula, a 700-foot precipice
which falls into the North Atlantic at the angle which a seabird
dropping falls to the sea. This cliff was rejected due to access
difficulties. Tom Patey suggested the Trolltinder Wall at
Andalsnes in Norway but we should have realised from a
cursory glance at a map that it was to be a non-starter. Tom
had assumed that the scanner, could get to if not a stone's
throw of the wall, certainly to within the statutory 5000 feet.
    It was spring when Joe Brown, Chris Brasher, Alan Chivers

and I arrived at Andalsnes. Snow still lay thick on the peaks and the shadowed valleys had not awakened from their winter slumber. We almost expected to find the trolls in residence. Chris, who is a great advocate of cross-country skiing, stated, "Well, lads, it's cross-country skis for this job; there's no better means of getting about in winter." He was addressing Joe and me – the title 'lad' doesn't seem quite fitting for Chiv in his more mature years – anyway he was to serve standing and waiting down below at base, with a walkie-talkie, whilst we stormed the heights.

"Crap," I said, with feeling. My view of cross-country skiing has always been that as a soft-shoe shuffle it may just help geriatrics to pass the time. It certainly does take time.

A long harangue ensued in which Joe played a passive role. He had done downhill skiing but no langlauf. Chiv smiled and puffed away at his pipe, an instrument which was later to save his life. Chris had his way, however. We were equipped with the long narrow skis and he also located an expert skier and guide to accompany us, who substantiated Chris's claims that cross-country skiing was the greatest thing since the Viking longboat.

We set off next day at the crack of dawn, or perhaps I should say at the seepage of dawn for it was a long-drawn out affair with the sun eventually breaking through when we were half-way up the mountain. It was then time to put on our skis, but as a long detour was proposed by the guide, to reach a point directly above us, I ventured to suggest that a route up the ridge ahead on foot would be quicker. This was dismissed by the Norwegian who was keen to be off on his boards, as was Chris, but both Joe and I favoured my proposed course of action, carrying our skis. We arrived on top ahead of them, much to their disgust. As they joined us I said to Joe in a throw-away line, "That was an easy way up, Joe. It is only a pity that carrying the skis held us back so much."

We had borrowed a large range-finder from the Norwegian army in Andalsnes which we set up on the summit and took various readings. But the scale of the Troll peaks was much greater than we had anticipated. Even had it been feasible to take the scanner up the precipitous track Tom Patey had suggested, the distance between possible camera positions and the Trolltinder Wall was too great for even our mammoth lenses. Back on the summit we unfurled the Union Jack and the Norwegian flag at the special request of our hotel manager, for this was Independence Day in Norway.

"Well," Chris said, once we'd had a bite to eat in the sunshine. "At least you'll be skiing down, Hamish. It will be a superb run."

"I don't think I'll bother," I said, ungraciously. "I don't go a bundle on langlauf skis for downhill, especially with my old climbing boots. I'd have as much control as a drunken driver in a dodgem car. I'll walk."

"Me, too," echoed Joe. "If I had my downhill skis and boots it would be a different story."

Shouldering once again our useless pieces of wood, Joe and I started off while Chris and our guide, in a series of whoops, disappeared down the way they had come.

With the heat of the sun the snow was now soft and treacherous. I noticed that Joe hung back.

"You want me to get avalanched first?" I asked.

"Well, bugger me, you've been on the snow since you left the pram. I'm a rock man myself. You know better than me if this porridge is going to stay where it dropped." It did.

A bit further down where the angle eased we decided to sit on our skis, using them as toboggans, and in this way we arrived at the bottom of the slope like ton-up Santas, much to the consternation of the other two who had just emerged from the pines at the bottom of their trail.

Later quests took us on a tour of the Western Highlands and Islands of Scotland where I showed Chiv and the others the possibilities of the Sgurr of Eigg, a castle-like mini peak of columnar pitchstone porphyry. The Sgurr was at one time fortified by means of a wall on its westerly aspect to enable the summit block to serve as a place of refuge for the locals during Viking raids, though some historians place the fortifications before the Norsemen. The face we were interested in was the Nose of the Sgurr, a vertical wall where, frighteningly, pitch-stone columns could be pulled out like loose organ pipes. We thought we would leave the organ pipes where they were.

Another objective which proved too difficult to reach with the scanner was the great grey gneiss 700-foot overhang of Stron Ulladale in North Harris, then owned by Sir Hereward Wake. Miles of knee-deep bog separated it from a convenient landing site on the coast.

A programme which did come to pass was on the Anglesey sea-cliffs at North Stack where three climbs were done simultaneously, Wen Slab, Tyrannosaurus Rex and the Spider's Web. Don Whillans would do Wen Slab and Joe Brown and Mac the Telly were to be suitably entangled in the Spider's Web, a route requiring astute rope manipulation. As Joe Brown had in the past been termed by the popular press as both the 'human spider' and the 'human fly', he was particularly suited to this route.

By this time I had built special equipment for Outside Broadcasts. I had, for example, a glass-fibre capsule left over from casualty evacuation which was adapted from an aeroplane jettison tank. This we used to transport cameras to difficult positions via the now well-proven cableway system; and with the assistance of Reg Phillips, a very able hydraulics research scientist, I had built a hydraulic winch which could be dismantled and had a capacity of 2000-foot of steel wire rope. These goodies we used at Anglesey. This O.B., however, almost ended in disaster. A storm (shades of Hoy) occurred the night before the transmission, and though I had taken the precaution of securing the cameras well above any potential danger from high seas, the sound equipment which was less portable suffered. We had been assured that gales were unlikely and besides the forecast was good. In the morning with an almighty swell still running in the wake of the storm we descended the cliff on the fixed ropes to inspect the damage. The platforms made from scaffolding were awash. One of these was breaking up, and eventually disappeared with

175

£15,000 worth of sound equipment while we were still watching it. B.B.C. engineers seem to thrive under such adversities
and the programme went on the air on time though initially
only two cameras were operating.

It must have been one of Chiv's worst moments. I had made
two cradles operated by tirfor winches for lowering the
cameras down the face. Selwyn Cox, a B.B.C. cameraman
who is also a climber, and Mo Anthoine were to use one and
Paul Nunn and I the other. Both Mo and Selwyn were apprehensive of their flimsy cages even though Joe and I had tested
theirs the previous evening. We had descended the cliff with it
by means of the two tirfor winches and knew thirty minutes
were necessary to get it down. Mo thought that my cages were
more suitable for canaries than climbers. He and Selwyn took
so long to descend to their positions that they were only halfway down when they should have been on the air. Meantime
Paul Nunn and I had brought our cage down to its operating
level and had started work for Chiv together with one cliff-top
camera. I had been apprehensive to say the least for there had
been so much to do prior to transmission that I had not had a
chance to practise with the large studio camera which we were
using. Fortunately the controls on this were much more
positive than on the minicam and it was a joy to use it, with its
electronic zoom and rock-steady control. That is, it was rock-
steady until one of us moved. Then the platform resembled a
cage shared by a hungry cat and one of Mo's canaries.

Eventually all the cameras were operating; John Cleare at the
Spider's Web and Mo and Selwyn were far enough down the
cliff to take part in the second transmission of the day. In spite
of the loss of the sound equipment from the platform the jury-
rig radio gear assembled by the engineers worked well. The
programme got quite good ratings and everybody was satisfied. The de-rig was a sedate affair, certainly compared with
Hoy, and there was no wind-up party as such. Mac didn't have
a rocket send-off, the nearest approach to this was the disposal
of my rocket-like camera capsule which we launched after it
was finished with from the cliff-top. It ended its days beneath

The author watches one of his glass fibre capsules used to transport a camera to difficult positions on the North Stack Outside Broadcast on Anglesey. Later £15,000-worth of sound equipment disappeared in a storm.

Hamish MacInnes, left, and Rusty Baillie at the camp site below the First Step on the Matterhorn Centenary Outside Broadcast.

The Matterhorn summit, author with camera.

the seething Irish Sea, entering the waves in a graceful parabola which would have done justice to a performing dolphin.

One of the stimulating aspects of doing an Outside Broadcast with Chiv is that we are always striving for the impossible. The impossible, so they say, always takes a little longer and we make this time allowance for our engineering colleagues to come up with some new solution to what appears at first sight an insoluble impasse. Such was the Matterhorn Centenary O.B. This was a projected programme to be transmitted live of the ascent of this spectacular 14,000-foot rock pyramid, probably better known to the public at large than Everest itself. 1965 was the centenary year of the first ascent by Edward Whymper. The accident which followed the first ascent was probably the most dramatic and tragic in the history of mountaineering. This tragedy in which Lord Francis Douglas was one of four killed caused an outcry that resulted in proposals to ban the sport. *The Times* asked: "Is it life, is it duty, is it commonsense, is it allowable, is it wrong?" Even today one can hear the echo of these sentiments after a mountain accident. The stigma of the affair was to prey on Edward Whymper's mind for the remainder of his days. Whymper, later reflecting on this loss of life, which brought him so much adverse publicity, wrote:

> Climb if you will, but remember that courage and strength are not without prudence and that a momentary negligence may destroy the happiness of a life-time. Do nothing in haste, look well to each step and from the beginning think what may be the end.

Just as well we didn't take his words too much to heart when we set out to do the O.B. programme of the Matterhorn, but optimists don't dwell too seriously on anything but a happy ending.

An O.B. of this magnitude had never been attempted before. The scale was immense compared to our previous British programme, or even the Aiguille de Midi where the convenience of a cablecar expedited the rigging. There is no cablecar up the Matterhorn; the only one fell about 2000-feet short of the Hotel Belvedere and the Hörnli hut, stopping at Schwarzsee. Chiv had to find out from his engineers if the minicams could transmit a signal, using them without cables over a distance of 4000 feet which was the distance from the summit of the mountain back to the Belvedere Hotel. Alan Roberts, the chief engineer, after doing some tests, assured Chiv that with reservations they would work, but after all, Alan pointed out, it is a different kettle of fish trying it an sea-level and at 14,000 feet. Cold and high altitude bugs could have a heyday screwing things up. But a nod is as good as a wink to Alan Chivers and he turned his attention to other pressing details. The O.B. slowly took shape. Without the help of the Swiss Army helicopters it would have been a non-starter. They ferried ten tons of equipment to the Belvedere Hotel with typical Swiss efficiency, taking up large generators as well as the delicate electrical gear without mishaps, setting them down on a blanket-sized ledge. This great mass of electronic gadgetry was reassembled inside the Belvedere Hotel. We didn't have a survey worth talking about. The mountain was still unclimbed that year when we arrived: it was plastered in snow. But the work went ahead and other camera positions were established at both Schwarzsee and the Görnergrat. The camera at the Görnergrat was on a railway flat car for it was essential also to have long distance shots of the mountain. John Cleare and I were again to operate the minicams and Rusty Baillie and David Crabb were our respective assistants. Davie was one of my instructors in Glencoe and was a strong but outspoken climber. One of his hobbies was geology which he practised with avid enthusiasm. Everything he did was coupled with a volcanic eruption of zeal, liberally punctuated with good honest Dundonian invective, fortunately this was usually incomprehensible to anyone not acquainted with the peculiarities of his patois. He had, however, a heart of gold and was really a good Samaritan in the guise of a Mephistopheles. One day Davie and I were travelling up on the cablecar from Zermatt to Schwarzsee. There was only one other passenger, a well-dressed man whom my companion suspected of being a 'hoch tourist'. The only thing worse than a high tourist or hill-walker in Davie's estimation was an Englishman and the combination of the two was too awful to contemplate. This chap was, however, Swiss; Davie made one or two pointed remarks about this unfortunate individual's appearance, from his virgin white socks to his natty William Tell hat. Later, however, when walking up to the hut from the Schwarzee with this Savile Row climber we discovered he was very fit. Imagine Davie's discomfiture when he discovered the identity of our new companion – Michael Darbellay, who in 1963 made the first solo ascent of the Eiger North Wall! He, too, was bound for the Hotel Belvedere and in the company of Hilti von Allmen climbed the Matterhorn North Wall during the Outside Broadcast. Hilte, unfortunately, was later killed in a skiing accident.

There were more activities at the Hotel Belvedere than the Outside Broadcast preparation. Demolition work had commenced on the adjoining Hörnli hut and workmen were now hard at it for the snow had just cleared at this altitude. They had to blast the rock foundations from time to time and this with the associated mess of a building site added to the general confusion. The hotel was overcrowded and what space was not taken up with equipment was utilised by the scanner crew, engineers and climbers of various nationalities. Everyone wanted to climb the Matterhorn that year. The Swiss government had declared 1965 as the 'Year of the Alps'. For the centenary anniversary of that first tragic ascent the authorities promised to 'close' the mountain. How, one may ask, can you 'close' a mountain? But they did in fact prevent all but official parties from going up the Hörnli route on the great day.

The four of us, Rusty Baillie, John Cleare, Davie Crabb and I, set up house and home under canvas on the ridge a short way above the hotel. Here we were out of range of the hotel's smelly dry closet, and the situation of the campsite commanded superb views of the peaks of the valley. We were also exposed to the elements, however, and one night we awoke to

179

a frightening high voltage display. It was a daddy of a storm and, with the death of two climbers struck by lightning in a tent in Glencoe fresh in my mind, I proposed that we should evacuate. This we did and witnessed nature's fireworks from beneath a large convenient boulder, while I held forth on the advantages of having a ridge pole in such a situation as it prevents, to some extent the body from acting like an electric fire element between the two end poles, and the consequent involuntary roasting.

Chiv was under a lot of pressure. As well as trying to co-operate with the Swiss director in such cramped and difficult conditions, our various rehearsals were abortive. On the first the minicams refused to work and on the second with a great deal of back-breaking work we got as far as the Solway refuge, a small bivouac hut halfway up the Hörnli Ridge. Here the snow was so deep, over ice, that it wasn't possible to go further. David Crabb gained instant fame in that last abortive live rehearsal. We were to the side of the normal route on an airy promontory and we had suffered a series of problems that day since leaving before first light, the most serious being the porterage of our equipment. Though we were both carrying 35-lbs each there was still enough left over for our two local porter/guides. What these two lacked in carrying capability was more than made up with their constant grumbling. I couldn't help comparing the situation with Whymper's exasperation with the two Taugwalders, Old Peter and Young Peter, who immediately after the accident which befell their party when coming down the mountain complained that as Lord Francis Douglas was dead, no one would pay their fee.

Davie was in a rare temper and as I was busy working on the camera, I asked him to deal with a query which came over the walkie-talkie from the Hotel Belvedere. Davie's radio voice was identical to his every-day brogue and his spleen was vented and relayed over the networks of Europe, though Telstar was used to relay the signal to America; I never did find out if his discourse on alpine weather, alpine guides and alpine broad-

casts ever reached the New World. That day on the descent we
had a further electrical storm. It was small-time stuff but
frightening enough. One of the guides who was carrying
expensive batteries for the cameras felt a burning sensation in
his back. Glancing behind he saw that his rucksack was on fire.
Not caused by any high-voltage discharge but by his crampons
short-circuiting the battery. The rucksack was dropped and
subsequently tumbled down the north face to be no doubt
gobbled up by some shark-mouthed crevasse and perhaps to
keep the bones of the late Lord Francis Douglas company.

It was the 10th July and the broadcast was scheduled for the
14th, the date of the first ascent. The whole thing was now a
gamble like Russian roulette with three rounds in the chamber
and the gun to Chiv's head. He may therefore be forgiven for a
slight lapse of memory, while going to the thunderbox, as he
called the hotel lavatory which functioned on a free fall principle
from the second storey of the hotel to the basement. Alan
Chivers describes the visit to the toilet:

I think I am one of the few people who can claim that at least
on this particular instance smoking was good for my health.

The regular visit each day to the thunderbox was an event
that we all delayed for as long as possible and on this
occasion I was making my way towards this little room
which, incidentally, was at the end of the corridor and hung
out over the side of the mountain: The floor was completely
exposed and about 50-foot below there were the Swiss
engineers blasting away at regular intervals in order to build
a new alpine hut. On this particular visit I was almost at the
door when I discovered I hadn't got any tobacco, and
smoking I regarded as an essential exercise, so I returned to
my room, collected the tobacco and was about 30-foot from
the door when there was a much larger explosion than usual
and I obviously hadn't heard the warning. The door of the
loo flew off and when the dust, splintered glass and wood
had settled at my feet I realised that had I been sitting on the
throne at that time, at best I would have been extremely

embarrassed by the incident, or at worst it might have proved fatal.

Chris Brasher was contracted to do the commentary on the climb and was to ascend the mountain with Hendrich Taugwalder, great grandson of the guide who had made the first ascent with Whymper. But Chris had not taken into account the effect of that scourge of mountaineers, which seems to manifest itself at altitude – piles. He was incapacitated and Mac the Telly had to take his place. When several climbers from Britain appeared in Zermatt I suggested to Chiv that he should immediately put them on the payroll as Sherpas. I knew them all well. Eric Beard that inimitable fell runner who had worked with us on the Old Man of Hoy was one. The others were Ian Martin, alias Fred Crumb, a member of the Rannoch Club who had a doss in a damp dark gulch below my house in Glencoe; also from the Rannoch Club was John Wright. Chris Patterson, a friend of John Cleare's was with them, and so was Dr. Mary Stewart, an American living in Glasgow and a mother of five. Mary is a tough and efficient climber who can carry as well as any man. They were all willing to help; now at least we had the person-power: only weather and conditions could stop us. Only the weather! The snow lay crisp and even. It had now improved and during the day the sun came out and our spirits rose if not our physical selves for there were no more rehearsals up the mountain. They were too depressing.

With advertising you can sell anything: the Matterhorn centenary programme was sold hook, line and sinker or perhaps I should say carabiner, rope and ice axe, to the public in a dozen countries. A press conference was held at the Schwarzee Hotel where the reporters seemed extraordinarily interested in how we were going to get the cameras up the mountain – so were we! We proposed to do this, we told them, by leapfrogging, that is, say, when John was filming on the old bivouac site used by Whymper on the lower reaches of the face, I should be in position higher up ready for Taugwalder and Mac the Telly to pass. By this time John and Rusty would have caught up, passed them and then got ensconced at a higher place still. At least that was the theory. Madame Yvette Vaucher who was then a Geneva shop assistant was to climb the north face with her husband, one of three separate ropes on that wall, and if she was successful in doing this she would be the first woman to do the climb.

The great day arrived and it was a fine one. The climbing conditions were good and our leapfrogging system appeared to work. Davie and I with Mary and Ian Martin assisting as Sherpas met the Vaucher party as they came down. They had jumped the gun by starting earlier than scheduled. But we did an interview with them in the full flush of Yvette's success. All she wanted then, she said, "was some salad, a lot of cake and a nice hair-do". She had worn plastic curlers beneath her climbing helmet during the ascent!

At John's highest point of transmission, above the shoulder of the mountain, his minicam gave up the ghost. This was bad news and we hurriedly agreed that both he and Rusty should come with my party to the summit and as soon as I had completed the sequence there they could dash (if you can dash on such terrain) back to the shoulder with my minicam to cover the descent, for Chiv wanted the approximate scene of the Whymper accident to be shown on the last transmission. It was an exhausting business. John and I didn't have any respite. Each country wanted ten minutes of live telly and we had to do one ten minute stint after another. As well as this we had to pack up the equipment and as soon as this was completed, sprint to the next location, passing Mac and Hendrich en route. We had been so busy with the problems of getting the transmissions out on time we hadn't even looked at the weather, until we were enveloped in cloud. As we struggled up the summit rocks, the grey mass crowded us like murky water. We hadn't the precise bearing for the Hotel Belvedere, or for that matter the angle of declination. I had taken the precaution a few days before of visiting a machine shop in Zermatt and making alloy poles to which the aerials for the minicams could be attached and angled to any position by utilising a swivel clamp. The sectional poles could be inserted in the snow or jammed in cracks in the rock. My aerial was now ready in position on the summit but without a precise direction for pointing it. We tried several times, using the walkie-talkie to zero in, but it was like that blindfolded parlour game of pinning the tail on the donkey. Luckily just one and half minutes before transmission a window appeared in the cloud and we saw the hotel sitting astride the ridge like a squat dwarf far below. One of the guides gave a yodel and I quickly swung the aerial round with the celerity of an ack-ack gunner firing on low flying aircraft from a mountaintop. We were in business.

The summit party's thunder was stolen by Mary Stewart who made an impromptu appearance for American viewers by saying hello to her folks and mentioning that she had carried a 30-lb load to the top!

That summit scene for me was by far the most gruelling. After the concentration of fifteen minutes holding the camera, I was almost flaking out. Davie helped to prop me up and in desperation I said to Chiv on the talk-back,

"You'll have to cut to another camera, Alan. I've had it." Fortunately, he did. As soon as I dropped down on the snow, shattered, John took the camera from my grasp. I remember thinking fleetingly of reports of some of my friends taking boots from climbers killed in a fall. With Rusty he set off down the fixed ropes, passing en route many of the official permitted parties, somewhat irate at this ungentlemanly behaviour. For it is a point of honour amongst the more stately of mountaineers that one shouldn't pass on a route, unless asked to do so. It is like blowing your nose at dinner with the table napkin. At one point Rusty came to blows with one of the guides, but there was a job to do and several million viewers waited for the next transmission.

On the way down Mac was doing his spiel about the 1865 accident whilst on a dog-lead rope held by the following Taugwalder, when he inadvertently slipped. This wasn't for the benefit of the viewers. It was quite genuine. In fact it only ended with a damp bottom for Mac, but it went over well.

This is what a live O.B. was all about. John was now suffering from my summit malady of keeling over through sheer strain from holding the camera for a prolonged period. Suddenly I saw that the large block of rock on which he was perched, about the size of a tea chest, was moving. Hurriedly I moved below it to keep it in place, but didn't mention this to John.

As soon as the transmission was over we all breathed a sigh of relief and John was pulled back on to the ridge where the Sherpas were brewing tea on a primus. I stepped aside and let his late perch keel slowly over and crash down the north face. We fervently hoped that on its 4000-foot journey it didn't encounter any humans.

It was late when we arrived in Zermatt and it seemed to be an anticlimax. The climb had gone well, but nothing had been set up for an evening meal. We stood around the fountain in the main street feeling like stranded tourists. Chris Brasher took this dilemma as a personal challenge and in fifteen minutes had arranged a gargantuan feast at one of the hotels. Beardie was on his best form as the mountain clown, but little did we know then that this was to be his last O.B., for he was later killed in a car crash. The evening which started as a damp squib developed with a bang, and ended with a splash, for later that night Rusty disposed of the owner of a night-club in a swimming pool which happened to be on the premises. Later still, he had a wrestling match with the local police in the main street. Zermatt was understanding, however; it had been a great day and the P.R. value of the broadcast to the Swiss was immeasurable. I remember thinking through an alcoholic haze of the battle of Zermatt at a time when I had first put on my climbing boots. Chris Lyons of the Creagh Dhu Club had told me of this fracas. It was of hard men in hard times just after the last war when the local guides had objected to the Scottish climbers, born and bred in the tough school of Glasgow's Clydebank. One of the causes of friction was the fact that the Creagh Dhu were doing climbs without the use of guides and a local belle, Madame Paulette, had taken the destitute climbers to her ample bosom and had made derisive remarks to the young blond gods as Chris called the aspirant guides. The difference of opinion made itself felt after one of the guides had put a firecracker in the trousers of a Glasgow lad. Chris and his friends, acting promptly, had thrown their pal into the fountain, the same fountain which we had been hanging around after coming down from the mountain. Later that evening the matter came to a head when the two groups met in a street. The aspirant guides were led by 'Mr. Five-by-five', a broad, short man, built like a large tree stump. The battle didn't last long, for the spearhead tactics adopted by the outnumbered Creagh Dhu paid off; Mr. Five-by-five was singled out by one of the boys and cried when he was punched. The most amusing aspect of that historic evening was at the end when Big Bill Allen, a six-feet-four, seventeen-stone Glasgow policeman, complained that his friends had been so fast that he didn't get 'a chance to hit onybody', despite the fact that the Club was outnumbered eight to one. At that precise moment a young man came over, grabbed one of the boys and started yelling at him. This was Bill's chance and he hit the man with such force that he cartwheeled across the street, under a café table to touchdown in a flowerbed. However, Bill was now pounced on by a charming but irate mademoiselle. It was her fiancé that Bill had projected so successfully and he had been offering only his congratulations to the valiant club for winning the battle.

Perhaps our stay in Zermatt didn't have the impact of that 1946 party but it did bring entertainment to a large number of people who enjoyed the immediacy of the live O.B. It wasn't the sort of programme that Chiv goes a bundle on, for the essence of a live O.B. is getting in amongst it with the mini-cams; this was impossible to do on the Matterhorn due to the scale of things. The public was now accustomed to seeing climbers eyeball to eyeball hanging on to cliffs by faith alone and perhaps the assistance of their fingernails, and the more easygoing pace of the Centenary Climb didn't have this intimacy. We had, however, pulled it off, how I don't know, and when I look back on the event I shudder; perhaps it was Russian roulette with only one empty chamber.

# 9

# St. Kilda

And if there's going to be a life hereafter
I'll fly back to St. Kilda by and by
As the dedicated defecating gannet
Passing on the message from on high.

There is not a lot to see upon St. Kilda;
Two dozen empty bothies and the Wall,
It is a dreary little dot of desolation
One hundred miles due west of buggerall.

I HAD JUST COMPLETED a rock climb on Buachaille Etive Mor in Glencoe with Dr. Morton Boyd and Lord Hawick. We were on Curved Ridge and stopped for a bite to eat beneath the Rannoch Wall, an elegant rock face with superb prospects over the Moor of Rannoch.

The Nature Conservancy Council owns many of the wild and lovely areas of Scotland and our conversation took us out to St. Kilda. Morton, as Chairman of the Nature Conservancy Council for Scotland knew everything that was worth knowing about this huddle of islands in the parlour of the Atlantic, and as I hadn't then been there, I questioned him closely on the group. In that brief conversation, while we sat and munched our sandwiches, admiring the great expanse of moor, I learned that there was a road up to a point at 1000 feet above sea level on Hirta, the main island, and that army landing craft went to and from the island at regular intervals.

Like most climbers I had heard rumours of fabulous cliffs, reputed to be the highest in Britain which plunged into a frothy storm-tossed sea, and birds in such numbers that they resembled falling confetti at an exuberant wedding.

"I'm not sure about the cliffs, Hamish," Morton said. "There are certainly plenty of them, but there's also a lot of vegetation. The St. Kildans, as you know, usually went down from the top on ropes to collect eggs and young birds." Morton, with Dick Balharrie of the Nature Conservancy, had ascended the famous gannetry of Stack Lee during one of their visits, as well as conducting regular sheep counts on the adjoining precipitous island of Boreray. "But if you're interested in going out there," he added, "let me know. I may be able to help."

Lord Hawick had an amused twinkle in his eye.

"Thinking of planning one of your TV shows on Hirta, Hamish?" he asked.

"Well, we're always looking for suitable subjects," I admitted, "but I don't suppose there's a snowball's chance in hell of doing an O.B. there."

Above us, on a difficult climb on the Rannoch Wall were two Glaswegian climbers and we gathered from their descriptive comments that the route was harder than they had expected. Lord Hawick was endowed with a very retentive memory and months later I was told that he entertained his fellow lords, in the illustrious House of that name, with a verbatim recitation of the conversation of those two climbers – expletive not deleted – and in a fair impersonation of a Maryhill dialect.

As we continued up towards the summit of the mountain, I resolved to do some homework when I got back that night. St. Kilda sounded very interesting to me, though it was difficult to imagine setting up an Outside Broadcast anywhere so remote in the British Isles. There is always something fascinating about an island, and in the following months I was not idle. At that time I was trying to set up a rescue flying squad in Scotland. This was to be a select group of rescue–climbers who could be flown by helicopter to remote cliffs and islands when there was a climbing accident. So I had a valid excuse to approach the R.A.F., with whom I work on mountain rescue matters, for permission to fly over the St. Kilda group in a training fighter to photograph the crags for identification purposes. My request was turned down, and my flying squad didn't get off the ground at the time, but a few weeks later a box of enlargements arrived which showed clearly every cliff in the St. Kilda group; the Air Force had done a thorough job.

At first glance the cliffs seemed superb but closer study revealed vegetation growing on the ridiculously steep faces and at the bottom of each precipice was a deep ribbon of white which only too clearly demarked the swell-like pack of snapping wolves I accepted as normal for that part of the world.

I contacted Chiv and outlined my researches to date, pointing out that it would be essential to have a survey before we could establish whether any of the cliffs would give the slimmest chance of an O.B. The most obvious cliff I told him was one called Conachair which was also the highest, though it looked to me as if it could win the award as Britain's most nearly vertical garden.

"But you never can tell," I said, "perhaps there's a route up the flowerbeds."

These islands have a strange magnetism for the footloose, or perhaps I should say, the seasick traveller. Why this should be is difficult to explain for they are wind bedevilled and for a large part of the year are in the stranglehold of the North Atlantic hurricanes. No swaying palms or maidens here; even to wear a kilt is to court disaster. Yet people have occupied Hirta since the beginning of history. No one is sure when they first came but there are the remains of prehistoric dwellings at Glenmore on Hirta which suggests that non-kilt wearing man was on the island for 2000 years. In 1930 the St. Kildans left forever and settled on other islands and on the mainland. At the present time Hirta is occupied by the army who man a tracking station to monitor rockets launched from South Uist in the Outer Hebrides; score keepers for a military game of giant darts. There is a jetty at Village Bay, the only habitation, and the army has its own pub, the 'Puff Inn'. The islands are owned by the National Trust for Scotland and leased to the Nature Conservancy Council. For centuries the group was in the hands of MacLeods of Dunvegan and the islands changed hands within various septs of the clan itself. There is a tale that the MacLeods of both Harris and Uist wanted control of St. Kilda. This was before the days of expensive litigation when gamesmanship superseded law and was much more expedient. A race from the Outer Hebrides to Hirta was suggested to resolve the ownership, a mere pull of some fifty miles. The first crew to lay a hand on the island was to gain possession. The Uist men were an oar's breadth ahead as they raced into Village Bay, but not to be outdone Colin MacLeod, who rowed for Harris, cut off his left hand and threw it ashore. That is why some MacLeods will tell you that there is a red hand on the clan coat of arms.

The St. Kilda society was an indolent one, at least as far as the males were concerned for it was the women who laboured while men gossiped. The island had its own parliament and such institutions are everywhere sanctuaries of idle chat. This body of cronies was fully representative, for the loquacious male population at least: they were all members. Here the day's work would be deliberated upon, for everything was on a communal basis. Some compared it to the law of Moses. Both work and the allocation of food were divided equally. Agriculture never went a bomb and the basic essentials of life came from the birds. They were culled in their thousands and air dried in the hundreds of cleats which cover the island like warts; turf and drystone chambers, the St. Kilda larder. Though small people, their appetites were apparently gargantuan – comparable to the native gannets. It was reported that in 1697 they scoffed no less than 22,600 birds in the course of the year. There were at that time 80 people on Hirta.

Religion held great sway on the island, especially under the censorious eye of the Rev. John Mackay. He arrived on St. Kilda in 1865; as the only person on Hirta with a timepiece, he held a monopoly and control of that plentiful commodity. He usually omitted to wind his watch and as no one else on the island knew when his service would start or finish (sometimes they would take three hours), the St. Kildans were always, on the Sabbath at least, kept guessing. They didn't dare miss church service – that would mean eternal damnation – and visitors reported that his sermons were models of monotony and endurance.

The other islands in the group are Boreray to the north and Soay to the north-west, separated from Hirta by a narrow channel. Soay got its name from the Vikings due to the sheep which then and now frequent it. They are found also on Hirta and Boreray.

Boreray, the highest point of which is 1245 feet, is a rock molar comprising various turrets and walls erupting from the edge of the continental shelf like a Neptunian castle. There is something wild and untameable about Boreray like a powerful Wagnerian theme. Close to it are its attendant trolls, Stac Lee, 544 feet and Stac an Armin, 627 feet; the latter is the highest sea stack in British waters. They stand stolidly alongside Boreray to the north and north-west respectively with their feet firmly planted on the sea floor, a sea which especially around Stac Lee is white for 300 feet with gannet droppings, for on this stack is one of the biggest gannetries in the world. Stac Lee always reminds me of my attempts to whitewash the house and my success in creating a 10-foot wide white moat! Boreray, with its guardian stacks, can be difficult to reach over the 'no man's land' of surf which muster round their skirts and even Village Bay on Hirta provides a get-up-and-run anchorage should an easterly wind blow.

> I often dream of going to St. Kilda
> The anchor's up, the boat's about to sail.
> Then I waken, almost chokin' with nostalgia
> And sit and quietly vomit in a pail.

It was a south-west wind which buffeted us as we left the navigator's labyrinth of the Sound of Harris and stuck the nose of the boat out into the worried furrows of the ocean one bleak dawn. The B.B.C. had hired a motor yacht for the voyage, a vessel, we discovered, more suited to the consumptive winds of inshore waters than the expansive Atlantic. Our crew were two professionals, John Gray, a member of the Glencoe Mountain Rescue Team and as able a man on a boat as ever was, and the skipper, a professional sailor from Oban. Our passengers were the old bunch, but on this occasion Joe Brown was missing, though he went to St. Kilda in a later survey. The party was a uniform colour, green, but in different hues. Chris Brasher because of, or in spite of the swell, clenched his pipe between his teeth as if it were a buoyancy aid. Chiv was distinctly unhappy, no doubt cursing me for ever suggesting such a hare-brained idea. Brendan Slanin, the chief engineer, B.B.C. Scotland, who weathered our earlier Hebridean tour with fortitude hadn't spoken for at least forty-five minutes and I gathered that he was frightened to open his mouth in case he lost more calories. Bob Portillo, another engineer, was equally silent and had a faraway look in his eye which wasn't nautical. Tom Patey, that irrepressible impresario, was unusually quiet and punctuated swallowing pregnancy pills, which he assured us were good for seasickness, with frequent periods hanging over the rail while he pretended to take an unusual interest in plankton. In reality he was feeding the residents of the Atlantic with porridge and toast and pregnancy pills. He looked at me after a masticated slice of bread had been distributed to the fishes and quoted Dr. Johnson balefully: "No man will be a sailor who has contrivance enough to get himself into jail, for being in a ship is being in jail with a chance of being drowned. A man in a jail has more room, better food and commonly better company." Any reply I may have conjured to this was stillborn for John Gray who had never been seasick before in his life asked me to take the wheel. It wasn't that the sea was particularly high, though the clinometer at the foc's'le door was colliding with its stops on each roll; possibly it was the combination of various unusual 'motions'. It took me about one and half minutes to lose control of the boat. One instant we were butting into the long sea from the south-west and next it was threatening to swamp us up the backside. I was exactly

The Wall of Conachair, St. Kilda.

Approaching the North Atlantic Wall: Alan Chivers, seated, Chris Brasher, Tom Patey, and Brendan Slanin, right.

Tom Patey, Alan Chivers and Chris Brasher consider camera positions.

The Pirate and his daughters in the Choyang valley.

180° off course. John took over again, muttering to the effect that he'd better drive in view of my strong homing instinct.

The foc's'le was in a mess; smashed bottles and tomato ketchup seemed to be everywhere. The chimney had become divorced from the stove and a fine film of ash settled on everything like the aftermath of a volcanic eruption.

Our St. Kilda landfall wasn't exactly a gladiatorial event but I expect that the army personnel were used to seeing sickly, bedraggled boggle-eyed passengers stagger ashore from what is after all one of the worst crossings in British waters. The Nature Conservancy Council through Morton Boyd had kindly given us the use of the factor's house for our 'holiday' and to this we now repaired, with bundles of salt soaked groceries and damp equipment – looking like survivors from the *Lusitania*. None of us relished the thought of sleeping on board and as there were not enough beds for everyone at the factor's house, Brendan Slanin and I volunteered to sleep on the kitchen floor, unaware that we would have nocturnal visitors. To some the St Kilda mouse is a large cuddly bundle of fur. Both Brendon and I found out to our cost the first night that it is also irresistibly attracted to warm sleeping bags and is often fearless of man. Mice are inordinately ticklish creatures as I was to discover, and Brendon found them so disturbing that the next night and for the remainder of our stay he preferred the aquatic torture of the bunk on the bucking yacht (otherwise he might have died laughing). I installed myself during the following nights on top of the kitchen table.

Upon exploring the island we discovered that the tarmac road went up almost to the summit of Mullach Mor, 1172 feet. This top is to the west of Conachair, 1396 feet, the highest peak on the island. The road had its own zebra crossing, evidence of some poor soldier's boredom.

We discovered that it was certainly feasible to take the scanner up the road, but it would be one hell of a job and would require the supplementary use of winches. The army also advised us about the difficulties with their landing craft, especially in the early spring. For transporting heavy equipment to the island they ran the landing craft up on to the beach at Village Bay. That is to say, if there was a beach, for each winter it is removed in the tempestuous seas and usually but not always it is deposited back on that otherwise bouldery shoreline in the spring. It is the only beach I have ever heard of that sensibly departs for its winter holidays.

The jetty at that time was only suitable for small boats, a scanner would have to get off a landing craft under its own power so that the jetty would be useless for our requirements.

"That is problem number one," Chiv said one evening over a dinner of eggs and beans and voicing our fears. "It doesn't take long to find them."

We did a brief survey of the top of the Conachair cliff, descending it as far as we dared, in dense mist or perhaps it was seafog. Chris Brasher with his orienteering know-how guided us unerringly to this point. Tom Patey, Chris and I went down beyond the last cleat which was stuck limpet-like to the upper part of the face, whilst the others stayed on the safer ground at the top of the cliff. We three, like blind men, cautiously eased our way down; it was very steep grass, then the face dipped in earnest to end abruptly on the lip of a draughty drop. We could sense that it was a hell of a way down to the sea but we couldn't see anything; we could hear the thumping of the surf like a double bass and the accompaniment of hundreds of singing seals, the St. Kilda sirens. It was an uncanny and unforgettable noise which plucked at our heartstrings as the singing of those mythical maidens must have beckoned to Ulysses, but we felt no need of a mast to lash ourselves to and stayed put! We dropped a rock; it seemed ages before we heard a splash. It was as if it had been stopped and searched on the way down.

We planned to circumnavigate the St. Kilda group the following day and it proved an 'all things bright and beautiful' morning. The less said about the creatures great and small of the night preceding the better. Over breakfast we discussed our proposed trip. Tom, who had done his homework on the island, was telling us, as he stirred the porridge, how the inhabitants of Hirta had requested medical aid by using the St.

Kilda mailboat. This was a block of wood with the centre hollowed out. Inside went a message; an inflated sheep's bladder was attached to it as marker. With the help of the Gulf Stream, the messages sometimes, miraculously, reached the west coast of Scotland but occasionally missed their target and were washed up in Norway. This method of communication was used right up to the evacuation of the island, though latterly just as a tourist gimmick. Tom was probably the world's worst cook; stirring porridge was the zenith of his culinary talents, or so I thought as I watched him, but that morning he even succeeded in burning it. When I wrathfully rebuked him upon the loss of my breakfast, instead of telling me that I should have done it myself, he quoted once more from his only source of reading matter at the time, the works of Dr. Johnson:

"'Oats', MacInnes," he said with a wry grin, "'a grain which in England is generally given to horses, but in Scotland supports the people.'"

"Your contribution this morning certainly won't support many!" I retorted. As he licked the singed lumps from the spoon, he remarked, "The St. Kildans used to clean their cutlery by licking it."

"When you two Scotsmen stop squabbling and deriding your ancestors," Chiv said, light-heartedly, "we'll get down to that ruddy boat again. There's nothing like roughing things after all this luxury and there's no reason why Brendon should have a franchise on it." Brendon was still being tossed about on board.

Well, we saw the island from the sea and the only cliff worth our attention as far as a possible O.B. was concerned was not the cliff of Conachair, but one round the corner, closer to Village Bay. This, Chris Brasher, with his journalist's flare, christened North Atlantic Wall. It was certainly impressive and so was the surf beating upon it that morning.

The next day we enlisted the help of the resident Nature Conservancy warden and the army, and with a flotilla of two large inflatable rubber boats in tow we hove to in the swell then

195

nudged on to a large shelf of rock at its base with the Zodiacs. The wall was all of 700 feet high, but ugly loose overhangs made us doubt its possibility as a climb for television. Such a route may take days not hours. We were all sorry we did not have the redoubtable Joe Brown with us for we felt that he would substantiate our worst fears. Tom was, as usual, optimistic. We found certain camera positions on the plinth at the base of the wall but these were not inspiring and, as I pointed to the upper section of a theoretical line, I told Chiv we would have to have mobile platforms like those we used on Anglesey, but for the North Atlantic Wall they would have to be capable of 600 feet vertical movement, not 60.

Meanwhile Bob Portillo had measured the distance from the top camera position back to where the scanner could be placed at the head of the road, and discovered that it was more than 5000 feet. This meant that we would have to take the huge vehicle down from the top of the road in the general direction of the cliff and across a swamp. I shuddered at the thought. None of us wanted to admit defeat but the deck was stacked against us. As Chiv said, St. Kilda was in a no-go state. We consoled ourselves by composing a bawdy song to celebrate our short stay on Hirta. An opening sample heads this chapter. Once we got into our stride there was no stopping us. It went on:

> And if you dream of counting sheep on Soay
> The Conservancy require a volunteer,
> The Trust have got a busy housing programme
> To build one roofless bothy every year.
>
> What happened to the little mice of Hirta
> Those pampered little mice so sleek and fat?
> We fed our furry friends on tins of Rodine,
> And introduced an undernourished cat.

There was a lot more. And so that Tom should not appear to our English friends to have the monoply in St. Kilda history, I told the true story of Lady Grange, the ill-fated wife of Lord Erskine of Grange who was banished to St. Kilda because she overheard a treasonous Jacobite plot while hiding behind a sofa. From St. Kilda she was shipped back to Uist with a rock tied to her feet for instant disposal, just in case an English warship hove in sight. Her husband's elaborate and macabre cover-up plan involved her ladyship in three funerals, first in Greyfriars Church in Edinburgh, then at Durinish on Skye, and finally at Trumpan on Skye. The last one was successful.

In some ways the St. Kilda O.B. took as many attempts to bury as Lady Grange. There were further meetings and I unearthed a firm who could lay an instant road or an airfield from trucks. These vehicles carried large drums of flexible alloy decking which unrolled beneath the truck as it reversed. Later, Joe Brown, Peter Crew and Tom Patey went to St. Kilda to do a further survey of the wall but their report was depressing. Joe felt, as we suspected, that it would take too long to climb, for after all an audience wants to see action not the infinitesimal progress of dangle and whacking vertically moving snails. They went to St. Kilda in the month of February, a time of the year when I declined the opportunity of renewing acquaintance with Hirta. My fears were well substantiated for they were marooned there and at home I listened in sympathy to the shipping forecast each evening with its monotonous repetition of storm force ten winds for Rockall and Hebrides. The boatmen from Harris who had taken them out there had prudently gone home and refused to return with such bad weather forecast. But the weather in fact was good on St. Kilda and after hearing the now usual "storm force ten imminent" Tom and Joe went to the top of Conachair, the highest point on the island and Tom lit a match and held it up still alight. But no one can be infallible, especially meteorologists. They were eventually picked up ten days later.

With up-to-date equipment it would be possible to overcome the technical difficulties of a St. Kilda O.B. now, but a suitable climb is still the difficulty for on these islands abounding with cliffs there is a conspicuous lack of suitable rock for

197

climbing which isn't either covered in Hebridean flora or gannet's guano. So St. Kilda got its final burial, but I often wonder if it will one day be exhumed and with the guano brushed from its ramparts, it may yet yield a harvest of excitement.

Joe and I, some years later, with other friends, went back to St. Kilda with permission to climb on Boreray. Permission which was more difficult to obtain than the rights to sell stocks and shares in the Potala of Lhasa, for some environmentalists, not those of the National Trust or the Nature Conservancy Council, felt that our presence for half a day on the cliffs would unduly disturb the birds, even outside the nesting season. Birds which for generations were culled in their thousands. Anyhow, it transpired that the cliffs were so covered in bird droppings that we would have required a sanitary inspector to lead our rope. So we returned to the mainland, achieving little on that final visit to this huddle of islands, but at the same time we had once more satisfied a need, for you come to terms with yourself on St. Kilda. Everyone needs a St. Kilda, an Ultima Thule, a place to get away from it all. The more sensitive, anonymous verse of a St. Kildan rather than our bawdy song imparts the feelings of those lonely island people and a way of life that is no more:

> Thanks to the Being, the gannets have come,
> Yes, and the great auks along with them.
> Dark-haired girl! – a cow in the fold,
> Brown cow! brown cow! brown cow, belove'd, ho!
> Brown cow, my love! the milker of milk to thee,
> Ho ro, my fair-skinned girl, a cow in the fold
> And the birds have come. – Glad sight I see.

# 10

# Yeti Again

Beyond eight paktset there is a hidden valley called
Khembalung, which is similar to Dewachan and to Potala.
To the west of Demet Snow Mountain and to the east of
Khumbu Snow Mountain lies this hidden valley. Again,
(the King) asked, 'Great Guru Rinpoche, when in the
future beings go there, what is the time that they should
go and what is the sign for the opening of its doors?'
[From the text on Khembalung of Guru Rinpoche]

I FIRST BECAME INTERESTED in the Hongu Valley in 1972 when
talking with Colonel Jimmy Roberts who was the Deputy
Leader of our first Everest South West Face Expedition.
Dougal Haston and I rejoined him at Pheriche when we came
off the mountain. Jimmy, with his blue far-seeing eyes, talked
about the Hongu which was just across the divide in front of us
and how, after he had returned from Base Camp on John Hunt's
successful 1953 Expedition, he had explored the Hongu and
Hinku valleys. He had climbed Mera Peak then, a long whale-
backed mountain of 19,000 feet which rises lazily from the
Mera La, the pass connecting the Hinku and Hongu. Of
course, native people had been going into these valleys for
years and they even took yaks and sheep over the 18,000-foot
Mera La. It seemed to be a real Lost Behind the Ranges place,
straight from the pages of James Hilton, and I resolved to go
there as soon as possible. I gathered from Jimmy that the north
end of the Hongu came right up to the Sola Khumbu watershed
at a point not far from Pheriche, but that the easiest access from
the north was over the Amphu Labtsa, a 19,000-foot pass. An
elevated doorway, the portals being the shapely tombstone of

Ama Dablam on the west and the ridge leaping up to Baruntse on the east.

After the successful Everest South West Face Expedition of 1975 I returned home suffering from the after effects of arguing the odds with a powder-snow avalanche. I had hoped to visit the Hongu that year, and though my ribs still hurt when I laughed, I returned to Nepal a short time afterwards. The region lived up to my hopes and I was excited by the wild country to the east of the Hongu. From the elevated grand-stand of the Mera La, valleys and ridges stretched like a white crested sea all the way across to the Arun valley, that great waterway and highway of Eastern Nepal. First, to the east of the Hongu there is the Sangkhua Khola, then the Choyang and the Iswa, which all flow into the Arun. Each of these great valleys represents a vast tract of country. Only a handful of people had been into the Hongu and Hinku then, and very few had been into the Sangkhua or the Choyang. Only three parties had managed to penetrate the head water of the Sang-khua and the same number had been into the upper Choyang. No expedition had succeeded, at the time of writing, in ascend-ing and exploring these valleys from the Arun. Here was a tract of country so wild that even the yeti would feel lonely; this was perhaps the very place to search for it. No one had managed to make a route from the Arun through to the Khumbu by this southerly line, though to the north a traverse is frequently completed by experienced parties from the Sola Khumbu over the Amphu Labtsa, West and Sherpani cols to the Arun. I was now determined to visit the Choyang, just as five years previously I had resolved to see the Hongu.

I first learned of the Lost Land of Guru Rinpoche from Dave Peterson who was then living in Kathmandu. Dave was one of the doctors on the controversial International Expedition to Everest in 1971. This expedition was renowned for the dis-cord of its members, pumpernickle and stone throwing but, let me hasten to add, Dave is about the easiest going person alive. He too had been into the Hongu and I mentioned to him the exciting possibility of exploring the Sangkhua and the Choyang from the Hongu. After Dave went home to the States he wrote saying that he was planning on taking a larger party back into the region the following spring, and that a colleague of his, a Buddhist scholar, thought that the upper Choyang could possibly be the Lost Land of Guru Rinpoche. Guru Rinpoche was an early Indian yogin who first took Buddhism to Tibet. He established retreats in remote places as sanctuaries for Buddhists in times of trouble.

Dave contacted me again after his expedition, saying that it was one of the most enjoyable trips he ever had, but didn't say much about the upper Sangkhua or the upper Choyang which his party had visited. His Buddhist colleague was obviously playing his religious cards close to his chest, and didn't want to divulge trade secrets.

A short time before this I had met Peter Hackett. Peter, too, was a doctor of medicine and was then based at Pheriche where a high-altitude research station has been established with funds provided by Tokyo Medical College. His main interest lay in the treatment of that high-altitude killer, pulmonary oedema and he enlisted my help in designing a portable, telescopic pressure chamber. He had visited the Hongu on two occasions; for him only the 19,000-foot Amphu Labtsa pass separated it from home. When I mentioned my idea of going into the area east of the Hongu, and to make a new route across to the Arun valley, Peter was dead keen.

Meantime I had suggested the idea to Joe Brown and Yvon Chouinard, who is probably America's best-known climber, as a compensation for an aborted Inca treasure hunt we'd been planning earlier. This too was something different from the normal climbing expedition and they were both interested. I now had a nucleus of four members.

As part of my everyday work involves planning films, I suggested the journey from the Arun to Sola Khumbu as a film to Pat Walker, then Head of Programmes of B.B.C. Scotland. As well as the journey I told Pat there was the possibility of a yeti investigation, but due to Nepalese sensitivity on this subject, I daren't mention it to them officially. The region is probably the best in the whole Himalayan chain for a full-scale yeti search. I also included the Lost Valley element for good measure, though I thought at that time it was the most unlikely one to materialise.

Pat liked the idea from the start and had already met Peter Hackett some time earlier when Peter visited Broadcasting House while we were working on the portable pressure chamber. In due course three members of the B.B.C. staff were selected to accompany us. All were friends of mine, having worked together on films in the past. Gordon Forsyth, the sound recordist, had been with Joe Brown and me in Guyana when we climbed the Prow of Mount Roraima. Robin Chalmers was to be the administrator, looking after the day-to-day running expenses of the B.B.C. and helping with directing; and Andrew Dunn, the youngest member on the trip, was to be our cameraman. A friend of Peter's, Dr. Joe Reinhard, an anthropologist who lived in Kathmandu, had such outstanding references and qualifications that it would have been impossible to take the field without him. This was later borne out: as well as speaking Latin, German, Nepali, Spanish, Raji and Kusunda, he was an authority on Shamanism in Nepal and for many years had been an avid procurer of yeti lore. He also climbed and was a member of the successful American Everest Expedition of 1976. I hadn't met Joe but later found him a very easygoing individual with a flair for getting the most out of the porters without causing offence, yet, at the same time putting a strict damper on their numerous fiddles.

With an eye for the box and the vast licence-paying public, I felt that in this age of emancipation at least two of the fair sex should be included in the party, but as no budding starlets offered their services we thought two scientists would fit the bill even better. We enlisted the talents of Dr. Cynthia Williamson, who is a mountaineer and a plant breeder and Dr. Elizabeth Rogers, a lecturer in zoology from Edinburgh University. Cynthia had been into the Hongu with me in 1975 and I knew that she acclimatised well but for some time we had trouble locating a suitable zoologist, until Elizabeth was found. Earlier I had been hoping to recruit an American girl who was recommended to me but whom I hadn't seen. I contacted the assistant curator of the California Academy of Sciences who knew the lady and I asked him if he thought she would be both fit and photogenic enough for our expedition. He was, however, on vacation when my letter arrived but eventually his reply in the form of a cable arrived. "If not too late, Jane is your girl." The Glencoe postman gave me a strange look as he delivered the message. Unfortunately, it arrived too late.

I met Vicomte Adolphe de Spoelberch many years ago when he first bought Alt na Feidh shooting estate in Glencoe. Ostensibly for part of the year at least he was my next-door neighbour. Later he extended his empire when he purchased Black Corries, the adjoining property to the east. There is in this time of Scottish Nationalism a resentment towards absentee foreign landlords in the Highlands, but in my opinion, if foreign ownership is wrong, it is at the government's door that blame should be laid and they should do something about it. Anyway, moor and mountain property isn't something which can be taken away in a packing case and installed elsewhere. Adolphe has a well-balanced attitude towards walkers and climbers on his land and feels that they rarely disturb his deer despite or perhaps because it is a popular area.

As well as being an avid traveller, Adolphe is a keen amateur botanist and a hunter. A hunter in the true sense; he will push off on his own into some far-flung corner of the Argentine which he visits frequently to hunt and eat what he kills. I can understand a hunter on these terms – one who takes on his quarry with slightly less odds in his favour. He trained as a barrister but on this expedition he was to be the shikhari, the hunting expert. At fifty-two he was the oldest member.

I had worked with Michael Palin of Monty Python fame on several occasions and had found him great company. Furthermore, he was fit and had a long-standing date with the Himalyas, which he had never managed to fulfil. We had been on an expedition together during a film shot partly in Glencoe on 'Crossing the Andes on Frogs'. Michael was delighted when I asked him to accompany us and he wrote by return. "Was this really an invitation to real-life exploring, lying on my breakfast table amongst my electricity bills and the latest VAT newsletter?" Later, however, business took its toll and he wrote, "a more mundane beast than yeti or even *Giganthopithecus* rears its ugly head at the end of the year. I refer to the common or garden Python film in the autumn." Michael just couldn't juggle the dates to suit coming with us and so, sadly, we were deprived of his rib-breaking company. No doubt some of our more down-to-earth friends in the climbing world thought that there were enough bloody comedians on the expedition anyhow.

Twenty years after Jeff Douglas and I had hunted yeti in the Central Himalaya and got embroiled with a Cursing Oracle instead, I was once again bitten by the yeti bug. There had been various reports of footprints over the intervening years but no authenticated yeti sightings. In March 1970 Don Whillans, photographed a trail of footprints in the neighbourhood of Annapurna; that same night he saw a creature which resembled an ape, bounding along on all fours. Don was sure he had actually seen a yeti and is still convinced of it. However, Pembatharke, a Sherpa who was Sirdar on the 1972 Everest Expedition and with whom I spent some time, was not so emphatic. Could it have been a Himalayan langur he had seen? This is a large leaf-eating monkey and, although it is not nocturnal, I have seen them close to the snow-line on several occasions. Could it have been serow, a Himalayan goat or antelope? Don doesn't think so.

Another interesting incident occurred in 1976 at 17,000 feet on Changabang, a peak in the Garhwal Himalaya. Peter Boardman and Joe Tasker had set up camp in an isolated region. During the night they heard a rustling as if something were rummaging in their food. It was. In the morning they discovered that a carton of thirty-six bars of chocolate was missing. Their nocturnal thief's visiting card took the form of a trail of prints arriving at camp, then leading off into the snow and oblivion. The individual prints were twelve inches long. It is interesting that the animal took chocolate which was covered in a plastic wrapping so there could have been no obvious scent from it. Bears are notorious thiefs, of course, and in North America the food bag must be hung from a tree branch out of their reach. But I hadn't heard of bears turning to crime in the Himalaya until this incident. If a bear didn't snaffle their chocolate, what did?

One of the advantages of an expedition with several objectives is that should one objective fail to materialise you can concentrate on another. Though the search for further evidence of the yeti in the Arun valley had emerged as the main aim of the expedition as far as I was concerned, there did seem to be obstacles in the way other than impenetrable jungle: impenetrable red tape! The Nepalese government are very touchy about the yeti and don't readily give permission to an expedition whose aim is to track it down. Mike Cheney, who was organising the porters for us and who is a director of Sherpa Cooperative in Kathmandu, warned me of this danger. So the other aspects of the trip now took a more prominent role. Just as well as it later transpired.

Nevertheless, I still allowed various enquiries for sophisticated equipment to proceed. My brother, who has feelers in the corridors of power in London, managed to obtain permission for us to take a 'Shrimp'. This is a doppler radar unit, the size of a half tin of biscuits which can send out a 6° beam and can record movement with great accuracy by giving an audible signal. This, we felt, would be ideal for monitoring animal movements at night. There was also the possibility of obtaining 'Tobias', a lightweight seismographical apparatus which is so sensitive that it can detect the movements of a tree root. I was amused to find that in dealing with the military establishments involved in the development of these exotic toys the names of the staff had a certain macabre similarity: Mr. Tombs, Mr. Mort and in another department Mr. Graves. When I told Mike Cheney about these gadgets, a letter came back by return, warning me about taking military equipment into Nepal. Such martial items would be frowned upon, I was told. Reluctantly, I had to decline the generous offer of these expensive detectors. Adolphe was not to be put off by such second-hand, unsportsmanlike remonstrances from Mike and was resolved to take his rifle.

We all arranged to meet at Heathrow prior to boarding a Biman, Air Bangladesh flight direct to Kathmandu. I nearly had a fit when I saw Adolphe. I didn't have any trouble spotting him amongst the mass of people milling around the terminal. He was head and shoulders above everyone else and above his head, thinly disguised by a blue stocking, was his rifle sticking at least two feet above his rucksack. It looked to me like an advertisement for a hijack but no one seemed to notice this strange appendage.

Very little is cheap in this world; certainly that cheap flight was a mistake. Not only were our knees pressed up to our chins for the duration of the journey, but the flight wasn't so direct as planned. We had to get off the plane at Dacca but our connection for Kathmandu had already left. I had the willies at Dacca airport because of Adolphe's rifle. Most airports in Asia are well stocked with enthusiastic, but emaciated porters – probably more so in Bangladesh, for planes are few and far between and they have to make the most of the limited number of available tourists. They usually focus on a specific item of luggage and clutch it as if it were their personal Sinbad until asked to carry it, or at least obtain some gratuity. One such porter with a betel-nut grin had a fragile but determined hand round the sock-covered barrel of Adolphe's rifle. He gave a sycophantic smile, no doubt contemplating a substantial tip and absently slid the stocking up the barrel, never taking his eyes off the benevolent-looking count. I dashed over and hurriedly pulled it down again before anyone noticed.

Eventually we got as far as Calcutta where we had to spend

the night. Though we got to Kathmandu the next day, not so our equipment, which was supposed to be accompanying us. It was destined to remain in a warehouse in Calcutta for a further ten days.

Meantime I had been thinking about Khembalung, the Tibetan name for the Lost Valley. I deduced that Peterson's colleague, the Buddhist scholar, had obtained his information on Khembalung at Thyangboche monastery. I knew that Peter Hackett had to pass the monastery on his way to Pheriche and I had asked him to call in and question the Rinpoche, the Head Lama. This he did and Yvon Chouinard, who had reached Nepal ahead of us, went with him. When we all met in Kathmandu they had good news on this religious front. The Rinpoche had a book on Khembalung, one of four called the 'Namden'. This volume describes the visit to Khembalung by a traveller called Milarepa in the eleventh century. The Rinpoche was enthusiastic about our quest and had it not been for the Mani Rimbu festival which is held in November, he would have come with us. Should we find the valley, he said, his order would be interested in establishing a monastery there. This was indeed good news and when I heard it I thought of another film I had worked on with Mike Palin and the other Monty Pythoners, 'The Search for the Holy Grail'. We were rapidly turning into religious sleuths with professional assistance all round. Yvon Chouinard had been a detective earlier in his career.

Khembalung is one of a number of 'beyuls' or 'hidden valleys', established by the Guru Rinpoche in various parts of the Himalayas. No one knows how many beyuls this Indian yogin set-up, but there could be as many as twenty. Various Buddhist historians as well as the lamas knew of Khembalung but didn't know its location. Rumours place it somewhere in East Nepal, possibly close to the Arun river. Not only are such 'Lost Valleys' difficult to find geographically, but it is said they will only be revealed when disaster strikes the outside world and they can only be 'opened' by an informed lama. Even if we found the site of Khembalung, its innermost secrets would not be revealed to us and it would perhaps appear to us uninitiated as any other common or garden forest clad valley.

For me Kathmandu has lost a bit of its romance. Once you have seen the temples and the bazaar and been deafened by the incessant hooting of the taxi and rickshaw horns, it loses its appeal. Should you select a cheap hotel, close to the main street, the cacophony of expectorating street sweepers provides a reliable if somewhat unpleasant reveille. Mike Cheney told me that I was requested to make an appointment with the Minister of the Interior. It was, he said, in connection with the objects of the expedition. Mike would go along with me. I was obviously going to be asked some pertinent questions and I went to the government offices with some trepidation. The Minister was charming however.

"I have been informed," he commenced, once the pleasantries had been performed, "that an expedition has been formed to search for the yeti. These rumours," he smiled benignly, "came via the United States." Then in a throw-away postscript he added, "I believe there are several American members on your expedition, Mr. MacInnes."

"Yes, there are," I agreed hastily, wondering how the gossip had spread all the way to Kathmandu. "But our expedition has many objectives, the most important of these is to make a good film and, as you know, Mr. Bal Krishna Shamra is your representative from the Nepalese Film Corporation. Certainly, if we come across tracks in the snow we would like to film them; that is surely acceptable?" And I continued, "But a further aim of our party is to see if we can shed any light on the existence of Khembalung, one of the Lost Valleys of the Buddhists."

The Minister was intrigued upon hearing this and questioned me about the beyuls. He concluded by offering us any help which his government could give should we require it. I think that even Mike, who no doubt had some misgivings at the start of the interview, was relieved at the way things had gone. Now the way seemed clear to start our journey; if we only had our equipment!

*Some of our Caucasus party with the Honoured Masters of Sport: the author and Eugene Gippenreiter are second and third from left, Abalakov, centre in tartan shirt, Paul Nunn, fourth from right, Peter Seeds, extreme right*

*On the way to the lost valley of Khembalung*

"There is no direct route to take when crossing rivers and rocks. You should explore the route exactly . . ."

[From the text on Khembalung of Guru Rinpoche]

Leaving Peter Hackett and Andrew Dunn to await the arrival of our gear, the rest of us set off eastwards, taking a flight to Baratnagar to start the footslog up the Arun valley. Peter and Andrew, once the equipment was located, were to charter a plane to join us, three days' march to the north at an airstrip called Tumlingtar.

We left the last dirt road behind us and were soon in hill country, brown baked hills shimmering in heat with great kites, the indefatigable scavengers of the east lazily observing us. There are certain games that explorers play when striding it out manfully in virgin country. For example, if you are way ahead and you take the wrong turning and have to backtrack, it is a matter of personal pride that those following should do likewise. When traversing the east bank of the Arun I made such a faux pas and knowing that the indubitable Joe Brown was hot on my trail I took to the jungle and returned to the point where I had made this error, about half a mile back. In doing so I left few tell-tale prints of my discretion. Gordon Forsyth, who was travelling with Joe – we usually split up into pairs for the day's march – marvelled at this pundit when he spotted that I had doctored some prints with a bunch of ferns.

After a sweltering trek, we languished by a river close to Tumlingtar airstrip, perspiring, swimming and listening with one ear to the crickets and the other for aeroplane engines; Joe Brown fished, as he always does where there's water, and the fish thereby provided supplemented the ubiquitous rice. Yvon recalled his adventures as a private eye and in Pakistan on his last expedition when he spent the night with some smugglers on the Khyber Pass. They were in trucks rather than on camels and didn't deal in opium or watches, but in fullsize, inflatable Marilyn Monroe dolls, complete in every detail, made in Western Europe. Yvon is probably best known for his contribution to ice climbing, for it was he, more than anyone who

*A rare thanka of the Guru Rinpoche, the Indian yogin who brought Buddhism to Tibet. The fierce beast right centre is a chuti*

pioneered the new school of ice climbing, the technique of ascending vertical ice using special curved ice hammers with slender picks and razor-sharp crampons. Before his personal 'ice age' he made pitons of chrome molybdenum steel, touring climbing centres of the western United States with a portable forge in the back of a van, selling his wares, hot from the anvil. He is now based in Ventura where he has his factory, which still sports the name he acquired with the property, the Great Pacific Iron Works.

Eventually, the Pilatus Porter arrived with Peter, Andrew and our equipment. Andrew was ill; he looked ghastly, white like the white of a hard-boiled egg. Peter had tried everything to cure him of his lurgi, a persistent dysentery, to no avail. There were discussions as to whether he should go back home; however, we decided to move slowly northwards to see if he would improve. A day beyond our camp site we met a native doctor, a herbalist, who examined Andrew on Peter's invitation and announced that he could cure him within twenty-four hours. He did, much to our amazement, with hot and cold compresses and herbs. We struck camp, another crisis behind us.

The town of Barabesi is an important market town of the Arun. There was a market in full swing when we arrived at the heat of noon. The town square was a cornucopia of fruit and Joe Brown and I flitted about like schoolboys in a tuck shop buying masses of cannon-ball-sized pomelo. These were a delicious grapefruit-like fruit and we were shown by enthusiasts, in the rapidly congregating crowd, the very specific way of peeling them. With no regard for etiquette we – that is, Cynthia, Joe and I – stuffed ourselves, juice streaming down our chins and the margin between the chuckling crowd and ourselves – we were squatting in the doorway of a shop – was rapidly being occupied by a rising wall of peelings. A well-dressed Nepali with that symbol of authority, an umbrella, cleared his throat of the inevitable Himalayan frog and addressed me.

"I am the District Commissioner, sir." He had to wait for

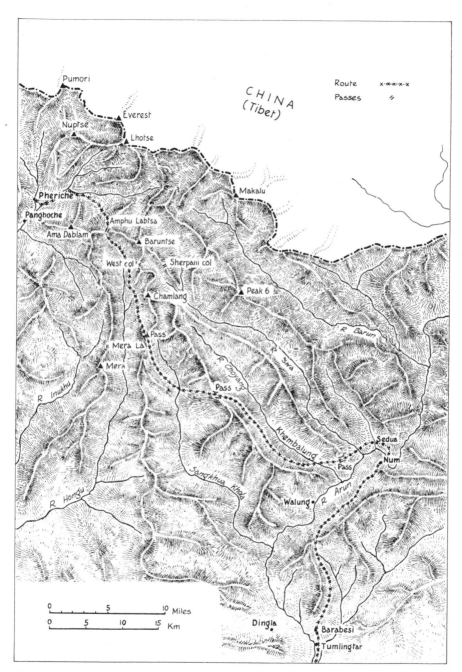

*A quest for Khembalung.*

my reply for several minutes until I had disposed of a mouthful of pith, but he seemed in no hurry, finding our appetite for the local fruit a compliment to his domain.

"Er, yes," I ventured, licking my fingers and wiping my Swiss army knife on my trousers, "pleased to meet you, sir," returning the compliment and offering a sticky hand.

"I have come to say that if I can help in any way with your journey, please don't hesitate to ask." He displayed fragile hands in a generous gesture. "I understand that you are from the B.B.C. and I wonder if you could tell me what has happened to Victor Sylvester?"

Later that day one of our Sherpas called Mingma, who was born close to the Choyang valley, told us that as a youth he had visited Khembalung, and had been through a sacred cave in the valley. This was exciting news for it was the first positive evidence which wasn't almost as old as Buddha. But could we believe the Sherpa? Although we listened to his tale with excitement, we also felt we should prudently take it with a few dixie fulls of salt. Nima, our Sirdar, hearing this tale from Mingma, told us that he had heard his grandfather talking about such a holy cave and how the old man had travelled all the way in pilgrimage to it from Namche Bazar, a journey over many knee-jarring passes. Obviously the holy plot was thickening.

A party of Germans passed by. They had been up to Makalu Base Camp and complained of enduring several weeks of rain, snow and leeches. Also, one of their members was, they said, "feeling tired" and had swollen legs. Obviously a case of pulmonary oedema, which they hadn't diagnosed. Peter Hackett licked his lips in anticipation, but the patient, an elderly man, had now almost recovered. It's interesting to speculate on why Germans more than other races are subject to this malady. My experience with German climbers has been disillusioning, I have found them badly organised and indeed many of their expeditions have ended in gripping dramas, usually due to a lack of planning.

The weather now started to get nasty and when it occasionally cleared we could see fresh snow on the mountains ahead. Makalu looked recently 'snowcemed', but we rarely saw the mountains; the Arun was living up to its reputation of being the wettest place in Nepal. Soon we came across leeches, or at least they came across us, an almost unheard of hazard in November, but they rejoiced both in rain and Anglo-American blood. Our clothes were continuously wet and we skated along slippery paths. Three days north of Tumlingtar we saw the Choyang for the first time across the vast trench of the Arun valley. It didn't look hospitable and I could see why it was supposed to be lost. It was enveloped in dense forest with the four-mile barrier of Chamlang at the top, forming a head wall to an altitude of 24,000 feet. Mists hung about the lower regions and we wondered what it had in store for us. Yvon woke that night with a leech in his nostrils. Andrew and Gordon were now busy filming with a dedication only seen in good film crews. Robin, as well as looking after the accounts, assisted by Joe Reinhard, was trying to discipline us to get the best possible shots.

"That was super, folks, but could you do it again – if you could avoid eating an orange when you're speaking, Hamish."

The country, despite the rain, was fascinating. In a part of the world which doubles its population every ten years, birth control has taken a major role in government propaganda. There were rather naïve billboards portraying a husband in bed, looking the soul of righteousness, lying alongside two small children, while his wife, ready for bed, but dressed in sufficient clothes to deter a determined rapist, holds up an admonishing finger as she turns off the light. The houses were scrupulously clean and the stories which we had heard of people dying from starvation in the upper Arun seemed far-fetched. Food was not plentiful: certainly there was not much to buy higher up the valley, but round Barabesi and to the east of that town, there was a great abundance of fruit. Oranges, delightfully small and easy to peel, cost as little as one rupee for fifteen and the monstrous pomelo continued to prove irresistible.

It is very difficult to instill in the minds of the Sherpas the need for hygiene. Indeed this is the case with most races in the east. Mingma, our cook, was no exception and a rather plump Sherpani, one of Mingma's minions, who was more of a camp follower than a porter, used to spend hours very carefully wiping the cutlery with a filthy teacloth. One of Mingma's cook boys, a nephew of Nima whom we called 'Smiler' was the only person in the kitchen staff that we could get through to, for speaking to Mingma about cleanliness was like telling a giraffe to wash behind its ears. One evening when giving Smiler instructions about boiling noodles, I added, "And, Smiler, boil those filthy tea towels as well." As I walked back to my tent there were howls of laughter from the kitchen boys; apparently they thought we were going to have the towels for dinner with the Chinese noodles.

We were now travelling high above the Arun river on a path which skirted the top of a ridge. It was raining when we arrived at a camp site, just off this ridge, overlooking a sweeping vegetated valley. Below the wide ledge, which was to be our camp, were fallow fields which ran out to the high tide mark of the jungle. The site was filthy, obviously it had been used very recently by a party which was not too obsessed with solitude when performing the functions of nature. Adolphe looked round, peering at these offending relics of humanity and using his long stick to gain more pertinent inspection.

"Yes," he said in his charming way, "I have come to the conclusion that these are German turds. Only Germans create such monsters!"

The village of Num is perched on the end of a ridge round which the Arun river snakes; the ridge and the houses resemble in some way the stern of a great liner, with the water 2000 feet below. Here we pitched camp the next night. We were surrounded by a green sea of forest. Valleys disappeared up into gorges at all quarters, each clad in dense jungle and representing a vast area. Battalions of yeti could roam here without being seen. Prints had been reported in the area, perhaps not amounting to regimental strength, but at least individual spoor. We were told this by a round-faced lama who had taken up residence in a hut close to where we were camping. He was being employed by the natives to prevent hail storms; they had had a disastrous fall of hail a few months previously which had ruined the crops and he now stood on guard preventing any further attack, no doubt invoking the assistance of various anti-hail deities with mantras. Though he only spoke fleetingly of the yeti, he did mention another animal called the chuti, which didn't register on me at the time. He also knew of Khembalung and of the cave.

The day before, whilst traversing the whale-back ridge to Num, we had spoken to a local who had denied all knowledge of the sacred valley and the cave, and it was only when Joe Reinhard came up with us and exercised his fluent Nepali that the matter was resolved. Apparently, there may be more than one Khembalung in the region, the Choyang one being the most important.

From Num we left the main trail, descending directly to the Arun river which we had to cross to reach the village of Sedua. It was a descent of 2,500 feet and we were ambushed by hundreds of leeches. The trail was almost impossible to follow and the final drop to the river was like the side of a high-rise block. Had we lost the way we would have had to abseil for the path with devilish ingenuity took the only line down the face. I was thankful to see that the spidery bridge across the river was made from steel wire ropes and not the bamboo or hazel twig variety in common use throughout the Himalayas. It was then a 4000 feet climb on the other side on tight-rope paths, criss-crossing in a multitude of steps, up through paddy fields.

It was raining at Sedua; I think it always rains there. This shower must have been a bit longer than usual; it lasted eighteen hours. We made good use of our squelchy stay for we met Norbu, a lama who knew all about Khembalung and the sacred cave; so the account by our Sherpa, Mingma, was true after all. He also had a copy of the Namden book which tells the story of Khembalung. He confirmed what Peter and Yvon had heard from the Thyangboche Rinpoche that several retreats had been established by Guru Rinpoche as sanctuaries in times of trouble, but there was little doubt, Norbu lama said, that Khembalung in the Choyang Valley was the most important. He volunteered to go with us. Norbu also told us more about the chuti.

"It is," he said, "a tiger-like creature, with a wolf-like head. It has four forward claws and one to the rear." All the stories about yeti, even in this yeti-infested area, are second- or third-hand, and you cannot find anyone who has actually seen one, though one of our porters said that he heard one calling. On the other hand, Norbu's father, with whom we spoke, had seen a chuti, as had other locals. It kills cattle, but not humans, and apparently they are found in the Choyang and Iswa Valleys. My old friend Dr. Wladimir Tschernesky believes it could be a striped hyaena. It is not perhaps really surprising that such a creature exists, for there are hundreds of square miles of forest for them to roam and there is no shortage of food. But it would be a daunting task to search for one when visibility is often restricted to a few feet.

We had been told that Sedua was a nasty place, the locals always quarrelling and unwilling to act as porters, or causing trouble if they did. Certainly I wouldn't choose to spend my summer holidays there, simply because it is so wet and the leeches would suck you dry. But the houses are picturesque, standing on stilts, as if about to march off to more congenial sites, but the stilts are used no doubt to combat rising damp. There is a further damp course in the form of flat stones between the top of the stilts and the base of the houses. The people were poor and didn't have much food to sell and what they had was at inflated prices. They are born traders and the older women would hang around for hours hoping to sell artifacts. Adolphe and Yvon were the big spenders, though how they envisaged carrying their loot over the passes ahead was a mystery to me. Adolphe had a yen for the ponderous silver ornaments which Sherpas and the Tibetans love so much, but to my mind these were more suited to weight-lifting Amazons or Sherpanis than to the womenfolk of the Western world.

Sedua, as I have mentioned, is leech-infested, and to go forth for a pee at night was courting a blood loss. Robin also contracted a bug and was sick outside his tent. However, there was no mopping up requirement here; rain and the hungry dogs sorted that. Joe, who had the knack of finding the expedition's supply of kukri rum and whisky, shouted across from his tent,

"Hey, Robin, come over and bring your mug. I've got the whisky but if you're going to be sick, bring your dog with you."

We had got to know each other pretty well by this time and we had interesting and invigorating conversations. Adolphe and Joe Reinhard would often be engaged in a serious discussion on folklore and philosophy, whilst Joe Brown told stories of his many expeditions. I had heard most of these on previous trips which made him a bit self-conscious about recounting them.

Robin is a charming person. Adolphe mentioned several times that he reminded him of Charlie Chaplin and indeed he does have that same sympathetic quality. Robin is a keen climber in his own right and a great lover of the outdoors, especially of the Western Highlands where he has a small cottage in the fastnesses of Torridon. It is a sort of Jekel and Hyde existence that he leads in some ways, for in contrast to the wildness of the Highlands his workaday home is in the confines of Glasgow's Maryhill, in the so-called 'Red Indian' district, where even if missiles don't come as arrows they do frequently take the form of bricks or part bricks. Robin, despite the fact that he lives on the second floor of a tenement has had his windows shattered in hostilities on several occasions. In the end he replaced the panes with bulletproof glass. Now he can give rebounding projectiles a wry smile as he gets on with his chores.

Gordon was still the well-scrubbed, spruce character I

remembered from our Guyana trip, though this time he had taken only one set of clothing; with my two shirts and two pairs of trousers, I now had the edge on him. He would on occasion, I noticed, give his clothes a surreptitious sniff to see if they required another wash other than the daily downpour. We were most impressed by Krishna Shamra, who represented the Nepalese Film Corporation. Shamra is a lawyer in Kathmandu, very lithe and fit, with a pill for every eventuality. Inoffensive enough you may think until he started taking prodigious quantities of garlic to help him, so he told us, to acclimatise. This was more apparent to Adolphe who shared a tent with him.

Yvon usually scampered along the trail barefoot and on his own. He liked to take in the 'atmos', as the film crew described the atmosphere of the country, without the distractions.

That evening we had an emaciated fowl for dinner and as we stood in the cook tent with water dripping everywhere the question of the bird's sex was being discussed, when Adolphe, in a voice well suited to a crowded courtroom closed the argument by observing, "I have just eaten the indisputable proof that the bird was a cock." It is true nothing is wasted in a Sherpa kitchen.

It was not going to be easy to reach Khembalung from Sedua. We first had to cross the Iswa Gorge, then a 12,000 feet ridge before dropping down to the Choyang. The trail from the top of the ridge down to the river hadn't been used for a number of years and no one was sure how long it would take us. Moreover, we would have to build a bridge to cross the Choyang river. From an aerial survey map I thought I had worked out an easier way into the Choyang, but this we were told wasn't possible; later it transpired that it would have been a better route. Meantime we were committed to bushwacking.

"You climb up to a jungle covered pass and come to a wide valley filled with jungle. The outer part is wide and the inner part is narrow . . ."
[From the text on Khembalung of Guru Rinpoche]

Two days from Sedua we reached the gorge of the Iswa, a deep cleft sporting the regulation turbulent chilly river. There was a dizzy descent down to the log bridge, a single tree-trunk perched between the overhanging walls of the defile with the water 150 feet below. Elizabeth almost had an accident at this bridge, when a primitive rail, a tree branch, gave way and fell into the river. Luckily she didn't.

Looking back at the descent from the other side of the river, the 1500-foot face we had come down looked impossible for the average mountaineer, let alone laden porters. We made camp that night above the river on a small island amidst paddy fields. It was dry.

In 1954 Charles Evans had reached the head of the Choyang valley taking the route which we were now following, but just ahead on the ridge to the west he had chosen a course parallel to the Choyang along the crest of the ridge. He had tried to descend into the Choyang but had been prevented by rhododendrons as impenetrable as steel wool. After what Joe would describe as a gruelling trip he reached the head-waters. I had been in contact with Charles Evans, before we left, and Joe, who lives near him in North Wales, had visited him. Charles thought that it might just be possible to find a way up the Choyang via the gorge itself, and Norman Hardy who was a member of that same expedition thought likewise. Norman is a New Zealander and when I contacted him he was enthusiastic about our proposed trip, having plans for a similar journey the following year. I had also managed to contact a plant collector called Stainton, who wrote the book *The Forests of Nepal*, and he thought it was feasible to find some way to the snow-line via the Choyang or the Sangkhua, the next valley west.

That evening I made a point of engaging two locals who knew the terrain ahead to act as guides and to cut a trail for our party. This proved to be a providential decision. Next morning we headed abruptly up the hillside and the last village, Walung, set on the steep face leading up to the ridge with fields of paddy and sweet corn, was a model village and looked as tranquil and fresh as a young schoolgirl. Bearskins were stretched on frames to dry and we discovered that the locals killed the bears, using a trap in the form of a large stone poised on a tree branch and triggered to a bait by rope. A small bearded native, describing how this was done, rolled on the ground, holding his head, depicting the state of the clobbered bear. Mingma, with an eye for business, had bought a bear's gall-bladder from this man. It is apparently much in demand as an aphrodisiac.

We followed our two guides up over the ridge to the watershed where there was a good path. As soon as we dropped over the other side for the final descent to Khembalung they lost the track. It looked to us like virgin country and we had to return to the crest. They now took us higher up the ridge to a clearing where some mani stones were lined up.

After a short rest here, we plunged down, more successfully this time, into the green hell of enormous trees and dense undergrowth; from time to time we did encounter a ribbon-like path. The two natives were what my Kiwi friends would describe as 'bloody bushrats'. One would weave his way through the undergrowth, as if taking part in a strange ballet, while the other as soon as the way was verified by the front man would slash a corridor through the jungle in a wave of destruction. We had trouble keeping up with these two stalwarts, they were such efficient trail makers, even though both were getting badly stung by giant nettles up to nine feet high with leaves a foot across and a sting like a cat-o'-nine-tails.

The forest was fascinating; incredibly lush with a wealth of flora, a mere patch of which would have kept a botanist ecstatic for weeks. Cynthia tried stopping to photograph specimens but had to give it up in case she was left behind, for this was no country in which to get lost. It reminded Joe and me of the rain-forest bordering the Mazaruni in Guyana. The two natives spotted a snake but it scuttled under a tree root. Later I saw another, under Cynthia's boot, but it didn't seem to object to this treatment and slid silently away as we crashed downwards. Our party was strung out and it was a miracle someone didn't get lost for there were several faux pas en route where we had to retreat up steep banks covered in dense bamboo. Eventually we arrived at the only flat place in miles, an area of about thirty feet square completely covered in the giant nettles. This was to be our camp site. It was so overgrown that it took the combined efforts of the Sherpas and porters more than an hour to clear it. On both sides the ground fell vertically away and Joe was astounded to observe that a bush which he was standing alongside was in fact the top of a fifty-foot tree. Below, through the canopy of the forest we could hear the throaty roar of the Choyang river and across the gorge on the far hillside we could discern some primitive huts with smoke curling up to join the mists. This was our Khembalung, or the village of Dobatak, as the guides called it. I don't think any of us had had visions of a Shangri La, least of all myself, but this joint I thought looked more like a damp Highland glen after the Clearances. However, there was no doubting its remoteness. It was certainly a place to get away from it all.

I suppose that over the years I've chalked up hundreds of leech bites and on the previous day, for the first time in my life, I had treated a leech bite on my wrist with antiseptic ointment. Following our ton-up guides through the jungle that day I hadn't much time to reflect on personal discomforts; I was too scared of being left behind. It was only when I looked at my wrist that evening that I was surprised to see it badly swollen. Red streaks ran up my arm and it was obvious that I had a rip-roaring infection. I was worried; so was Peter when he saw it and he immediately put me on a course of antibiotics, hoping that it would arrest the trouble. There was little hope of getting carried out from that part of the world should one of us have an accident, and this was constantly preying on my mind. I swallowed my antibiotics with dedication.

Next day, in true Baden-Powell tradition, we built a bridge over the Choyang river. Nima played a prominent role in this operation, dressed only in swimming trunks and belayed with a climbing rope by two Sherpas. It was a colourful and relaxed exercise; the structure crossed the river in two spans, linked by a large rock midstream. Mingma the cook, always keen to partake in trades other than cooking, immediately fell off a slippery rock into the icy water, much to the amusement of his fellow Sherpas. A well-built native had come down the hillside from Dobatak on the other side of the river. He had the bearing of a warrior, fierce dark eyes and was promptly nicknamed 'the Pirate'. I noted that (unlike Mingma) before he jumped on to the slippery boulders he threw fine gravel on them for traction. A simple operation perhaps, but to me at least it portrayed a man with commonsense – someone to take along, which we later did, together with his two charming daughters.

By midday the bridge was completed and we all crossed it safely, and later in the afternoon arrived at Dobatak where we camped close to the huts we had seen the previous evening. There were just two families living there; they seemed healthy and had about thirty-five cattle, a few sheep of a strange vintage, goats and an enormous truculent bull.

The holy cave we were told was half an hour up the hillside in the forest beyond the house of the resident lama. In the house adjoining this holy man's lived the local witchdoctor, or shaman. He acted as a spiritual healer and complimented the role of the lama in many ways. There was not much to see in this lower part of the Choyang. The gorge, which extended for fourteen miles to the headwaters, looked a hopeless proposition, being heavily wooded with the sides rising in places 10,000 feet to the ridges on either hand. It was obviously beyond our resources to force a way up the floor of the Choyang, as it would need a big back-up of porters and food, but we discovered upon questioning the locals that the ridge to the west, on our left, as we looked up the valley, had a track along its crest. The valley on the other side of this ridge, the Sang-khua, is also unexplored. We were told the yeti lurked there, revelling in splendid isolation. The route along the ridge climbed to 16,000 feet in places before it gained the headwaters of the Choyang. From there we knew that it was possible to get into the Hongu valley, then over the 19,000-foot Amphu Labtsa pass to the Sola Khumbu. Joe Brown was heard to remark that evening as we sat around the campfire: "When do we get to the place where Hamish knows where we are?"

The day after we arrived at Khembalung a ceremony was arranged at the cave. Our friend Norbu from Sedua was standing in for the resident lama, who was away. He prepared a hundred butter lamps and an enormous brew of chang, the native beer. For a change the morning dawned fine but the Choyang felt like a damp, cold greenhouse as we made our way up the trail to the lama's house. It is situated in a tranquil spot, a place eminently suited to contemplation, with views on so rare a day as this out over the Arun and back up to the snowy topcoat of Chamlang. Now, preceded by musicians, we carried on up the hillside through a corridor of bamboo into deeper forest, stopping on the way to pick sprigs of the holy juniper which grew close to an 'om mani' wall – a long cairn of flat stones each inscribed with the Tibetan prayer 'Om Mani Padme Hum'. The shaman, or oracle and the lama called a halt under the shelter of a rock overhang decorated with carvings and there we were asked to take off our boots. "This'll kill me," I muttered, and Adolphe complained that he couldn't prattle about in bare feet either due to an ankle injury, but nevertheless we complied with the lama's request. Just ahead and partly hidden by creepers and prayer flags on long bamboos was the cave mouth. It looked more like the entrance to the underworld, but somehow emanated an air of tranquillity. This was possibly induced by the incense carried on a dixie lid by the shaman. We were told that it was customary to wash our feet at the holy stream which pranced down close to the prayerflags and after doing this we went inside. Though we had been travelling through country almost entirely made up of mica schist, here it was limestone. Inside, the cave dipped down steeply and we could see inside for some forty feet to where it narrowed; the floor was strewn with large boulders. I could also see the dim outline of a large trident bedecked with old prayer flags and a bell. To the right close to a stone wall was a natural shelf with Buddhist carvings on the rock. This ledge served as an altar and there was another, smaller trident. I thought to myself of the lines of the Khembalung text:

> In that cave there is a female Lu [serpent deity]
> so you should do a Lu Tor for her.

We had been told by Norbu that the cave had been used as a place of pilgrimage for hundreds of years and that Guru Rinpoche had endowed it with certain 'residents', spirits of men who would come to the aid of believers and those seeking refuge. Those who had not sinned could travel through the cave unscathed, emerging lower down the hillside. Those who lost the way reached a lake where an aggressive chuti lurked. Nima told us that pilgrims had in fact lost their way in the past and had perished. This later piece of information was only gleaned from him reluctantly when I asked him why he had taken my personal climbing rope along. After a prolonged ceremony at the altar, we were asked to contribute a few rupees and then our procession, mostly of porters and locals, about fifty in all, descended into the depths. They rang the bell on the trident as they passed. I was fortunate enough to be close to a Sherpa who had been with me on Everest in 1972 and 1975 whom we'd nicknamed 'Nippon Wide', due to the very broad Japanese rucksack he used in 1972. Nippon Wide had a pressure lantern, so I had a good view, or rather good illumination for one could hardly describe scraping along on one's stomach and thrutching through letterbox-sized slots as viewing. At one point the great human centipede ground to a stop; a wrong turning had been taken. The lama with the celerity of a sewer rat had scampered ahead and left us humans floundering in the labyrinth. It was, we discovered, difficult to put fifty people into reverse in a confined passageway, especially when some three languages are being spoken. Eventually this was achieved and we continued downwards to the local equivalent of the Acheron, an icy cold stream in which I at least had to crawl, nursing a throbbing arm. After about twenty mintues we

*The Old Man of Hoy*

emerged in daylight and I was not sorry. I don't like caves at the best of times but hemmed in fore and aft by humanity, I find it positively claustrophobic. Joe Brown and I came to the conclusion that the cave was a fraud, for we have both sinned unrepentantly over the years, yet we escaped the revenge of the chuti. Perhaps it only works on true Buddhists.

"That was bloody awful," I complained, as I crawled out, "like the Glasgow underground in the rush hour."

"It was smashing," said Joe. Joe revels in the things I dislike most, from creepy-crawlies to breakfasts of dhal. We had not yet finished with the god business that day, for the shaman, who was the absent lama's next door neighbour, had been invited to our camp to hold a spiritual cure. Dr. Hackett was suffering from dysentery. We all felt, so to speak, that he should get some of his own medicine. When the shadows were suitably long and the fire blazing to the right proportions, the shaman stole silently into the camp dressed in red robes and accompanied by his assistants and a drummer. There was much drum-beating, mumbo-jumbo and eye rolling. It was good theatre and we enjoyed the evening. Only a shaman could have arranged a dry night in the Choyang. When he felt the attention of the audience waning after a few hours, he announced an interval, and I certainly wouldn't have been surprised if the Pirate's daughters had come round selling icecream. Afterwards he re-entered his trance, an extremely difficult state to achieve with Andrew's cine camera literally six inches from his nose. Presently he announced through a medium, the cymbal clapper, that it was imperative for Peter to give a suitable donation to one of the local deities at first light; thereafter he would be cured.

Despite a shortage of porters, for we had paid off a lot at the camp as many of them wished to return home, we set off the next morning up the steep hillside leading to the ridge. Norbu lama who had taken ill also returned to Sedua. Nima and another Sherpa waited at the camp for further porters to arrive.

It wasn't an exacting day; very few days were. Somehow the expedition crocodile, or perhaps I should call it a tortoise, just

*Author in the cage operating a camera on the Anglesey Outside Broadcast. The climbers are on Tyrannosaurus Rex*

couldn't manage a full day's march. A good path angled up the face of the ridge through large trees and we obtained fleeting views across the Choyang. There were several clearings which were occupied by red-robed lamas: these were retreats for meditation. Joe Brown and Yvon had gone ahead that day in an endeavour to coax the porters on for a few further miles. However, as I was taking up the rear of the group I was surprised to find the porters preparing camp at one of the clearings made by the lamas which was only two hours' march from Khembalung. We were annoyed about this 'lightning' strike and as they wouldn't budge we eventually had to go on up the trail to fetch Joe and Yvon. The tents were pitched on the small mud patch like cars crammed on to a cross-channel ferry at the height of the tourist season. That evening a lama who was portering for us had gone back to our camp at Dobatak for a further load. He came face to face with a large bear on the trail. The Himalayan bears can be extremely dangerous and I have seen natives badly mauled and even killed by them. However, the bear seemed to respond to the screams or perhaps the prayers of this holy man, for it took off into the bush.

The next day this same porter, following behind Adolphe, who was up front, again came face to face with a large bear. Adolphe, who had heard some rustling in the undergrowth, hadn't seen the creature when he passed, but it jumped out in front of the lama who screamed with enthusiasm. Adolphe, taking out his knife, rushed back down the trail to the terrified man, but the bear, no doubt perturbed by the charging count, turned tail and fled. Later, recalling the incident, Adolphe told us that he had "heard the bear bristling in the bamboo shoots".

There is no doubt that the Choyang is wild territory by any standards. Despite this the trail was good; it was used in summer for taking sheep to high pastures at the head of the Sangkhua. It makes one reflect on the ethics of exploration. There are very few places where the human foot hasn't ventured. Yet the white man has such a high opinion of himself that his second-hand visits are termed 'exploration'.

Three days from Khembalung we reached the snow. The

transition was sudden, stepping from a shower into a snow storm. One moment we were following a channel cut through bamboo and the next we rose into a full-scale blizzard. It certainly took us unawares for although we knew that we were approaching the snow-line which was abnormally low, the drop in temperature was alarming and we huddled under a large overhanging rock which afforded little shelter as it faced windward and the blowing spindrift. Joe Brown and Peter Hackett managed to warm up a very young porter suffering from exposure. Yvon, Joe and I were worried. We had been on enough expeditions to know that our predicament could very quickly be transformed into a disastrous situation and we didn't want any corpses on our consciences. None of the porters was clad for this sort of weather. Most had bare feet and the snow was now lying deep.

I did a quick recce a bit higher up the ridge with the Pirate and Joe Reinhard and fortunately found a camp site a few hundred feet away. As we had plenty of tents we bundled all the porters into them. These coolies or porters normally sleep out in the open, even in quite bad weather, but this was out of the question in the prevailing conditions. We were all bitterly disappointed; we knew that if the weather didn't clear up and thaw rapidly, there was no way we could go on. If we did push ahead, some porters would have surely died or at the very least have been frostbitten. We decided to sleep on it before taking any drastic action.

The morning dawned fine and the whole Himalayan chain awoke in brilliant splendour. We could see the way ahead now, snaking along the ridge which climbed from where we camped at 13,000 feet to two peaks. Beyond this was the wall of Chamlang with shapely Peak 6 out on its right flank, and mighty Makalu behind. Beyond that again was the loneliness of Tibet. Away to the left I could see what was to me familiar country. The Mera La and the peaks of the Hongu. It was tantalisingly near yet not near enough. We just couldn't gamble with human life. Anyhow Nima announced that the porters wouldn't go on, which came as no surprise to us for it was obvious that the difficulties were going to be so formidable that it would require a fully equipped mountaineering party to continue. We decided on a course of action. It was clear that only one or two of the climbers in the group could press on; the others would have to go back. Joe Brown had been having trouble with his back for the past few days which ruled him out, and my arm, though getting better, had obviously sapped my strength and I was having adverse side-effects from the antibiotics. This left Yvon, Joe Reinhard and Peter Hackett. By donating various items of equipment we managed to equip four porters and two Sherpas to go with them. The cook and Nima rapidly sorted out food for their journey, which we estimated would take about eight days. Within an hour this spearhead group set off, picking their way through the snow and we watched them as they got smaller and smaller with mixed feelings. I had planned this journey two years previously and we were now within four days of where some of us had been before in the Hongu. It was therefore a bitter disappointment not to have gone with them.

They did complete the journey by crossing the head of the Sangkhua and thence to the Hongu. On a very remote section they came across a set of tracks. They went to the brink of a cliff and then continued again from the bottom. Had this creature, most probably a bear, climbed down?

The early tale of trapped Tibetans eating their boots in the Hongu before they perished was a bit too close to reality for their liking, for the food was desperately short and the going hard and dangerous in the deep, fresh snow. The porters were so shattered carrying the heavy loads in these conditions that they lay down in the snow, saying that they couldn't go on. On the eighth day they dropped down in an exhausted state from the 19,000 feet Amphu Labtsa pass to reach the Khumbu. Half a day's march away was Peter's research station at Pheriche. Their journey was over.

> Go to the secret place without remaining attached to one's own country.
> If you cannot go there because of rain or avalanches, then you should
> make smoke of black dog dung and the hardened sap of a tree.

# 11

## Stop–Go on the Eiger

A climber has fallen, but why let us mourn?
For each one that dies, there are two to be born.
Ready to rise at the Führer's command,
To conquer or die on the grim Eigerwand.

[Dr. Tom Patey]

THE GREATEST CLIMBING OUTSIDE Broadcast of all time was first mooted in a tiny tent in the Western Cwm of Everest during the 1972 South West Face Expedition. I was sharing this canvas box with Dougal Haston. We hadn't spoken to each other for over three hours but this was quite a normal state of affairs between us. There was no point in talking if we didn't have a great deal to say. I put down a chess problem in disgust, taking deprivation of oxygen as an excuse for my shortage of grey cells. I thought of going over to the main tent where a game of scrabble was in full swing. I could hear the laughter and the ensuing argument as Mick Burke tried to use a popular but disallowed four letter word in common use on expeditions. I decided against joining them and my thoughts strayed and after about ten minutes I said,

"Hey, Dougal, how far is it from the 3.8 window on the Eiger North Wall to the Hinterstoisser Traverse and from the 4.2 window over to Death Bivouac?" Dougal looked up from his book, a treatise on Freud and regarded me with a jaundiced eye, having been dragged down from a higher plane.

"Probably within the 5000 feet, if that's what you are thinking." He knew of course that I was thinking about a possible Outside Broadcast on that mountain.

229

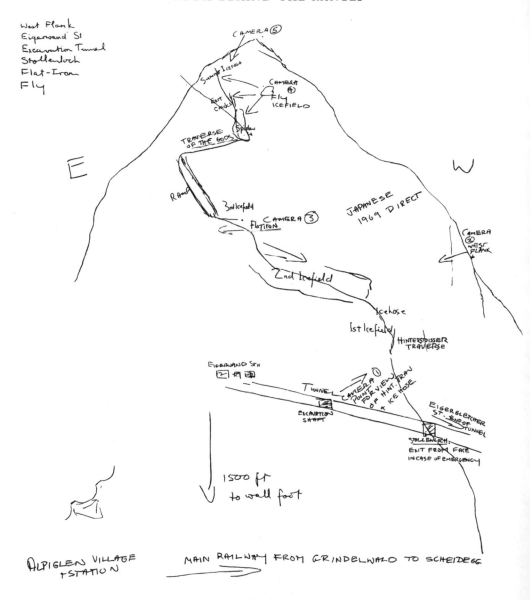

*The first plan for an Eiger Outside Broadcast, devised by the author and Dougal Haston while sharing a tent at Camp 2 on the 1972 Everest South West Face Expedition, and sketched on the spot by Dougal Haston.*

"And how wide is the tunnel?" I asked. "The Jungfraujoch railway tunnel?" He put down his book for he knew he was going to be pestered and within minutes he, too, realised that there was a possibility, remote as it at first seemed, of such a scheme being feasible.

Making a movie film on the Eiger was difficult enough, a British party with Leo Dickinson as cameraman had done this, but to contemplate staging a live TV broadcast was, some people thought, the height of lunacy. The cameras were large, the camera cable heavy and how could one keep schedules on the Eiger North Wall? That was the ammunition of the critics.

A few years previously such a project had been mooted by the Swiss, flying a public relations kite. Then it had been quite ridiculous, for the cable runs from the cameras to the scanner were only about 1000 feet. It would have been a case of 'hello, chaps and goodbye' as the climbers set off for the hill. Other shots could only have been gleaned from large telephoto lenses, for we couldn't have used the cameras on the wall at all. But the more Dougal and I discussed it, the more we felt that the idea was within the bounds of reality. A few days later when I returned to Camp 1, I wrote to Chiv back in London:

*Everest South West Face*,
Box 224,
Kathmandu,
Nepal.
3rd October, 1972.

Dear Alan,

I trust you are back home again after the Olympics. No doubt you know that Chris Brasher will be on his way out here shortly to write for the *Observer*. We shall try and take care of him!

The reason for this letter is that no doubt Paul Faux will be thinking of another climbing Outside Broadcast in the next year. Joe Brown, Don Whillans and I had a holiday in the Shetlands before I left and though we managed to get some

231

good climbing there, we didn't see anything of merit for a broadcast.

You will recall that some time ago the Swiss approached us regarding a possible Eigerwand programme which we all thought at the time was 'no-go'. However, at present I am climbing and sharing a tent with Dougal and I have gone into the matter with him. The solution could possibly be the month of October. During this month there are long settled spells and though the days are shorter it is not too cold. I will go into the difficulties of coverage of the ordinary north face route, a two to three day climb: two minicams on face, one at the Fly [see Dougal's book, *The Eiger*] and the other on the Flatiron just below the Bivouac. The Fly camera can have cable runs back to the summit in a direct line more or less. The Flatiron camera can have its cable from a window on the wall [Gallery Window, Eigerwand Station] which is approximately 1800 feet below the camera position. The Flatiron camera has vast coverage of the icefields and a canopy could be provided for possible stonefall. This position also covers the Death Bivouac. Camera and camerman could be put in position hopefully by a helicopter. The Fly camera is a more diffficult situation but fairly safe. The camerman can abseil down to it or can be lowered by chopper. These two mini-cam positions are the most difficult in the whole operation, but are not terribly dangerous as adequate stocks of food, etc., can be established at each place. There would be no other cameraman on the face except for the summit icefield man who would cover the last few minutes of the climb. This camera would share the same transmitter as the Fly camera to send back the signal to Kleine Scheidegg. This unit could be located in a tent on the summit of the Eiger (regular chopper flight).

To sum up the coverage would be as follows: *Icefields*: Flatiron minicam with large zoom. *The Traverse of the Gods, The Spider Exit Cracks*: would come under the Fly camera. *The Summit Icefield*: would give summit cover (probably this would be the Flatiron minicam taken up by helicopter).

There are many positions for the bigger cameras below and there is no need to go into these, but the whole climb can be captured by long lenses from below.

*The West Flank*: it is possible to have a camera here (see drawing) with a cable run to the scanner in the ventilation shaft of the railway tunnel.

For the lower part of the face a camera at the window close to the Hinterstoisser Traverse could get this as well as the Swallow's Nest Bivouac. This would also deal with the approach to this point which could mix in with the long lens shots from below.

With, say, two cameras below by the hotel there could be a total of seven covering the climb. However, I would suggest that a further camera could be used to great advantage in a helicopter, using the same transmitter feed back as for the Summit and Fly cameras as these won't be in use until the end of the programme.

I can just hear you say, "Now, my lad, where is my wee scanner all this time?" My answer: "In pieces". Well, not quite. It could go up on the railway to the Eigergletscher Station and there be put in the underground-siding. Due to its size the tunnel couldn't take the scanner, even if the low loading freight cars were used, but a partial de-rig is possible or the scanner could be left at the Eigergletscher Station and a cable run up to the window at 3.8 and then on to the Eigerwand Station to eventually get to the Flatiron position. The cable run to the West Flank would also be about 3000 feet. There is mains power at the Eigergletscher Station and line of sight to Interlaken from either the windows or close to these positions for sending the signal out.

I think that this could be seriously on now, Alan, doing it along these lines. I would suggest that you contact J. Schmid at the Swiss Tourist Centre in London to get the weather reports for the last six years or so for October. The Swiss, I know, would co-operate re the railway, helicopters and perhaps even with accommodation. The cost could be cut down using three separate climbing parties, the United

233

Kingdom, Swiss and, say, German. Cameras would be reasonably static and it would not be too difficult to get optimum use out of them. Three bivouacs could be shown with the cameras and by doing the standard route speed would lend interest to the programme. I feel sure it could be a real 'cliff-hanger', with the minimum of risk – only two climbing cameramen on the face. Enclosed is Dougal's sketch and what I have in mind regarding coverage.

Best wishes to all and excuse the typing. I am at Camp I at the moment, but that is no excuse so I'll just blame Chris Bonington's typewriter.

Yours, Hamish.

Chiv must have done a somersault when he received this letter. He realises of course that I dwell in the realms of lunacy for a large part of the time, but it says a lot for him that he didn't just put my epistle in his 'never-never' file, but saw a glimmer of light at the end of a long and tortuous tunnel, which was to prove longer and more tortuous than that of the Jungfraujoch railway. Delicate feelers were put out by the B.B.C. to the Swiss Government and they gave an unreserved 'Maybe', and a definite 'Yes' to a feasibility study.

The Hotel Bellevue at Kleine Scheidegg squats with schwiezerdeutsch self-assurance at the foot of the Eiger North Wall, fed by hundreds of tourists disgorging from trains from both Grindelwald and Lauterbrunnen each day. At night they retreat to their respective villages while the hotel seems to shrink within itself as if afraid of the hours of darkness. Not many tourists stay at the Kleine Scheidegg overnight, the building sleeps; even the North Face is more vocal, giving the occasional cough of a stonefall or avalanche.

The Eiger climbers' pub is the nondescript Alpiglen, down the railway line towards Grindelwald, sheltering under the very petticoats of the North Face. It is here that for-real climbers gather then steal off silently at dead of night to make what for many is regrettably their last climb. For the Eiger has claimed many victims and is well-named the 'Ogre', an ogre who doesn't always kill cleanly in a fall or an avalanche, but often slowly freezes his victims to death on some lonely bivouac ledge. The history of ascents and accidents too numerous to recount here has been well documented in a host of books for those with a taste for the macabre in literature.

I first made acquaintance with the Eiger North Wall in the summer of 1957. I wrote to Chris Bonington who was then commanding a tank crew in Münster to ask him if he fancied attempting the first British ascent of the face. He did, not then realising that on the twelve ascents hitherto there had been fourteen fatalities, not an encouraging debut for Chris's first alpine season! However, he seemed to have unfounded confidence in my ploys and we arranged to meet in Grindelwald. This didn't prove easy. With due deference to my birthright I am abstemious to the point of ridiculous brevity when sending telegrams, especially overseas ones. I sent Chris a cable from the outskirts of Glasgow, saying, "Meet me Grindelwald 7 July Manx Norton." I should have known that Chris who is ignorant in mechanical matters would have no idea that Manx Norton was a thoroughbred racing motorcycle. Chris didn't have much luck in tracing this elusive Manx Norton, though he asked people if they had heard of him or seen him. Eventually we did meet up full more of enthusiasm than good sense. I discovered that Chris had no duvet or bivouac sack but I gave him a spare bit of plastic that I had for covering the motor cycle and an old pullover. The only description we had of the route was a postcard I had bought in Grindelwald.

Our attempt on the wall was brief. We climbed the easy lower section and found a suitable overhang under which to spend the night, but by the time good Swiss are thinking of an aperitif clouds had started to build up like a traffic jam. Instead of settling down for the night we decided to beat a rapid and ignominious retreat, the best decision either of us have made before or since.

Next day we set off for the more conducive peaks of Chamonix where a few days later we read of the drama of the Claudio Corti accident on the Eiger North Wall; they must have started on the climb about the same time as us. Corti's friend Stefano Longhi died from exposure and Corti was winched to safety. Erich Friedli was one of the brains behind this rescue, where for the first time long steel cables were used for hauling Corti to safety. Erich was later to work with us on the Eiger television project in an advisory capacity and became a very good friend of both Dougal and myself.

"Will you walk into my parlour?" said a spider to a fly:
"Tis the prettiest little parlour that ever you did spy."
[Mary Howitt, 'The Spider and the Fly']

It was a large party that assembled at Kleine Scheidegg for that first survey in the summer of 1973. Various things had already been established; the Swiss had perfected the art of de-rigging a scanner for their coverage of ski races so this obviated the need for the B.B.C. to engage in this complicated exercise, though the B.B.C. engineers did establish that they could in fact do the de-rig should the need arise. It also appeared that we could make more use of helicopters than we had anticipated, for by this time injured climbers had been plucked up by winch wire from such places as Death Bivouac and it was therefore quite feasible to put cameras off at such positions.

Even so, I don't think that Fritz von Almen who then owned the hotel believed that we seriously hoped to make a live broadcast from the wall. Competent people, he said, had attempted to make movie films on the climb in the past but had failed. He didn't acknowledge the British 16mm film of the North Face. Fritz was the great entrepreneur of the North Face; he had never climbed the route but was an assiduous telescope addict, acting as self-appointed guardian to the wall. Every movement of climbers was seen through his telescope.

Some of the Swiss TV representatives were old friends; 'Guggi', Werner Guggisberg who was the chief engineer on the Matterhorn Outside Broadcast was a delight to work with and he was destined to take over the main engineering role on the present project. As well as being a talented technician he was venturesome and willing to try anything within reason. He told us about a new type of lightning-proof tent which he had on the drawing board for housing equipment on the West Flank. Werner Wetterli, as the senior representative of Swiss Television, was no less enthusiastic but his feelings were very much tempered by the sentiments of his bosses in exalted places and by the Swiss Government. A programme of the magnitude of the Eiger was of national importance and prestige to the Swiss. But they couldn't risk a national scandal, for if there was an accident during the broadcast, there would be much criticism. They were trying to keep their cake and eat it, with true Swiss reserve.

On this initial survey, which was really a feasibility study, we hoped to make some transmission tests from various points on the wall, as well as to inspect the positions on the West Flank. A number of B.B.C. engineers under the diligent eye of Alan Roberts had driven out from the U.K. with equipment and had fitted out a small transmitter station close to the Bellevue Hotel. They soon established that communications to and from the 3.8 window were very good indeed.

Dougal and I had already met Günter Amann, the helicopter rescue pilot. It was Günter, a German by birth and an ex-Luftwaffe pilot, who with a local Swiss, Herr Kaufmann, had first succeeded in lifting climbers off the wall using the helicopter winch. This technique had been pioneered by the British during the Second World War and before its application in the Swiss alps had been used with great effect on the peaks of Chamonix. Günter is a slight, quiet, unassuming man who likes to think out all his moves. Although he isn't a mountaineer, he probably sees more of the hostile parts of the Alps than most climbers.

Basically, two types of helicopters are used in the Swiss Rescue Service: the Alouette and the Lama. The Lama at this time of writing holds the world's altitude record of almost 41,000 feet. It is also the only helicopter that can lift its own weight. It looks as if it has been hurriedly assembled with left overs from a large Meccano set, but once airborne you can feel its woomph and the effortless ease with which it can hover in the most vicious downdraughts.

Using Günter's Lama workhorse we dropped off at various points on the West Flank and there seemed distinct possibilities there for camera platforms. Because of the great distance across to the Ramp and to the Traverse of the Gods from the Flank, Guggi seriously thought of using an astronomical telescope in lieu of a camera lens, mounted on a reinforced concrete tripod. Using long ropes we checked the distance down to the Rotstock from the position of cameras three and four, which was within our 5000-foot cable limit, for it was in the tunnels of the Rotstock that we now hoped to place the scanner tapping the power supply to the railway. It all looked very encouraging, but there was a pile of homework to do. Guggi, for example, wasn't at all happy about the risk of cameras being struck in a lightning storm and the possible catastrophic results.

It is inevitable that with an exercise of this size the secret should leak out. Chris Brasher was one of the opponents of the Eiger idea. He had considered with us the proposal to do a live climb of the wall a number of years previously at the suggestion of the Swiss, but that was before the great revolution in technique of both helicopter rescuing and winching and the long cable runs which were now possible to the cameras. Chris still held to his earlier views, despite these advances. Several anti-Eiger reports appeared in the Sunday papers with reference to danger and accusing us of playing to the sensation-mongers' gallery.

During that next winter I took part in a winter climbing film on Ben Nevis. I suggested to Alan Roberts and Chiv that this climb would be a good test bed for the Eiger sound equipment which had been specially developed in the meantime. The film, 'The Ice Climb', was an ascent of Astronomy, a hard winter route on the north face of Ben Nevis and the radio mikes which we wore transmitted both day and night, for we had to bivouac on the route. One tends to forget these 'personal bugs' and the sound recordist must sometimes feel like a priest at confessional. They worked well anyway.

It went without saying that Dougal would be one of the climbers on the Eiger Outside Broadcast. Chris Bonington, who is a first-class non-stop commentator was also an obvious choice. Chris is such a prolific talker that once in a joint TV appearance with Nick Estcourt, Nick never got a single word in during the transmission. To be able to talk, especially in 'grip' situations, is one of the most important qualifications for an Outside Broadcast climber. Climbers are ten a penny who can do these sort of routes, but few have the gift of conveying to the mass audience their feelings and emotions. The programme could accommodate one quiet man like Dougal; he provided good contrast to the others, but not a whole group of alpine Trappists. Chris, in the company of Ian Clough, had also made the first British ascent of the normal route on the Eiger and Dougal, as well as doing the original route with Rusty Baillie a few years before, had been in the van of the dramatic ascent of the Harlin Direct on the Eiger where John Harlin had fallen to his death.

The broadcast was planned for the autumn of 1975, by the original north face route. Also that year Chris had arranged to have a second attempt on the South West Face of Everest. The problem was, could we fit the Eiger in before we departed, for it was to be a post-monsoon expedition? Chris thought we could if the three of us flew out immediately after the programme was completed, so plans were made for a September ascent of the wall.

Meantime surveys continued. Being lowered by winch wire became as familiar to me as abseiling. Back in Scotland I did many rescues using a helicopter winch and it was old hat to me. Not so for Dougal, and his initiation was on the face itself at the Flatiron just below Death Bivouac. That morning we had a late and casual breakfast and by the time the main stream of tourists had been conveyed by those arteries of humanity, the Grindelwald and Lauterbrunnen railways, we had our cram-

pons on and were boarding Günter's Lama. We had with us
sound equipment for tests at Death Bivouac, and we also
proposed trying out the radio mikes in the proximity of the
chopper to see if it would be possible to obtain 'talk-back' with
the helicopter hovering close by. This trial was necessary to
establish if we could get any conversation from the climbers
during the climb when the camera would be mounted in the
helicopter.

It was a fine morning but we didn't believe in putting our
heads on the Flatiron or any other Eiger chopping block. We
had enough equipment with us either to climb up out from
Death Bivouac or to retreat across the Second Icefield.
Weather, we knew, on the Eiger was like a spider, one moment
it would be 'come into my parlour' and the next hell could
break loose.

The landing site was big enough for a pair of size nine boots
and a convenient piton at waist level was within easy reach to
clip on to. A few days previously Günter had made his first
rescue from this point. The ever-vigilant Fritz von Almen at
the Bellevue had heard cries and contacted the rescue service, it
turned out to be for two uninjured Swiss climbers. The
contrast of being flown from the spongy comfort of the luxury
hotel to the sterile vertical desert of the wall was startling, to
say the least. Here in the shadow the cold gripped us like a
tourniquet in spite of our warm clothing. The whirlibird
departed, dropping down sideways in an elegant but frightening looking sweep and we felt terribly alone.

"Well, Jimmy," Dougal said, lapsing encouragingly into
Glaswegian, "welcome to this charming hostelry. It has, as
you see, one of the finest outlooks in the Alps and a history to
compare with your pad in Glencoe."

Several of the MacDonalds from the infamous seventeenth-
century massacre had been butchered at my backdoor at home
and it seemed a natural progression of thought to enquire of
my genial guide if the ledge beneath an overhang, a rope's
length or so above was Death Bivouac. It was, and we climbed
the unstable snow to see if anyone was at home. There wasn't

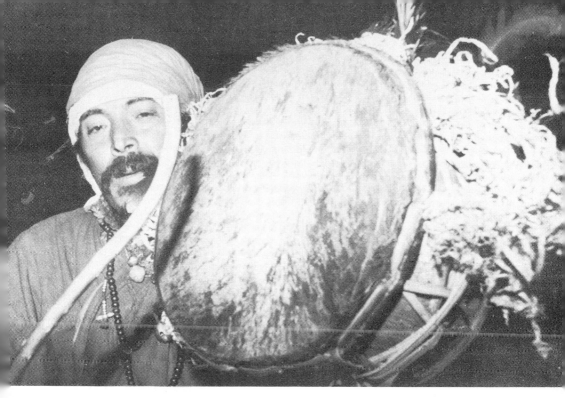

The shaman led us into the pilgrimage cave. Sinners had to beware of the chuti.

Altar ceremony in the cave.

Birth control poster in the upper Arun valley.

An aerial view of the Eiger, showing the West Flank, centre: F is the Fly; S, the Spider; D, Death Bivouac; E, the point where Clint Eastwood was lowered over the face when he cut the rope; R is the Rote Fluh; KS, Kleine Scheidegg.

much there: a few rusty tins, broken lengths of rope, pitons in the wall above, each no doubt with a story to tell. It was well protected by the overhang and I realised that with a good supply of food, a camera crew could, as I had thought, weather out a storm here, at least with tolerable comfort. It was also in a super situation to cover climbers approaching across the top of the Second Icefield. There was a good position close by to watch their departure to the Third Icefield, as well as a reasonable outlook to the Ramp, that steep icy corridor which is one of the hardest sections of the climb and is the key to the Traverse of the Gods and the upper part of the face. We went out on to the Third Icefield for a way and then returned. The talk-back equipment worked well, and we were in constant touch with Alan Roberts' engineers back at Scheidegg. The remaining thing to do when the helicopter returned was to test the noise level as it approached our two-boot ledge and hovered above us. We descended to this and Günter approached.

"If you go up second," I shouted to Dougal, "I'll do a count-down for them back at Scheidegg. You keep talking as well, for we're on different circuits. It will at least give them an idea if they can make out any intelligible speech."

"O.K., Jimmy," Dougal said as the winch wire hook descended. It must have been a natural survival instinct on Dougal's part, for when the hook was within his reach he grabbed it, clipped it to his harness and was lifted. As he rose, Günter took the chopper out and down the face in what looks like a graceful descending curve but which is terrifying for the victim on the end of the wire. Shortly afterwards he came back in and picked me up. Dougal never really gave an explanation for his precipitate action but as far as the radio trial went, it was conclusive: there was no way anyone could be heard above the din of the helicopter gas turbine.

We were back for lunch. We met Fritz as we entered the hotel. He had seen us earlier that day wolfing down our bacon and eggs as if they were trying to escape, and seeing us again dressed in our climbing clobber, besplattered with ice, he condescendingly asked if we had been amusing ourselves on the nearby Eigergletscher.

"Tourists," he said, "enjoy going out on the ice," and added rather acidly, "But they often get into trouble."

"No, no," Dougal assured him in his usual quiet, dead-pan way, "we've just been up to the Third Icefield from Death Bivouac." I saw a lump appear in Fritz's throat and I could imagine him saying to himself, they're making a fool of my Eiger!

That trip to Death Bivouac was certainly stimulating. But I had a niggling thought at the back of my mind. This had manifested itself while we were eating a bar of chocolate on the ledge of the Bivouac, I didn't say anything about it to Dougal at the time, but the following day when it was the turn of the Fly to receive me, these doubts were more than confirmed. Günter had been somewhat apprehensive about dropping me off at the Fly. The Fly, I should explain, is a tiny snowfield high up on the face above and to the right of the Spider. It was christened during the first ascent of the Harlin route, and comprises a small, high angled snowfield, like a sheet of note-paper balanced on top of a picture frame, truly isolated in a hostile position. I had earlier rashly suggested to Chiv that it might be possible to establish a camera position on this place and even to take a generator there to keep the electronic camera warm. I later regretted this optimistic prediction; I regretted it the moment I was lowered the full length of the winch cable, at an altitude of about 12,000 feet. There was nothing beneath my crampons except the distant meadows of Alpiglen and the faint ribbon of the Kleine Scheidegg railway line. Günter eased me towards the face and I started to spin. It was a rapid spin and I soon became very dizzy indeed, as if emerging from a ten day bender and vainly searching for the aspirins. Usually a spin can be stopped by leaning back and splaying out one's legs and arms, but this technique just didn't work and as well as this, I started a small but progressively increasing pendulum motion. This, too, is common when out some 35 metres on the end of a winch wire suspended from a moving helicopter. Both swinging and spinning I felt more like a season ticket holder on a merry-go-round than one on Eiger business. My task was to take photographs of the Fly and the view towards the Ramp, but I had no ambitions to unclip from the winch wire. I touched down and instinctively drove my terrordactyls into the ice and I gratefully felt the front points of my crampons bite into the hard surface, like teeth into a firm apple. Dougal, who was peering out of the helicopter doorway with the winchman, informed Günter that I was safely down. To avoid danger from stonefall, Günter took the chopper horizontally out from the face and I could tell from the engine noise where he was positioned. A frightening thought ran through my mind: if I came off, the thin winch wire would never hold the shock load of a fall. I quickly took the photographs and gave a rapid signal indicating that I had paid my respects to the Fly. Günter didn't need any prompting. Stones were falling round the helicopter; the proximity of the Spider was obviously not the place to take one's favourite aunt, even for curds and whey!

In the bar later over a bottle of that great Swiss wine, Dôle, I put my alternative proposition to Dougal.

"How about the Japanese Direct route instead?" I asked.

"The direct?" he quizzed.

"Yes, I gather there isn't so much stonefall, just the odd shower. It's also closer to the West Flank and situations such as the overhanging red wall of the Rote Fluh and the upper reaches of the climb are safe yet dramatic for camera positions.

"Uh huh," he agreed, "there's something in that." So we discussed it at length and both became enthusiastically infected by the possibilities of this change of plan. It was an obvious choice and we didn't know why we hadn't considered it seriously before, though we had talked about it on Everest.

There hadn't been a British ascent of the Japanese route, but we realised that a direct line to the right of the face would lend itself better to the West Flank cameras simply because they were closer. The main drawback we saw was that the climb itself takes up to five days.

When I broached this dramatic change of plan with Chiv, he

was obviously taken aback. It was of course a major change of policy but when I outlined the problems we had on the Fly and the aspects in favour of the Japanese direct, he too saw the sense in the scheme. We could cover the route with the minimum of risk, the weather wouldn't have such an influence on the programme and the exposure on the climb itself was, if anything, even more sensational than on the original route. Later the Swiss wholeheartedly fell in with these views; after all, this would give the climb much greater credence, especially with the climbing public and would deflate the critics' accusations of film and be damned.

After that extensive survey in 1973 we returned home once more to chew upon our respective technical cuds. There was, as Chiv put it, still a lot of talking to do over the 'nuts and bolts', but things at least were looking promising. A further visit to Scheidegg was planned for the summer of 1974, with the final transmission scheduled for September 1975.

# 12

---

# The Eiger Sanction

Between the acting of a dreadful thing
And the first motion, all the interim is
Like a phantasma or a hideous dream:
[*Julius Caesar*, Shakespeare]

FATE, THAT IMPARTIAL FOOTMAN of both God and the Devil, is never far away. He gave me his undivided attention one Saturday when, on the sea cliffs to the south of Edinburgh, a rock caused a trivial looking impact injury to the side of my leg, close below my left knee. For such a miniscule bruise, about one inch square, it seemed inordinately painful. In fact it caused me so much pain that I called at the out-patients department of the Edinburgh Royal Infirmary. But it wasn't the day for slick service and as I waited my conscience caused me temporarily more discomfort than the injury and with a gait more befitting Long John Silver, I left. I was getting as soft as some of those cream puffs I rescue, I told myself; climbers who, in the words of Huan Findlay, a local farmer and member of the rescue team, "complained of twisted eyebrows". But by Monday morning I was still in Edinburgh and the pain was so intense that I returned to the Infirmary, knowing that in Glencoe X-ray facilities were non-existent.

Dame Luck, not to be outdone by the Devil's Advocate, now took a hand in events and a friendly woman doctor, whose sons were keen on climbing, realising that I wasn't calling with a twisted eyebrow, gave particular attention to this innocent-looking injury and a quick X-ray confirmed her

245

suspicions: she didn't tell me just then, but I had gas gangrene. Within minutes I had a circle of doctors round my trolley. Donald MacLeod, whom I later got to know well, made the announcement as the senior surgeon present. He told me the worst in no nonsense words and added that he would have to operate immediately. As a throw-away line to cheer me up he added that from the three cases he knew of at the Royal Infirmary one had lost a leg, one had recovered and one died.

It was difficult to describe my feelings at the time. I had been exposed to life and death situations on many occasions but these had usually been in the heat of the moment or carefully calculated when I knew the odds, not lying helpless on a trolley like a side of beef. I felt numbed, if not chilled, and recalled how a short time ago we had been investigating reported calls for help in the Lost Valley in Glencoe when some of our team were watching through binoculars two climbers (not those we were searching for) on a nearby cliff. Wal Thomson, one of the team, exclaimed, "He's off!" Sure enough we could see with our naked eyes the inert bundle of the leader at the base of the rock face of Gearr Aonach, with his second still on the belay above.

Within fifteen minutes we were alongside the fallen man; he had regained consciousness. I asked him, "Can you move your legs?" for he was lying in a strange way which I didn't like.

"No!" he replied; his voice had an edge of panic to it and I remember the expression on his face when he realised that he was paralysed from the waist down. Some months later Willy Elliot, one of the rescue team, called in with a newspaper cutting. It read simply "Climber takes his own life". The poor lad had committed suicide; he had our sympathy. All this went speeding through my mind as I lay within that semicircle of white coats.

"Well," I said eventually with resignation, "if you can't save my leg, leave it where it is; I might as well go to the Pit with it."

Donald did save my leg and my life and my sixteen days in the Infirmary I spent writing a thriller which helped to take my mind off the 'discomfort' (there is no pain in Donald's wards).

While I was sitting up in my hospital bed devising oil boom skulduggery on a West Highland sea stack, Dougal was involved with fictitional foul play of a similar nature as climbing adviser to Clint Eastwood in the filming of *The Eiger Sanction*, much of which was shot on the North Wall. I hadn't become involved myself, being fully occupied with the B.B.C. Outside Broadcast, but I had recommended two of my instructors as assistants. When I was still just hobbling around at home I heard from Martin Boysen, who was also working with Dougal, that one of them, Dave Knowles, had been killed by a rock fall on the West Flank. I was shocked for I had known Dave since he and his twin brother had first come to Glencoe years before. They had both been in our rescue team. Two days later the Swiss-American climber Norman Dyrenfurth rang from Kleine Scheidegg.

"Hamish, I wonder if you could help us out. Clint Eastwood has asked me to contact you to see if you are willing to come over immediately to take charge of the safety aspect of the film." He told me that things had ground to a halt and it was costing them £25,000 a day just to keep the unit on location.

"I can hardly walk, Norman. I'm fresh out of hospital and recovering from a secondary infection. I'm not exactly a bundle of energy just now."

"There is no need for you to walk or climb anywhere, Hamish. We'll supply helicopters for your use. Have a think about it and give me a ring."

"Right, I will, Norman, but I'll have to contact Alan Chivers at the B.B.C. for I am due to go out to Kleine Scheidegg next week anyhow for a meeting on a TV project."

"Well, just come out that bit sooner," Norman suggested. "You can still have your TV meeting. We'll juggle with the film programme accordingly."

Next day I took the plane to Zürich and caught the last train up to Kleine Scheidegg late that evening. Martin Boysen and John Cleare were the first people I saw as I got off the train. I was introduced to Clint and his producer, Bob Daley. Clint and Bob suggested that we should meet after dinner and discuss the whole project and how it could be completed without further loss of life.

My immediate reaction on meeting these two men was one of relief. Both were people who talked straight, 'spade men' without frills. The unit, I discovered, was a company of big men with George Kennedy, who also played a leading role, Clint, and Mike Hoover, a cameraman; all were well over six feet and the 'high altitude' sound man made them all look small.

As well as advising on safety, I later discovered that my know-how in rigging and setting up difficult shots was to be called upon and I looked forward to working with the crew. Martin and Dave had been standing in for Clint and others in various climbing shots; not that Clint couldn't do these particular sequences, but he was usually busy with some other take. Indeed, I can't recall him shirking any particular nasty aspect of the film, but certain difficult pitches required some-one who knew how to move easily, not jerkily, on rock or hard ice, without the thrutching movements someone without experience would inevitably make. Martin Boysen can of course move as easily on a difficult climb as a sailor up a companion ladder and his build was similar to that of Clint. John Cleare was working with Mike Hoover as a cameraman in these sequences. As well as the normal Hollywood crew there were specialists. Mike Hoover is a climbing cameraman of great talent and had shared the same ledge as Dave when the rock fall hit them. When I arrived he was still bruised and shocked by the incident. Later, when we had our meeting Clint drawled in his easy way,

"I'm sure glad you made it, Hamish, we'll go along with anything you say."

For the first few days we worked round the lower part of the Jungfraujoch railway tunnel at the Rotstock where tunnels give access to the lower part of the face and there is an assortment like a well-stocked grocer's shelves of gullies, buttresses and rock walls for the cut-away shots. Clint wanted to film on the face itself, on the Rote Fluh and even higher up at Death Bivouac. Although the Rote Fluh gave us adequate protection from stonefall, access to the bottom of it via the Difficult Crack was not without the odd sniping rockfall. I insisted that only climbers and Clint himself should go up to this point. Clint went along with this. I also suggested that there should be no filming higher up on the wall and this decision, too, was agreed to and welcomed by everyone.

But there was one sequence which required a bucketfull of exposure – climbers' jargon for a hell of a drop – preferably near the centre of the wall. This shot entailed Clint hanging from a rope from an overhang. Clint, never underselling a take, felt that somewhere near the 4.2 window on the Harlin Direct would be a suitable location. The 4.2 window is a hole at the end of a tunnel where debris from the Jungfraujoch tunnel was chucked out. It leads on to the face and at this point the wall falls away in an enormous drop. Using the tunnel for access did not involve the objective dangers of climbing up to that point and I agreed to have a look at it. Though I had been down from this point before with Dougal on our B.B.C. surveys, I was equally impressed by this second visit. The corridor from the tunnel to the door, 'the door to nowhere', was lined with ice like a cold chamber. I was with Chic Scott, a Canadian climber, and Bev Clark, a friend of Dougal's from Leysin. Above the entrance the rock rose in an overhang and over this in monotonous regularity avalanches and stonefalls thundered down.

The next day the main group was working on the Eiger glacier and my presence was not required. Chic and I took the workers' train up to the 4.2 window.

The train clanged to a halt on the steep 1 in 4 gradient and Chic and I got out with our ladders and drills; the day's work was about to start – an unusual day's work. After a cup of coffee for it was only 6 a.m. we opened the door to nowhere and clipped on to the ropes which had been fixed in place the previous day. Instant exposure can have a strange effect on one. We moved in a matter of seconds from the claustrophobic ice-cramped tunnel out on to the draughty fastness of the wall. I had a plan for engineering this particular shot which entailed hoisting a steel canopy to the lip of the overhang high above the door to protect Clint from stonefall as he hung directly beneath it. I proposed to make this steel umbrella in the form of an open ended pyramid with a base about two metres square. This necessitated good anchorages. The drilling of bolt holes was the work programme for that day. We put the ladders in position so that they reached to a point close to the lip of the overhang and there Chic and I spent the day hammering star drills. It wasn't exactly pleasant for we were occasionally drenched in the spindrift from avalanches and though we were safe enough, it was disconcerting to feel them breathing down our necks. It was a period of bad weather in the Alps, with piles of snow on the higher peaks, which resulted in the outpourings from the battlements above us.

The following morning I went down to Interlaken to get the canopy under way and with this in mind I made tracks to a small engineering shop recommended by Norman Dyrenfurth. I spoke to the foreman, asking if it would be possible for them to make a steel umbrella.

"Umbrella?" He repeated in English for I am sure that he thought that I had used the wrong German word. "There is a place, sir, that makes umbrellas in Berne, but not in Inter-laken."

"No," I insisted, "not an umbrella for rain." Quickly I drew a sketch of what I had in mind.

"Ah!" he said, beaming, "a canopy for your fire, not an umbrella. An umbrella is for keeping off ze rain. Zis is for keeping up ze smoke."

"Yes, but this is a canopy or umbrella for keeping off showers of rock. I want it for the Eiger North Wall." He paled and I thought he was going to hit me with a spanner he was holding. He obviously thought I was taking the piss. Then he exploded in a paroxysm of laughter and shook his way into the office like a blancmange. I could hear him telling a colleague about a "verrückt Engländer" who was wanting a bomb-proof umbrella to climb the Eiger. Later, however, the matter was resolved and I managed to convince him of the reality of the project. We discussed the construction of the canopy at length and designed it so that it could bolt together on location. We estimated that it would weigh about 350-lbs when assembled.

Next day I returned to the overhang and just as we were going out of the window, an especially large stonefall, about equivalent to the contents of a couple of big dump trucks, descended. This caused boulders to ricochet almost into the doorway itself. I realised that even with the umbrella the set-up was too dangerous. Reluctantly I had to tell Clint that the 4.2 sequence would have to be abandoned. I think then he must have felt depressed, for the gods seemed to be against his film. *The Eiger Sanction* was fraught with almost as many problems and tragedies as was the first ascent of the North Wall.

> A sickening jerk tore the rope from his grip –
> Out sprang the piton, away flew the clip.
> Out in a giant parabola he flew –
> A small hurtling object outlined in the blue.
>
> [Dr. Tom Patey]

We eventually did the umbrella episode, without the umbrella, high on the West Flank, close to where Dave had been killed, but actually overhanging the North Face. I had suggested this position to Clint as an alternative as soon as I had raised my objections about the 4.2 window and he said that was fine by him but he didn't think Dougal would go a bundle on it. Mike Hoover also thought this location ideal, so I tackled Dougal that afternoon. It was apparent that he wasn't wanting to work on the West Flank because Dave had been killed nearby and he now thought the rock too dangerous. Though Dougal may have appeared to many as the hard, inscrutable man of the mountains, as non-committal as a sphinx, deep down he had strong and sensitive emotions. I probably knew Dougal as well as anyone in later years, for we spent a lot of time together, and

I was aware that a motor accident for which he was responsible and which involved a fatality many years ago in Glencoe still hung over him as poignant as any hair-hanging sword. I had once asked him why he never drove, forgetting for the moment this tragic incident in his life, for he travelled very widely giving lectures, and being dependent on other people to drive must have been frustrating.

"Would you drive after what happened to me?" he asked. And recalling the accident, I saw his point.

He agreed however to come up and have a look at the West Flank position with me for, as I told him, I had studied the overhanging section of the wall at this point for the television Outside Broadcast with Guggi, the Swiss engineer. Guggi and his associates had agreed that this part of the Flank was as safe as can be expected on such a rickety mountain. Dougal and I flew up with Günter and landed by winch wire. The Flank at this point resembles the rounded top of a large submarine. We went over to the lip of an overhang.

"This is the place I had in mind, Jimmy." We lay on our stomachs and peered over the awesome drop. The wall slipped away underneath us so that we couldn't see it for quite some distance until the overhang eased to the vertical and swept towards the 3.8 window. The initial drop was over 2500 feet, with another 2000 feet of less steep stuff tagged on before it ran out on to the meadows.

"If we chuck the dummies off from here," I said to Dougal and dropped a small stone as I was speaking, "they won't touch anything for about 3000 feet and then only in passing until they reach the toenails of the mountain." The stone as we watched it got smaller and smaller until at pinhead size it seemed to dissolve.

"The rock does seem solid enough," my companion agreed, "and the drop big enough to allow you time to write your will as you descend. Hunky-dory for the dummies, but how do you propose Clint should fall when he cuts the rope?"

"I'll put one ladder out from where we are lying, like a diving board," I explained, "so that the end is about 25 feet

252

clear of the face, and then put another one vertically up from here so that the bottom of it rests on the diving board ladder. The top of this vertical one will be connected to the end of the horizontal one where Clint will be by ropes and it will also be guyed back on to the ridge behind us. We'll put in a couple of expansion bolts to hold the Flank end of the diving board ladder in place on the rock face here behind us." I pointed to the flat tabletop rock surface behind where we lay. "It will work on the cantiliver principle."

"It sounds crazy to me," he admitted, "but that's your pigeon. I agree, the place does seem O.K."

The contraption was ready for the next afternoon. When Clint and Mike Hoover landed they must have been taken aback when they saw the Heath Robinson structure. Both had to go to the very end of the horizontal ladder. Clint must weigh over 14 stones and Mike about the same. As they moved out over the drop the ladder bent like a cheap ruler, but both were roped. Clint was tied to two safety ropes, belayed by Dougal and myself. The scene which we were going to shoot represented part of the episode where Clint was to hang from the end of a rope (which had snagged on the overhang above the Gallery Window of the Eigerwand Station). In the script two ropes were thrown to Clint from the Gallery Window by rescuers and these were the ropes which Dougal and I now held. In lieu of the snagged rope we had one which hung directly from the end of the ladder. Clint had to cut this while hanging from it, thereby freeing himself so that he could swing down on to the face held by the two rescue ropes. Dougal and I were on stances back on the Flank and when we had lowered Clint thirty feet from the end of the ladder he tied on to the 'snagged' rope which he was to cut. Mike was spreadeagled on the end of the ladder with the heavy camera pointing down the 'snagged' rope at the actor.

"Are you tied on yet, Clint?" I shouted.

"Yeah, I'm on. Wait till I get this knife out."

In Clint's position most people would have mental kittens. If he is a mountaineer, then he will probably feel as Dougal and I did: O.K. for Clint – he's a hero, but not for me, Jimmy. I felt at the time I had taken everything into consideration, but Clint in his no-flapping way, like the true professional that he is, saw two problems. Once he had cut the rope, what would happen to the knife as he fell? It had to be razor sharp, but he felt quite rightly that he would tend to clutch the knife as he fell. This could be highly dangerous. But there was no way round it and in the end he resolved to concentrate on dropping it as soon as the rope parted. Also the sudden departure of 14 odd stones from the diving board would, as Isaac Newton had so wisely pointed out many years ago, have an equal and opposite reaction. Mike would be the victim of this whiplash and the ladder would of course spring upwards. Mike prepared himself against this contingency.

It was all over bar the cutting and Clint yelled up, "Hey, guys, is this safe?"

"It's safe enough," I shouted, "but I wouldn't do it."

"Well, if it's safe, let's get the darn thing done. Ready, Mike?"

"Ready."

"Here goes."

The Swiss army knife bit through the Edelweiss climbing rope and Clint plummeted down to swing like a yo-yo beneath the overhang. A few seconds later I called,

"You O.K., Clint?"

"Yeah, sure, I'll come up now." He soon appeared up the rope using Jumar climbing clamps. Mike, after the sudden upwards flick, was pleased with the shot. It was a winner.

Next day we were back up again, this time to drop the three dummies from the end of the ladder.

The dummies represented Clint's ill-fated companions in the film whose rope didn't snag. Their fall was spectacular to say the least. Watching them spiral down thousands of feet had an uncanny reality about it. It was like seeing one's life racing away to its termination. Dougal and I had similar thoughts, for he said, "Makes you think, Jimmy."

I agreed. "But we both know doctors who smoke."

After we had dismantled the diving board and flown back to the hotel, I suggested to some of the guides that they should recover the dummies, using the helicopters, but they didn't seem to be in any mad rush, thinking no doubt that it wasn't worth the risk. As I felt partly responsible for both this scene and my three dumb friends, I resolved to do the rescue job myself. I suppose it is an old anti-litter instinct I have with years of clearing bodies from the hills back home. Anyhow, I didn't want future generations of climbers, as they started up the North Wall, to find these grisly left-overs of mass entertainment. As the others were to film on the Rote Fluh the following day, I decided to collect the dummies in the morning. Using Martin Boysen as a spotter at the bottom of the Rote Fluh, I flew in with Günter to the lower reaches of the face and started hunting. We found one dummy without any trouble. I went down on the winch wire and clipped it by a short length of rope to my harness. Martin, using his walkie-talkie, was then able to direct us to the others.

"The other two are under that overhanging section, Hamish." He came over loud and clear on the walkie-talkie. "More towards the West Flank and up a bit. See that long patch of snow?"

"Ye-es."

"Well, it's about there."

"I see them," I replied above the din of the chopper and proceeded to direct Günter with hand signals. I was still hanging on the winch wire but up at cabin level beside the winchman like a haunch of mutton on a butcher's hook. Meanwhile, dummy one, weighing a mere 80-lbs, was dangling from my waist, spiralling in a very realistic fashion. As we had suspected that the scene of recovering the dummies could look rather gruesome, we had arranged before setting out to put down on the meadow and to stow the dummies inside the machine before returning to base.

The position of dummy two was not so good. It was on a very steep, unstable scree beneath an overhang down which water pranced in a constant shower. I was lowered again and tied the frayed end of the 'quiet man's' rope to my harness and as dummy number one had descended with me, it was now straining on its leash further down the slope. I gave the signal to be airborne again but Günter in the meantime had spotted the last of the three fallen stars, poised on the very lip of a wall. He took me there at the end of the wire. I felt like a crane driver as I placed the two dummies with precision beside their forlorn and mutilated companion, so that they wouldn't continue their journey to Alpiglen when I landed. Martin and the others above must have had a grandstand view of the whole affair and probably thought the operation was as mad as I did just then. The last body had a greater length of rope attached to him and I tied him to his co-star, the one with the second longest lead, instead of on to my harness. When I was lifted to the helicopter, the first body was just clearing the deck and we were some twenty feet higher before the second one was airborne and a further 70 feet before the last reluctant body took off. All hung like a string of sausages from my harness and I felt as if I was being pulled apart in this airborne tug of war. I never found out why we didn't land on the meadow as arranged, but we didn't, and flew over Kleine Scheidegg just as a train from Lauterbrunnen was arriving and another from Jungfraujoch was due to depart. Word of our macabre air cargo flashed through the trains like sheet lightning and masses of humanity streamed out for a look. There is nothing like human suffering and the prospect of blood to excite *Homo sapiens*. This after all is what they supposed Eiger climbing is all about.

The same day we recovered the bodies, I had to help with a sequence where Clint was to make a spectacular pendulum across the Rote Fluh wall. It involved a running action across the face while hanging on the end of a climbing rope. When climbing, it is used to get from one line of faults to another. The first filming sequence on this was done by Mike Hoover who was alongside Clint, but it was also necessary to obtain other shots from the helicopter which could be edited in with Mike's. I was in the helicopter with Dan Meyer, the operator of the Westcam. This is a device for obtaining rocksteady film

*Above* Dougal Haston being lowered to the Flat Iron on the Eiger OB survey. The overhang right is part of the Harlin Direct. *Below left* Dougal at the 4.2 window on the North Wall. *Below right* Dougal climbing up to Death Bivouac from the Flat Iron landing point.

The Eiger: Chick Scott at work at the umbrella anchors on the Harlin Direct.

Clint Eastwood ready to cut the rope while filming *The Eiger Sanction*.

from a helicopter in flight. The camera is set on a gyroscopic mount and the whole unit contained in a protective sphere about five feet in diameter. Part of the perimeter of the sphere is transparent to allow the camera to operate. It can either be used at the side of the helicopter or beneath. Both mounting points have disadvantages. With the side mount the manoeuvring of the helicopter can be made much more difficult. If it is slung beneath the skids, a special ramp is needed for landing. We had it slung beneath us for this occasion; the shot Clint wanted entailed coming up the valley towards Grindelwald and the Eiger, and the mountain would appear bigger as we progressed until just the Rote Fluh filled the frame and then just Clint hanging on a rope on that nude red wall.

That was the theory, but we couldn't get it to work. It is of course impossible to look through the viewfinder of the Westcam by normal means as it is under the chopper so a small electronic camera does this for the operator. Inside the helicopter the scene is displayed on a monitor. In those days the monitor gave a black and white picture and it just wasn't possible to locate Clint on the wall, as his clothing, a yellowish colour, took on the same colour texture as the rock when it was converted to monochrome. Günter took the helicopter so close I could almost have given Clint a sandwich had I had one with me. Here we could frame him but not further out. It was a difficult situation and I wasn't sure what to do for communications were not the best. In an effort to save weight I had suggested the previous night to Dougal that the signal for the sequence of the pendulum to start on the Rote Fluh would be a series of flashes from a strobelight that I had given him; we had a prearranged code of signals worked out. However, when we discovered that it wasn't possible to locate Clint with the Westcam, I suggested to Günter that we should lower a walkie-talkie to Chic and Bev who were at the top of the Difficult Crack. We went back to Kleine Scheidegg and I dashed off to my room to grab 500 feet of 5mm line and an extra walkie-talkie, with the helicopter engine still running. In minutes we were back hovering high above Chic and Bev who were looking up at the belly of the helicopter wondering what the hell was going on. When they saw a Father Christmas parcel descending 500 feet from the heights, Bev assumed that I was sending them a gift of a bottle of wine. The previous night he had produced an excellent Gletscher wine made close to his home in Leysin. He was disappointed when he discovered that it was a walkie-talkie that came spinning towards him. Chic grabbed it and just as he started to unclip it I dropped the 500 feet of cord, thinking it could be useful to them on the Rote Fluh. The result of this was that it wrapped itself around him as it fell so that he was trussed up like a spider's dinner. With the walkie-talkie was my note asking them to get it up to Clint "as if on an urgent journey to the bog". In half an hour I was speaking with the boss.

"Is it possible to reverse the film, Clint?" I asked. (I had been thinking meantime.) "We can get you on the monitor when close in, but we just cannot locate you on an approach shot. If we pulled out the way we came in, surely the labs could do a reversal job on the film?" Clint thought for a minute and from the helicopter I could see him considering it as he hung on his rope.

"Yeah, sure, that should do it," he agreed. "Let's try it." During all this Clint was in a mind-blowing situation, though safe enough – Dougal, Martin and the lads saw to that. The wall angled inwards then continued as near vertical as damn it; you would certainly lose your small change if it came out of your pocket, and it wouldn't stop until well past the 3.8 window 2000 feet lower down. Yet despite this, when he started to do the pendulum – in reverse, so to speak – he had the presence of mind to look in the opposite direction to where he was running in a great arc across the wall, so that when the film was printed he would then appear to be looking in the right direction. Not many climbers who are used to such acrobatics would have relished running 'blind' in such a place.

One of my last memories of *The Eiger Sanction* was filming a shot which didn't involve any of the actors, but would show the North Wall in all its prodigious savagery. I had suggested we take the helicopter up to 15,000 feet and make as rapid a descent as the Lama could do in safety. Günter had consulted his tables and suggested that about 4000 feet per minute would be his limit.

Günter, the cameraman and I got aboard the next day and climbed effortlessly to our required altitude. Once the summit was framed on the monitor Günter took the chopper up even higher and asked if we were ready. We were and we dropped. It was a weird feeling; things suddenly went quiet. On the monitor the top of the mountain came into view, then the summit snowfields and the Spider with his Fly out in the parlour on his right. The wall grew in stature; it was like panning down the body of a great fat woman until she filled the monitor and our view. We plummeted down like a peregrine. I didn't think we would ever slow up, but I knew when we did, for the machine started to vibrate, then to oscillate like a tuning fork. The floor shuddered and it was as if we were in a tumbler polisher; perhaps a washing machine would be a more appropriate comparison for the perspex misted up. Still we kept descending. To me the odds seemed against effective braking when dropping vertically 4000 feet per minute, but Günter of course had the altitude difference calculated to the last millimetre. Now there was nothing to see. The Bellevue which we were level with a short time before had disappeared as if spirited away in a fog. We were of course further out from Scheidegg over the valley of Grindelwald with plenty of good empty space beneath the seats of our pants, but there was just nothing to see; only the monitor showed the countryside. Dan obligingly gave Günter a view of this by panning his camera for the Westcam hadn't misted up. In a few minutes the condensation had cleared but the rise in temperature had been considerable and we slowly made our way back to our landing ground at Scheidegg, still clutching our large egg.

As my job on *The Eiger Sanction* was drawing to an end, Chiv and Chris Bonington and my other B.B.C. television colleagues arrived to finalise details of the Outside Broadcast.

The 1975 transmission dates were fixed, the climbers selected and the endless work we had all put into the project over the past three years, on and off the mountain, looked like coming to fruition at last. But that winter the Swiss Government vetoed the project. It was said at the time that the dates for transmission would clash with a Swiss national holiday, but it was clear that, knowing the Eiger's reputation, the Swiss had got cold feet. It was a bitter blow for us all, but especially for Chiv. The Eiger climb was to be his last Outside Broadcast, the finale of a long and successful career. As he said, he could either have gone out in a blaze of glory or slunk into retirement following the greatest flop of all time.

Good ideas don't die easily and by 1977 the Swiss Government had had second thoughts and some more money was injected into the project by an offer of a joint deal from the American commercial network Trans World International. I had to return to the Japanese Direct route without Dougal now, for he had been killed in an avalanche accident close to his home in Leysin a short time before. But there was some good news of a new lightweight camera being developed. The microcam, would weigh a mere nine pounds, complete with transmitter. It was as yet an unknown quantity but we'd come a long way from cumbersome monsters of the Old Man of Hoy. Once more, schedules and climbers were arranged, but somehow the Eiger always manages to hit back when it's least expected. In the summer of 1978 I had a phone call from Chiv, just back from the World Cup in Argentina.

"Hamish," he said, "TWI have pulled out for financial reasons, we're back to square one – at Base Camp!"

I told myself as I shoved my obese Eiger file to the back of a shelf to grow cobwebs, that the O.B. resembled the current Stop-Go of the British economy.

It's difficult to think bigger than the Eiger. It represents the ultimate in man's aspirations and folly. It is always news and usually bad news: bad news is news and as such it seems to be irrepressible. Only three months elapsed when word came that again the O.B. was in a 'go-state' and the whole thing swung into gear again. "Can you come out for another survey?" Chiv asked me.

"Sure," I replied, "I'll look forward to that. One thing Chiv, we can always say that we started on this project as relatively young men."

There's no doubt that the Eiger demands its pound of flesh, both physical and mental. We will be working at the limits of technology and of course the final trump card will be played by the Eiger herself, for there's no saying what weather will be in the parlour when we call on the spider and fly with the greatest climbing circus of all time.

> We shall not cease from exploration
> And the end of all our exploring
> Will be to arrive where we started
>
> [T. S. Eliot]

# Index

yeti
  yeti hunt in Central Himalayas,
    107-9; yeti hunt in Arun valley,
    201-2, 204-5, 209-28; detector
    equipment, 205-6; evidence for
    existence of, 94-8, 103, 105,
204-5, 215, 216, 222; Nepalese
sensitivities towards, 201-2,
205, 206, 208

Zermatt, 110, 111, 112, 178, 182,
183, 185, 186